Edexcel DiDA

Diploma in Digital Applications

Using ICT

Elaine Topping
Ann Weidmann

Contents

1 Preparing for DiDA

Digimodule

Look around you – you are surrounded by information – in the post, on the bus, in the classroom, everywhere! Most of this information is presented using ICT – posters, letters, presentations, websites, and much more. Look again at some of these publications – is the information communicated effectively? They have all been created by people who can use ICT but what makes the difference? Some of these people have thought more carefully about **who** it is for – the audience – and **why** it is needed – the purpose.

In Unit 1 you will learn how to make the best use of ICT tools to produce publications for different purposes. These will include paper-based publications such as letters and leaflets and screen-based publications such as web pages and presentations. If you already have a range of ICT skills and you want to apply these skills in effective ways then DiDA is for you.

DiDA is 'hands-on' – very little can be done away from a computer. This is good news for you but you must learn about the risks of using computers for long periods and how to keep yourself safe. You will produce many files as you work on this unit and you will learn how to store your work sensibly so that you can find it later on.

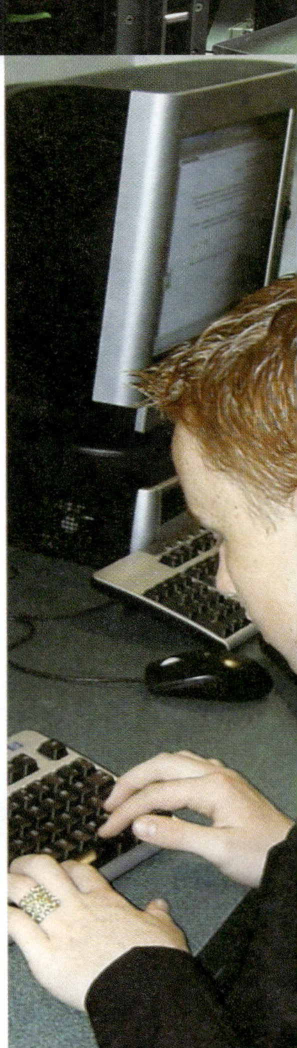

In this chapter you will learn:

- ***what qualifications you can get as a DiDA student***
- ***how DiDA units are assessed***
- ***how to use this book and CD***
- ***what you need to learn for Unit 1***
- ***how to keep you and your work safe***

1

What is DiDA?

DiDA is a suite of qualifications consisting of a number of different units, each worth one GCSE. The qualification you get depends on how many units you complete. At the moment you can get an Award, a Certificate or a Diploma.

Achieving the Award

Unit 1: Using ICT is the basic toolkit for DiDA. If you work through this set of materials and you can apply your ICT skills effectively, you will be eligible for the **Award in Digital Applications (AiDA)**.

Achieving the Certificate

The **Certificate in Digital Applications (CiDA)** can be achieved by adding any other unit to Unit 1. The optional units are shown in the table.

Unit	Title	In this unit students learn how to:
2	Multimedia	gather digital assets – sound, images, video, animation etc – and combine them to create multimedia products
3	Graphics	produce effective images for screen and print
4	ICT in Enterprise	put ICT to work by planning and promoting an enterprise

Further units will be offered in the future.

Achieving the Diploma

The **Diploma in Digital Applications (DiDA)** is achieved by completing Unit 1 plus any three other units.

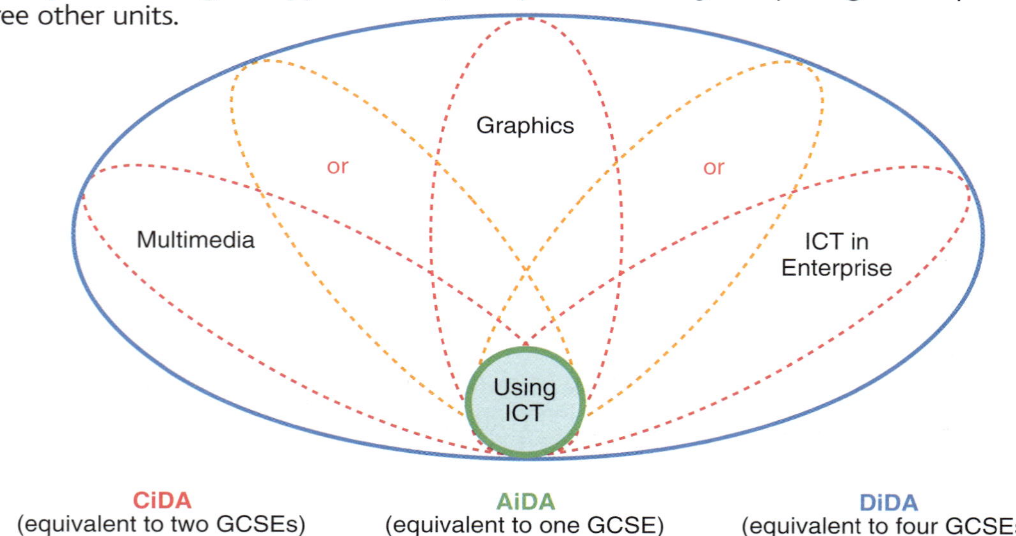

What's in DiDA? This diagram shows how the qualification works for the first four units issued by Edexcel. You may be able to replace any of Units 2, 3 or 4 with other options in the future. Watch the animation to see how everything fits together.

How difficult is it?

You can take each unit at level 1 or level 2. This is one of the things that makes DiDA special – if you are very good at, say multimedia, but not so good at graphics, you can do the different units at different levels. You will get an Award, Certificate or Diploma at level 1 or level 2.

How is DiDA assessed?

DiDA students do not have to sit in rows in an exam room – there is no formal exam. Instead, you will have around 30 hours at your centre to work on a project set by the exam board. Once you have completed the work needed for a unit you will tackle the SPB (Summative Project Brief). Each SPB is published as a website – all you will need is a link to access it on-screen. It is not a soft option – you will have to work hard to complete everything on time – but you will be able to demonstrate your ability to apply your skills by developing publications that are creative, effective and fit for purpose.

So what will you have to do?

The SPB for Unit 1 will have a scenario and a series of activities based on it. You will use ICT to develop a range of publications for different audiences and purposes, both on-screen and in print. Have a look at the specimen SPB published by Edexcel to get an idea of what is involved.

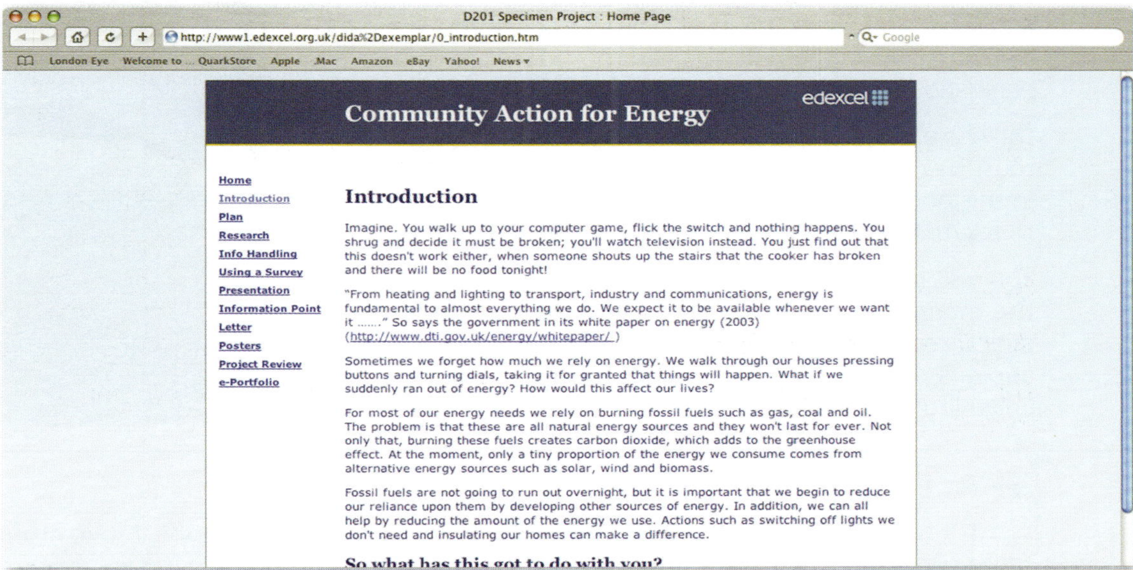

You must bear in mind that DiDA moderators don't like paper! The final stage of the SPB is to create an electronic portfolio (eportfolio) to demonstrate your achievements. This will allow others to view your publications on-screen and see evidence of how you produced them. Your eportfolio will be marked by your teacher and checked by a moderator.

What grades can you get?

All DiDA units can be awarded at four levels – Pass, Credit, Merit and Distinction. They are all equivalent to GCSE grades, as this table shows:

GCSE grade	DiDA Level 1	DiDA Level 2
A*		Distinction
A		Merit
B		Credit
C	Distinction	Pass
D	Merit	
E	Credit	
F/G	Pass	

As you can see, there is an overlap between the two levels. A distinction at level 1 requires the same level of work as a pass at level 2.

How do you use the ActiveBook?

DiDA is all about digital applications and these materials reflect this fact. There is a printed book for you to read but there is also a CD containing a number of digital resources. You may be reading this paragraph in the printed book or on the screen. For text like this, it doesn't really matter but before you read on, open the CD and look at the home page and tabs.

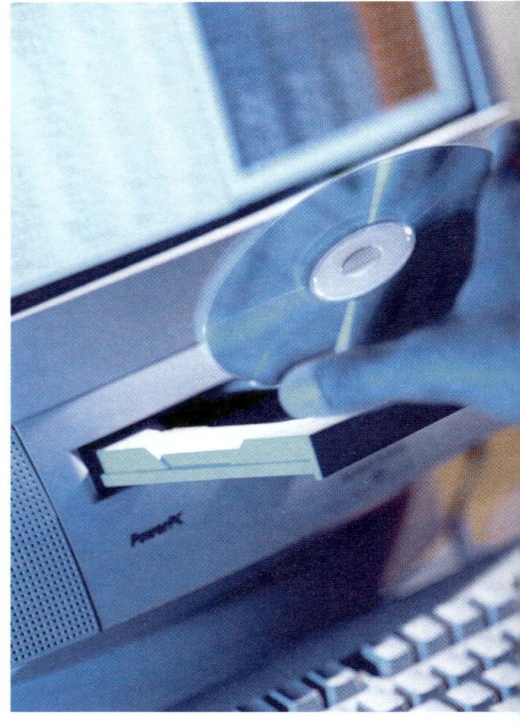

ActiveBook

The most important item on the CD is called the 'ActiveBook'. This is a digital version of the paper-based book.

You will see that the pages of the ActiveBook *look* the same as the printed version – but there is a big difference!

The ActiveBook is interactive. You can control where you are and what you are doing at any time. You can move around by using links in the text. You can move forward or back a page and search for a page using the tools in the ActiveBook.

DiDA is a computer-based course and most of your work must be done using a computer. You can read about a topic in this book but there will be points at which you will need to use the CD for further information or for activities.

You will have noticed that this symbol appears in the margins of the book. This indicates that there is a digital resource in the text nearby. The symbol also appears on pictures. Clicking on the text or the image links you to a resource.

Activity 1.1

Try it now. Click on the ActiveBook tab and open the ActiveBook. Move around the ActiveBook, check out different links and then find your way back to this page.

Can I do this?

A section called *Can I do this?* allows you to check that you have the necessary skills before continuing. For each skill, you will be offered two options:

- 'Tell me' – to take you step by step through a process.
- 'Test me'– to check that you know how to do the skill.

For example, this is an extract from *Can I do this?* in Chapter 5. Try clicking on each one to see what help is available.

You can also use the Skills List on page 176 to check your skills.

Can I do this?

Using database tools, make sure you can:

Create a new database table

Create new fields in a table

Enter sensible field names

Select suitable data types

Change data types

Select field sizes and formats

Change field sizes and formats

Enter simple validation rules

⏩ Activity 1.2

Have a look at some of the Can I do this? sections in the ActiveBook for help on the skills you should have. Also go to page 176 in the ActiveBook and click on some of the skills and page numbers given.

Activities

Needless to say, activities require you to do something! Sometimes you will do this on your own, at other times you will be asked to work in groups.

Many of the activities make use of digital resources provided on the CD. For example, you will be given a database to work with in Chapter 5. Each of these resources will be accessed via a hyperlink indicated by the [hyperlink symbol] symbol nearby.

8 Creating a presentation

Can I do this?

Using presentation tools, make sure you can:

Create slides	Crop and resize images
Create and use a master slide	Include animation
Use lines and borders	Include sound
Change colours	Insert links
Import and position images	Create transitions
Align text and images	

TALKING POINT 8.8

What else can you do to make sure that the slides are error-free?

⏩ Activity 8.10

Use your storyboard to create the presentation for the management committee at Oasis. Use information from the folder as well as multimedia components of your own. Your presentation should last for 10 minutes and you should prepare speaker notes to accompany the slides.

Making it more than just a slide show

No matter how well designed the slides are, a presentation is only as good as the presenter. You must practise your presentation in front of a test audience. Make sure that you know what you are going to say for each slide so that you can look at the audience when you are speaking. Don't keep turning round to look at the slides behind you and avoid just reading the speaker notes.

Sound enthusiastic about what you are saying and **never, ever stand there and read the slides out bullet by bullet**. The audience can read the slides for themselves. Your job is to fill in the details and get the full message across effectively.

Getting the timings right

Your audience will have been told how long the presentation will last. When you are practising, check that the presentation is the right length, allowing time for questions if appropriate. Don't talk for too long without involving the audience in an activity or a discussion.

You must also test your presentation to make sure that animations, sound and transitions work as intended. Use the prototype to get feedback from a test audience.

Other uses of presentation software

Scrolling presentations run without user interaction. These are often used in public areas such as a leisure centre reception area or an exhibition. Passers-by can stop and watch as much as they like.

132

Getting the message across – targeting a known audience 8

Newsletters

First impressions

Whereas a report is likely to be read by the audience even if it is not very exciting, a newsletter is optional reading. If it is not designed well, they probably won't bother. It will come as no surprise that you cannot design a newsletter until you have answered these questions:

- **Who** it is for? How old are they? What sort of writing style can they cope with? Why are they interested in your topics? How much (or how little) do they already know?
- **Why** is it needed? Its purpose should be clear at a glance.
- **What** should go in it? Concentrate on what the audience will want to read, not on what you want to write about. They are not necessarily the same thing! When you design the pages, you will need to make sure that more important items stand out.

TALKING POINT 8.9

Look at these newsletters and comment on:

- *Audience and purpose*
- *Number and size of pages*
- *Colours (full colour/2 colour/b&w)*
- *Balance of text and images*
- *Title*
- *Writing style*
- *Content*
- *Use of white space*

133

Talking Points

Everything you do for DiDA is concerned with communicating information. Your publications need to be fit for purpose, suitable for the audience and purpose. You will only be confident in this if you have looked at and discussed the work of others. Talking Points allow time for discussion with others in your group – to find out what they think and why you don't always agree.

TALKING POINT 1.1

You have had a chance to look at some of the features of the ActiveBook. Why do you think we have produced a pack that has a printed book and a CD? How do you think it would be best to use the materials? When will the printed book be useful?

Tackling The Project

The final page in most chapters is called **Tackling The Project**, where you will practise the skills you need for the SPB.

You will collect evidence of what you have done and store it in folders. Eventually you will learn how to create an eportfolio so that you can select the best of your work to showcase your achievements.

What else is on the CD?

The Project

The Project is a mini website, just like a real Unit 1 SPB, and it has the same type of structure and content.

There are two main differences between **The Project** and an SPB:

- you will work on sections of **The Project** as you complete each chapter. For the real SPB you will have at least 30 hours at the end of the course to concentrate on it.
- you don't have to produce a complete project plan for **The Project** because you are told when to tackle each section. For the SPB you will need to carefully plan your work so that you complete everything within the time allowed.

Activity 1.3

The Project is just like a website with links to various materials you will need. Click on The Project tab and have a look at The Project brief just to get a feel for what is in store, but don't try to make a start just yet! Check out the different types of links.

The Digimodules

Your teacher will introduce each chapter using a digimodule. This is a multimedia presentation which can be used on an interactive whiteboard. It covers the main areas of the chapter and allows time for group discussion. There is a link to each digimodule in the ActiveBook on your CD, so that you can re-visit them at any time.

Activity 1.4

Go back to the first page of this chapter and click on the digimodule symbol. This will allow you to view parts of the digimodule for this chapter.

The other tabs

- **Go Online:** This tab takes you directly to the Edexcel DiDA course website where you will find links to all the websites mentioned in this book.
- **Help:** This tab explains how to use your CD. You can search on key words to find the information you need.

Zoom tools

Some of the pictures of publications shown in this book are quite small. If they change colour when you move the cursor over them in the ActiveBook, then they can be made bigger. Click on the item and it will enlarge so that you can see it more clearly. To return to normal size, click on the cross in the top right hand corner.

You can also zoom in or out on any part of the ActiveBook at any time by clicking the magnifying glass symbol on the tool bar.

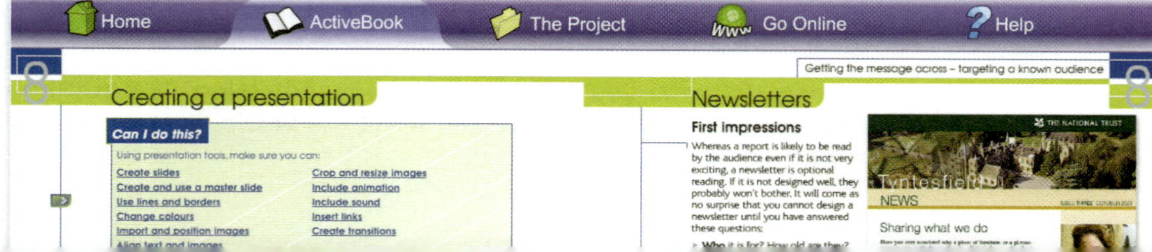

What do you need to learn?

You should by now have some idea of what DiDA is all about but what do you actually need to learn? DiDA has a specification which sets out exactly what is required. There are three sections for DiDA students to read themselves:

1 What you need to learn

DiDA is all about applying your ICT skills to present and communicate information as effectively as possible. You will learn how to select the most suitable type of publication, content and style for a particular audience and purpose.

First you will need to gather the information you need. You will learn how to find, select and store information that is already available.

You will also learn how to gather new information yourself using methods such as interviews and surveys and by using cameras and other equipment.

You will practise good design techniques so that you can present information in a range of publications, and learn how to make use of feedback to ensure fitness for purpose.

You will learn how to design, develop and test an eportfolio – this is not only for the SPB, eportfolios are becoming more and more popular with employers and colleges. Some people think that we should all have one!

TALKING POINT 1.2

Look at section 1 'What you need to learn' of the specification. What do you know already?

2 Managing your project

The success of a project depends to a great extent on how well you plan it. You will learn how to produce a project plan and use it to keep a check on your progress and meet your deadlines. You will also learn how to carry out a review of a project to evaluate how well you have done.

DiDA students spend most of their time using computers and the final part of this section covers things you need to do to make sure that you keep both yourself and your work safe.

TALKING POINT 1.3

Look at section 2 'Managing your project' of the specification. Why is it so important?

3 The ICT skills you will need

This section includes all the ICT skills you will need and the types of software you should be able to use.

Activity 1.5

Look at the ICT skills list in the specification and see what you know already. You may surprise yourself!

... and the rest

The rest of the specification for Unit 1 is intended for teachers and moderators although you might want to look at the marking grids later on to see what will gain you marks.

What are standard ways of working?

DiDA is all about using ICT effectively. Section 2.3 of the specification is called *Standard Ways of Working*. It deals with things that we should all consider when working with computers including health and safety and file management.

Bad and good habits

How do you work safely?

You should already know some of the rules about working safely and there is plenty of information out there on how to organise your workspace and time so that you reduce health and safety risks. It is so easy to get into bad habits if you are not careful.

▸▸ Activity 1.6

Open the questionnaire. Use it to identify any bad habits you have got into when using a computer. Decide what you are going to do about them. Choose as many as you like. Remember that changing one thing might mean that you have to change others. Save your completed questionnaire and call it Safe Working. After a week, check to see if you are still working safely.

Working safely questionnaire

file:///Users/robbriggs/Desktop/Working%20safely%20questionnaire.htm

London Eye Welcome to QuarkStore Apple .Mac Amazon eBay Yahoo! News

Working safely questionnaire

Is this you?		What can you do about it?	Planned action	Follow up
Do you work at a computer for long periods?	☐	Take regular breaks – at least 15 minutes away from the computer every two hours	☐	☐
		Take a short break from typing and looking at the screen every 10-15 minutes	☐	☐
Do you sit for long periods in one position?	☐	Take regular breaks. Get up and move around	☐	☐
		Use an adjustable swivel chair	☐	☐
		Move the printer away so that you have to get up to reach it	☐	☐
Do you lean forward rather than use the chair backrest?	☐	Check position of back and seat of chair Use the backrest for support	☐	☐
		Make sure there is enough leg room	☐	☐
		Check readability of screen	☐	☐
		Get an eye test	☐	☐
Do you sit with your body twisted?	☐	Make sure there is enough leg room	☐	☐
		Use a swivel chair	☐	☐
		Arrange workspace in a U shape	☐	☐
Do you sit with your shoulders hunched?	☐	Relax your shoulders	☐	☐
		Lower the work surface or keyboard	☐	☐
		Lower chair armrests	☐	☐
		Raise the chair	☐	☐
Do you strain your neck to look at the monitor?	☐	Adjust the monitor height so that it is at eye level or slightly lower	☐	☐
Do you twist your head to the side?	☐	Move the screen so that it is in the centre of your view	☐	☐
Is your lower back not supported by your chair?	☐	Check the height and angle of chair back	☐	☐
		Use a lumbar cushion	☐	☐
		The chair back should only lean back if the seat moves with it	☐	☐

It won't happen to me!

Have you ever lost important ICT work and had to do it all again? Do you think that it won't happen to you? If you don't take precautions, it almost certainly will – and there is a good chance that it will be your fault!

Take a look at this pie chart showing the main reasons for work being lost.

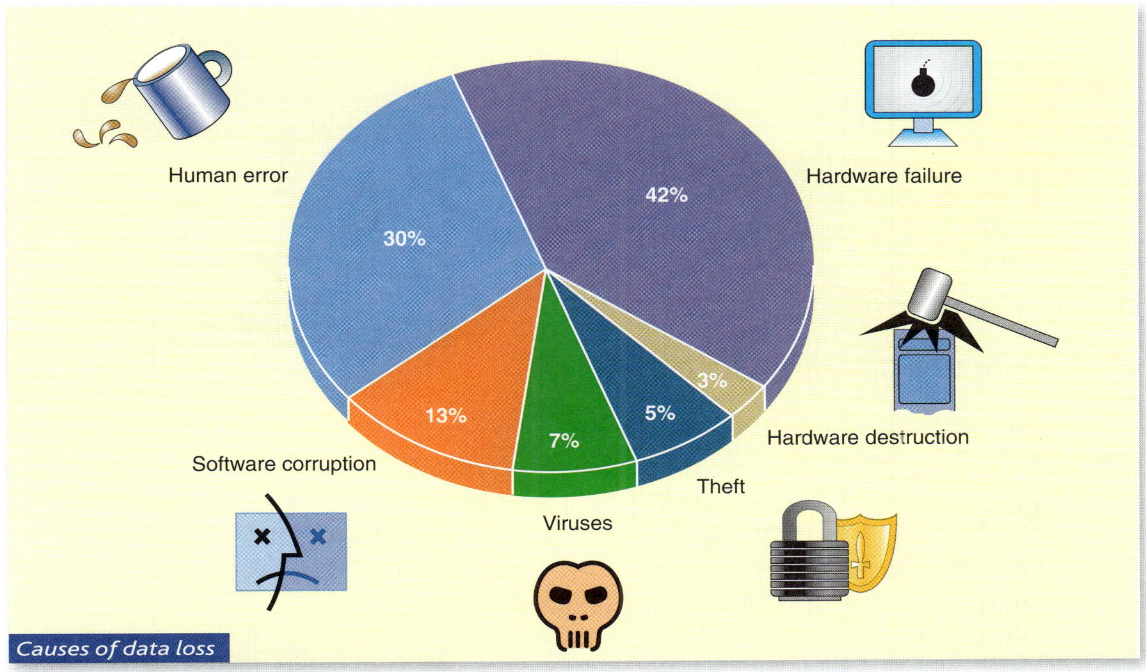

Causes of data loss

Let's look at some of these in more detail so that you can think about what you should do to protect your work.

Viruses

Viruses are programs that run without you realising it and do things that you don't want them to. Why do people write them? To cause trouble, for fun, for revenge, for a challenge, to make use of programming skills.

Every time an anti-virus company finds a cure for a virus, virus writers seem to be ready with another one.

Many do not cause any serious damage but some are designed to corrupt your software or destroy your files. Anti-virus software is very good at preventing viruses from attacking your system provided that you keep it up to date.

System destruction

Imagine that you arrive at your school or college one morning to find that a fire has destroyed the entire computer system and everything that was stored on it.

Hardware, and everything stored on it, can be destroyed or damaged by flood, power surge, fire, lightning or equipment failure.

Hardware failure and software corruption

However hard you try, things can still go wrong. Hardware and software can let you down at crucial moments and work can be lost. Other people can deliberately corrupt your software and files.

Human error

When working under pressure it is very easy to make mistakes.

Around a third of all data loss is our own fault. Have you ever:

- overwritten a file with another one by using the same name?
- forgotten to save something and lost it because the network crashed or there was a power cut?
- lost a file because you couldn't remember where you put it?
- lost a disk or memory stick that you saved a file on?
- forgotten to make a copy?

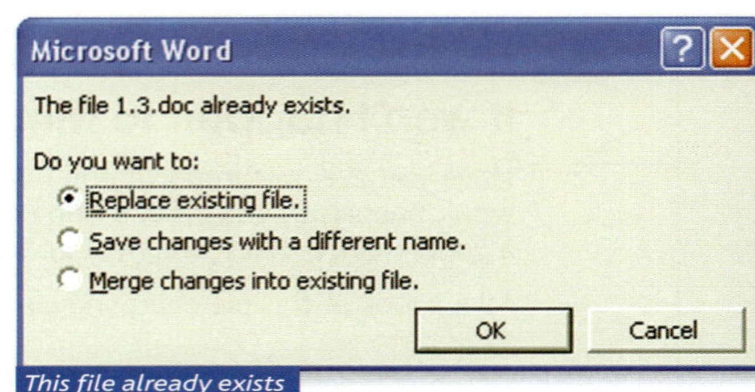

This file already exists

Do you want to save changes?

What can you do about it?

Backing up

Make backup copies of all work you want to keep. It is no good simply making a copy on the same hard disk as the original file. Make a copy somewhere else. Make regular backups – every time you make significant changes to a file that you would not want to do all over again.

Never overwrite your only backup with the next version.

Passwords

Use passwords to protect your system or user area and your folders. Keep your passwords private, even from your friends!

Anti-virus software

Use anti-virus software. New viruses appear every day. Make use of features such as automatic update to ensure that your system is protected from the latest viruses. Scan the system regularly and scan emails and all new files.

And finally …

Avoid sharing portable devices such as memory sticks and don't download files from unknown sources. Viruses are often sent out as attachments to emails. Don't open attachments from unknown sources; delete them and empty the recycle bin.

TALKING POINT 1.4

Discuss what measures are taken in your centre to keep ICT work safe.

How should you manage your work?

Can I do this?

Using file management tools, make sure you can:

Create folders and subfolders
Move around a folder structure
Find a file by searching
Save a file in a folder or subfolder
Copy a file or folder
Move a file or folder
Delete a file or folder
Use passwords for logon and folders
Change a file or folder name

Clearing the clutter

'I can't find my file'

Do you recognise this situation? As a DiDA student you will realise that organising and storing your work is just as important as creating exciting publications. You need to use your ICT skills to keep your work safe so that you can always find things when you need them. How should you go about it?

The answer is to clear the clutter! The more organised you are, the more time you will have to work on a project rather than wasting it hunting around for missing files.

Every time you save something with a new name, you create a digital file. It's where you save it that counts.

Operating systems like Windows provide an easy way to organise digital files in folders. Decide on different categories, create a folder for each category and make sure that you save files carefully in the correct folders. *There really is no excuse!* If you store everything in one folder, it will be just the same as rummaging through piles of paper.

Don't save unnecessary files – you need evidence of what you have done and perhaps one or two draft versions but not a different copy for every few minutes you spend on something.

What folder structure should you use?

There is no simple answer to this. Some people have folders for different types of publications – letters, memos, presentations, etc. Others create a folder for each different aspect of their work, with subfolders if necessary. In the example below the Publicity Manager of a leisure centre has folders for each area of his work. He has created a subfolder for each edition of the newsletter.

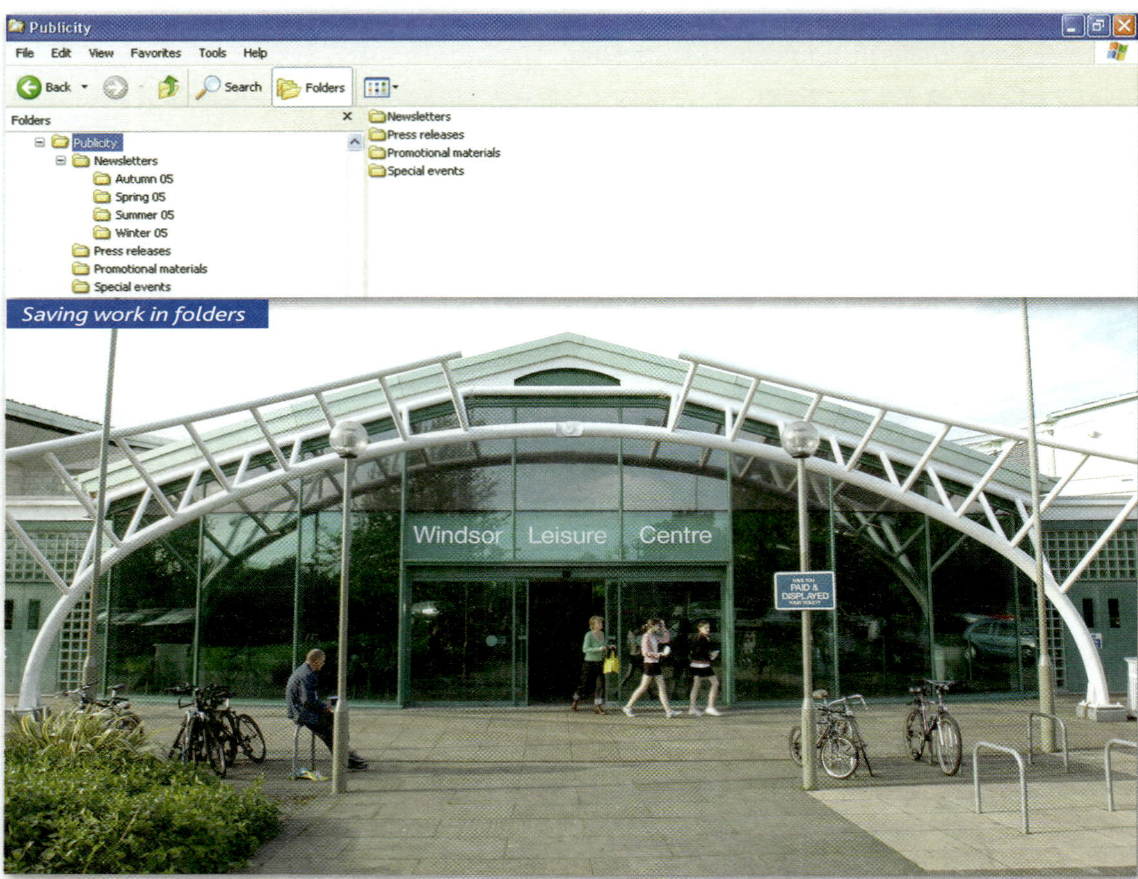

Saving work in folders

You will certainly need a structure to store files that you produce as you work through these materials. Your folder structure should suit the way you work – it will not be the same as everyone else's.

Whatever structure you come up with, make sure you use it. Whatever you do, don't be tempted to save files straight onto the desktop and think you will move them later.

What should you call your folders?

There is no point in designing a logical way of organising your work if you still can't find things easily. You need to use sensible file and folder names. If you look at the example above you can get quite a good idea of what the folders are for even though you don't know anything about the person who created them.

Use names that tell you enough. In the example above, the folders identify categories such as Newsletters and Special events.

Keep them simple. Use abbreviations to keep folder names short but be careful that they make sense. For example a subfolder called Final Publications could perhaps be shortened to FinPubs but FP is taking things too far.

TALKING POINT 1.5

The table shows a list of folders on a PC. The list of contents is not in the correct order. Can you identify the correct content for each folder?

Folder Name		Content of folder
CustServ		Accident book for each department and first aid manuals
XmasParty		Activities for a school induction week
Accidents		Bookings and posters for a Christmas party
5 July		Bookings and posters for a college prom
Party		Files relating to homeless people in a city
Homeless		Flight and hotel confirmations for a holiday in the Caribbean
Induction		Images and articles for the fan pages of a pop group website
FanPage		Letters to customers whose central heating is due for a service

Are all the folder names sensible? Are there any that you are not sure about? How would you improve the names?

▸▸ Activity 1.7

Take a look at your user area if you are working on a network or at your own computer at home. Is everything stored in a logical way? Do the folder names make sense or do you need to open some of them to see what they are?

Rename any folders where the meaning is not clear.

What should you call your files?

The rules are much the same for files as for folders. Avoid general names such as letter1.doc, letter2.doc, image.jpg, etc. Use names that give some idea of the content of the files. Consider using dates or version numbers in the file names if you have different versions.

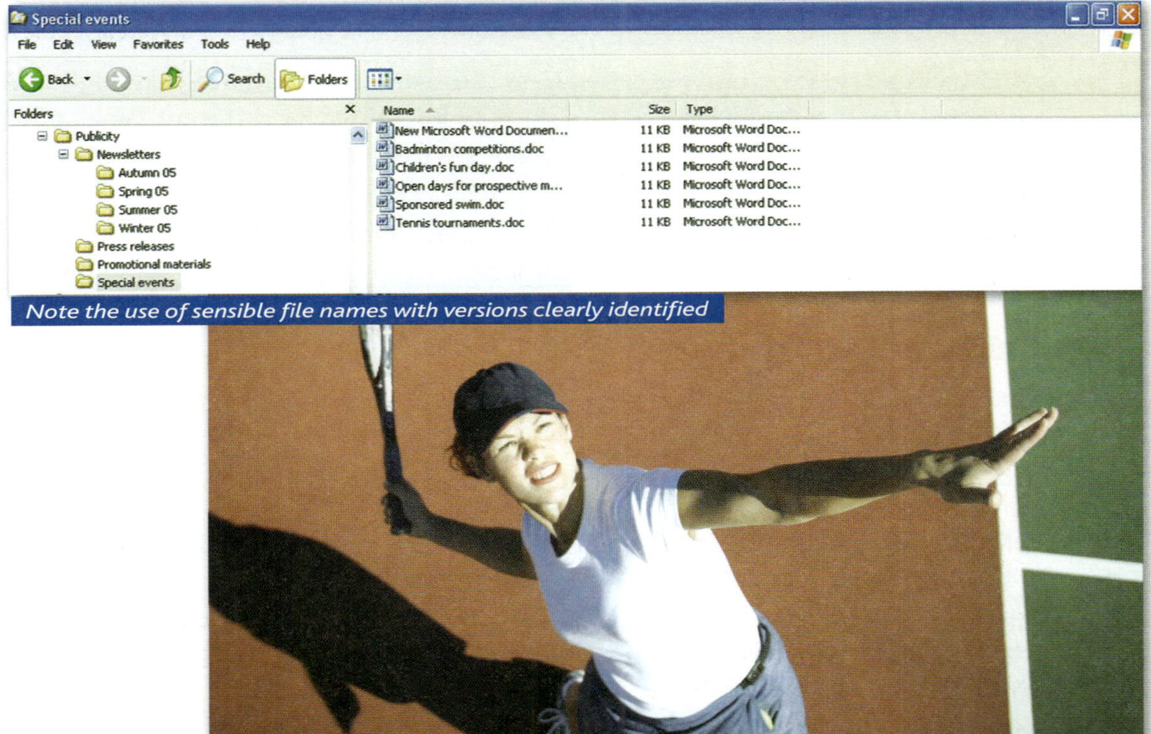

Note the use of sensible file names with versions clearly identified

▶▶ Activity 1.8

Take another look at your user area if you are working on a network or at your own computer at home. Do the file names make sense or do you need to open some of them to see what they are? Do you have the same files in different places? Or old versions of a document that you don't need any more? Have a go at clearing your clutter now!

Once you have tidied up your user area you should be ready to create some more folders for your Unit 1 work. Each chapter contains activities that require you to create or improve documents and other files.

Looking for a file

▶▶ Activity 1.9

Create a folder structure to store the work you will produce for the activities in this book. Don't worry about THE PROJECT – we will give you a structure for that.

Start by creating a folder called Unit 1 or something similar. You might want to separate final publications from draft publications, or different types of file. Another possibility is to create a separate folder for each chapter. The important thing is that you know exactly where to look when you need something. Remember that you can change the structure later if you find that it does not meet your needs.

Independent working

Once a topic has been introduced, you can work at your own pace using the ActiveBook, accessing additional resources and activities by clicking on links.

Successful DiDA students will be confident enough to apply their ICT skills independently but this does not mean that you should work alone! On the contrary, you should continually seek opinions and get feedback from others on what you are doing. You and your peers all want to do well and this is the best way to help each other out.

Although you will gain more marks on the SPB if you do most of the work independently, there are also marks for making use of feedback and for publications that show a good sense of audience and purpose.

Introducing SPBs

In the end, the final grade you get for Unit 1 will depend on the quality of work you produce for the SPB. THE PROJECT is very similar to an SPB in the way it looks and works.

Activity 1.10

THE PROJECT brief is on your CD. Open it now. You will see that there is a menu to the left of the Introduction. Read the information below and try out the links.

Just like an SPB, THE PROJECT is a mini website and you should not think of it as a series of pages in a particular order. The menu appears on every page and allows you to move directly to any section of THE PROJECT.

Menu	
Home	
Introduction Plan Project Review Eportfolio	The first set of menu items link to pages that introduce THE PROJECT and to the planning and completion of THE PROJECT.
Gathering info Research Creating a database Using the database Conducting a survey	The second set is concerned with research and gathering information that can be used in the final publications. All projects will include these three methods of obtaining useful information – using information sources such as the internet and the media, extracting information from a database and carrying out a survey. What you do in this section will depend on what publications you are asked to produce.
Attracting attention Flyer Poster Making information available Web pages/info point Leaflet Targeting a known audience Formal letter Presentation Report	In the third section of the menu there are links to details of a range of publications you must produce. You must make sure that you understand what is required before carrying out your research.

You will need to start by reading the whole project brief so that you have a complete picture of what is involved.

1 Tackling THE PROJECT

P

As you tackle each section of THE PROJECT, you will produce files – publications and other evidence. Not all of this work will go into your eportfolio – you will need to select items from everything you have stored. It is essential that you can find each file easily when you need it. If you organise yourself at the beginning, it will make your job much easier.

Read the introduction and the plan section of THE PROJECT.

You need to create a folder structure for your work on THE PROJECT.

You should:

- Create a folder called THE PROJECT.
- Create three folders called Gathering info, Publications and Review – as shown in the diagram.
- Create subfolders for Publications and for Gathering info. You might decide to create a separate subfolder for each publication or you might divide the publications up into different types as we have done.

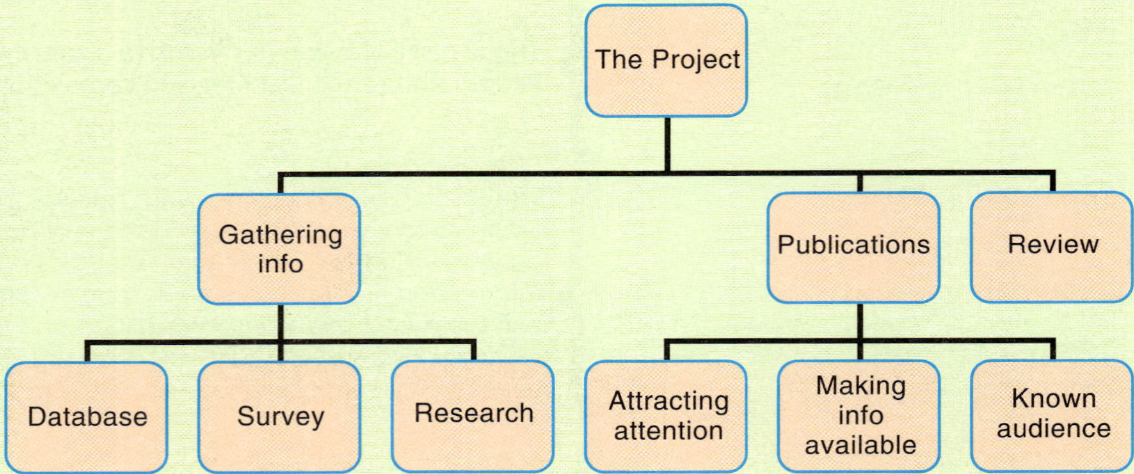

You may want to break the structure down further – for example the Survey folder could contain separate folders for the questionnaire and the spreadsheet. It is up to you. What matters is that you are organised and can find things later. You should be prepared to add more subfolders later if you feel that folders are getting too full.

2 Who, why, where, what, how?

Digimodule

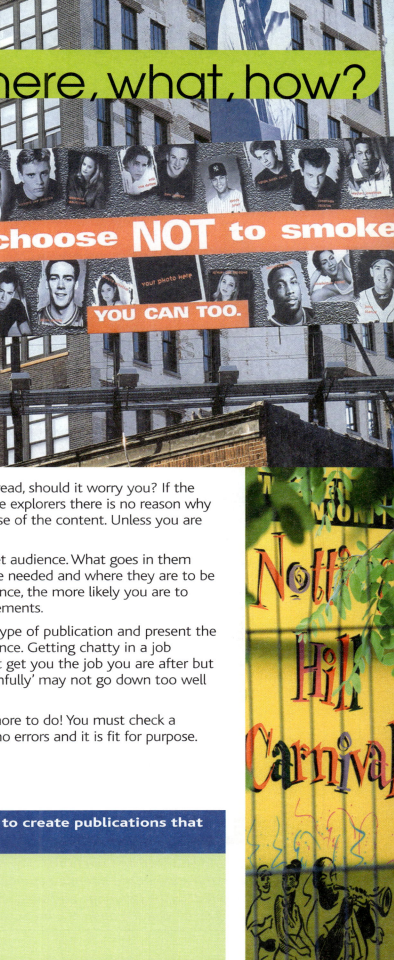

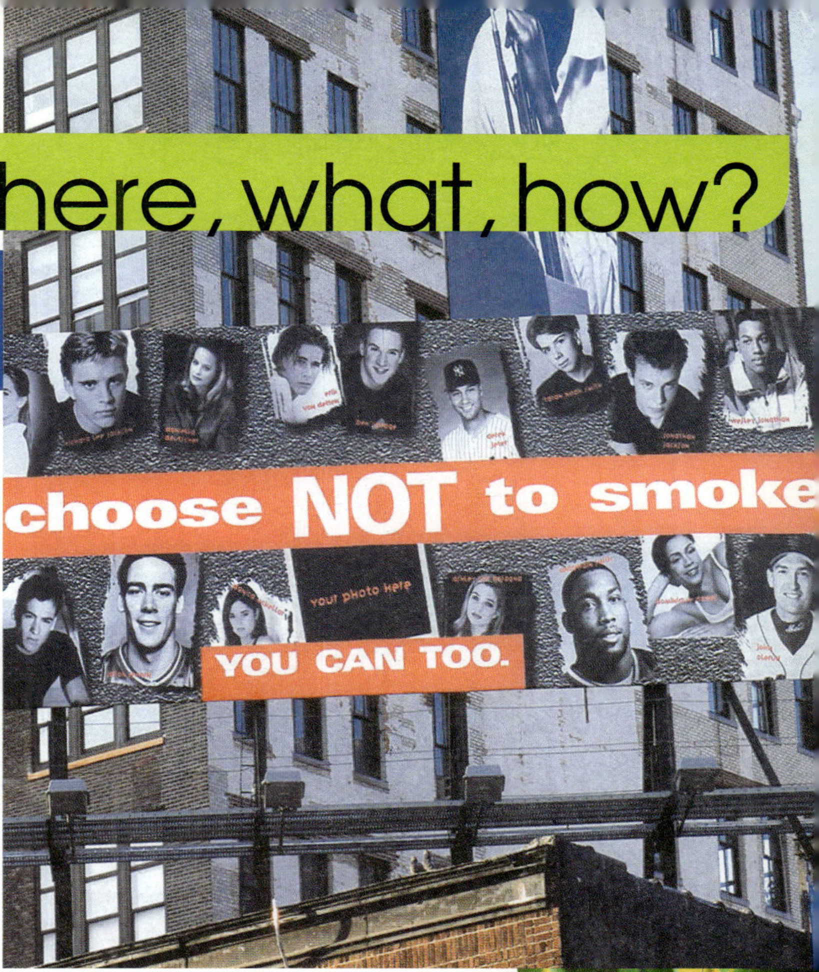

If you cannot understand something you read, should it worry you? If the publication is intended for a group of space explorers there is no reason why you should be able to make complete sense of the content. Unless you are about to take off into outer space, that is!

Publications must make sense to the target audience. What goes in them depends on who they are for, why they are needed and where they are to be used. The more you know about the audience, the more likely you are to produce something that meets the requirements.

You also need to be able select the right type of publication and present the information in a style that suits the audience. Getting chatty in a job application letter to an employer may not get you the job you are after but a letter to a friend that ends in 'Yours faithfully' may not go down too well either!

Even if you get all this right, there is still more to do! You must check a publication and make sure that there are no errors and it is fit for purpose.

In this chapter you will learn how to create publications that are fit for purpose by deciding:

- ***who the target audience is***
- ***why the publication is needed***
- ***where it is for***
- ***what must go in it***
- ***how you should go about it***

2 Who is it for?

Every time you find yourself presenting information to others, you need to be clear who those others are so that you can choose the most suitable type of publication, content and style. The people your publication is intended for are called the target audience.

Look at this screen from a story intended to teach interactive reading to children.

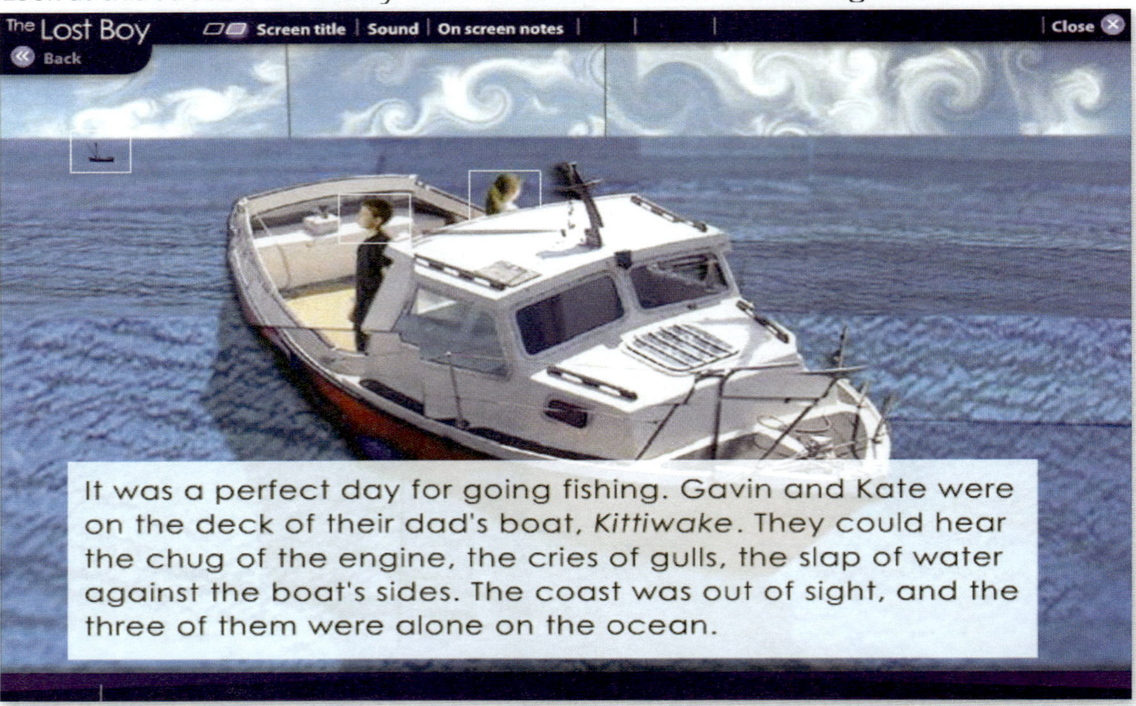

The Lost Boy
Back
Screen title | Sound | On screen notes
Close
It was a perfect day for going fishing. Gavin and Kate were on the deck of their dad's boat, *Kittiwake*. They could hear the chug of the engine, the cries of gulls, the slap of water against the boat's sides. The coast was out of sight, and the three of them were alone on the ocean.

Do you think the language, content and style are suitable for the purpose?

TALKING POINT 2.1

Look at this document that is displayed on a noticeboard at an ice rink.

Ice Rink Rules

1. Please skate in a clockwise direction around the ice rink. Do not skate across the ice. Do not go back against the flow of skaters.
2. Any medical condition that may be affected by skating must be reported to a steward before skating.
3. Skates must be removed before leaving the rubber mats around the ice rink.
4. Climbing on the barriers around the rink is not permitted.
5. Smoking, alcohol, food and drink are not allowed on or near the rink.
6. Dangerous behaviour should be reported to a steward immediately.
7. Abusive or anti-social behaviour will not be tolerated and offenders will be asked to leave.
8. Children under nine must be accompanied by a paying adult skater at all times.

Would you stop and read this? Why not? Discuss the content and presentation of it and think about the intended audience and purpose. Who is it for? Why is it needed? Is the language and style appropriate? Will this catch the attention of the audience? Will the audience be persuaded to read it?

The more you know about your target audience, the easier it is to produce a publication that is fit for purpose. To find out more you will need to ask questions like these.

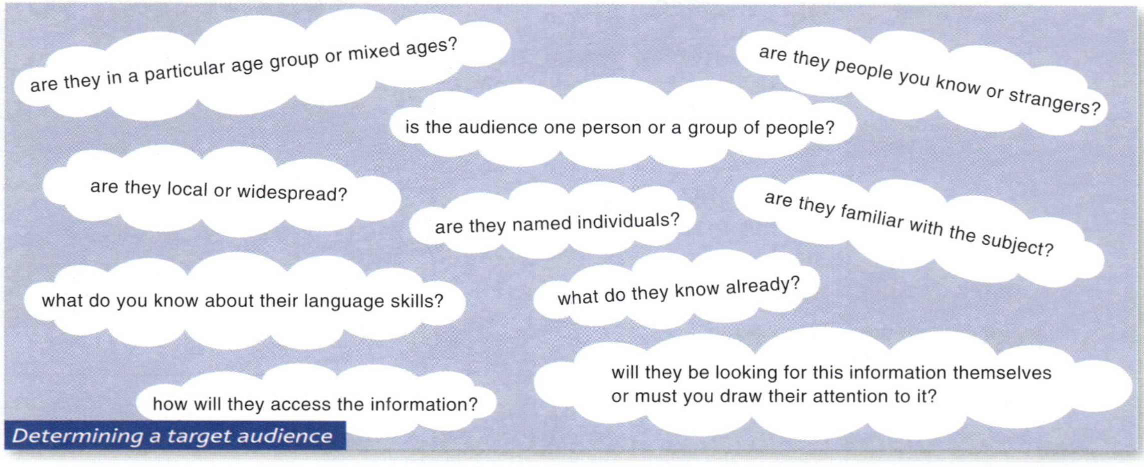

are they in a particular age group or mixed ages?
are they people you know or strangers?
is the audience one person or a group of people?
are they local or widespread?
are they named individuals?
are they familiar with the subject?
what do you know about their language skills?
what do they know already?
how will they access the information?
will they be looking for this information themselves
or must you draw their attention to it?

Determining a target audience

Once you are clear about your target audience you will know which types of publication are suitable and which can be rejected.

TALKING POINT 2.2

By looking at each of the publications below and the questions in the box above, try to work out the likely audience for each.

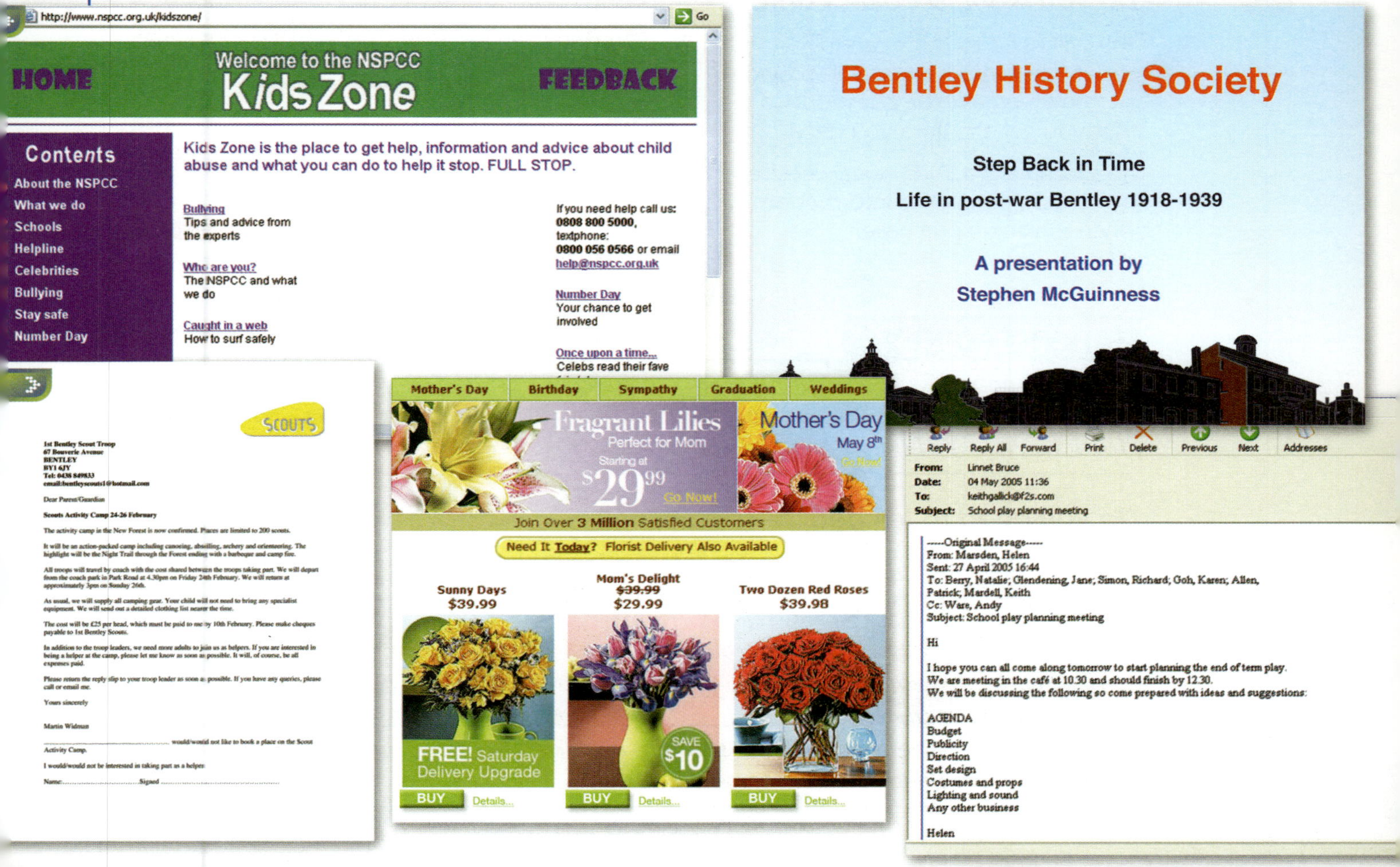

http://www.nspcc.org.uk/kidszone/

HOME | Welcome to the NSPCC Kids Zone | FEEDBACK

Contents
- About the NSPCC
- What we do
- Schools
- Helpline
- Celebrities
- Bullying
- Stay safe
- Number Day

Kids Zone is the place to get help, information and advice about child abuse and what you can do to help it stop. FULL STOP.

Bullying
Tips and advice from the experts

Who are you?
The NSPCC and what we do

Caught in a web
How to surf safely

If you need help call us: **0808 800 5000**, textphone: **0800 056 0566** or email help@nspcc.org.uk

Number Day
Your chance to get involved

Once upon a time...
Celebs read their fave

Bentley History Society

Step Back in Time

Life in post-war Bentley 1918-1939

A presentation by
Stephen McGuinness

SCOUTS

1st Bentley Scout Troop
67 Bouverie Avenue
BENTLEY
BY1 6JY
Tel: 0438 849833
email:bentleyscouts1@hotmail.com

Dear Parent/Guardian

Scouts Activity Camp 24-26 February

The activity camp in the New Forest is now confirmed. Places are limited to 200 scouts.

It will be an action-packed camp including canoeing, abseiling, archery and orienteering. The highlight will be the Night Trail through the Forest ending with a barbeque and camp fire.

All troops will travel by coach with the cost shared between the troops taking part. We will depart from the coach park in Park Road at 4.30pm on Friday 24th February. We will return at approximately 3pm on Sunday 26th.

As usual, we will supply all camping gear. Your child will not need to bring any specialist equipment. We will send out a detailed clothing list nearer the time.

The cost will be £25 per head, which must be paid to me by 10th February. Please make cheques payable to 1st Bentley Scouts.

In addition to the troop leaders, we need more adults to join us as helpers. If you are interested in being a helper at the camp, please let me know as soon as possible. It will, of course, be all expenses paid.

Please return the reply slip to your troop leader as soon as possible. If you have any queries, please call or email me.

Yours sincerely

Martin Widman

.... would/would not like to book a place on the Scout Activity Camp.

I would/would not be interested in taking part as a helper

Name:................................Signed ....

Mother's Day | Birthday | Sympathy | Graduation | Weddings

Fragrant Lilies
Perfect for Mom
Starting at $29.99 Go Now!

Mother's Day May 8th

Join Over 3 Million Satisfied Customers

Need It Today? Florist Delivery Also Available

Sunny Days $39.99 — FREE! Saturday Delivery Upgrade — BUY Details...

Mom's Delight ~~$39.99~~ $29.99 — SAVE $10 — BUY Details...

Two Dozen Red Roses $39.98 — BUY Details...

Reply | Reply All | Forward | Print | Delete | Previous | Next | Addresses

From: Linnet Bruce
Date: 04 May 2005 11:36
To: keithgallick@f2s.com
Subject: School play planning meeting

-----Original Message-----
From: Marsden, Helen
Sent: 27 April 2005 16:44
To: Berry, Natalie; Glendening, Jane; Simon, Richard; Goh, Karen; Allen, Patrick; Mardell, Keith
Cc: Ware, Andy
Subject: School play planning meeting

Hi

I hope you can all come along tomorrow to start planning the end of term play.
We are meeting in the café at 10.30 and should finish by 12.30.
We will be discussing the following so come prepared with ideas and suggestions:

AGENDA
Budget
Publicity
Direction
Set design
Costumes and props
Lighting and sound
Any other business

Helen

Why is it needed?

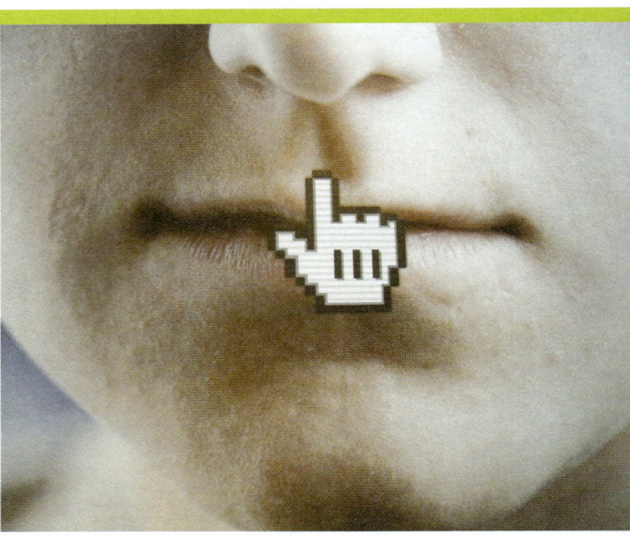

Once you are clear about who a publication is for, you need to think about why it is needed – the purpose of what you are doing.

There are a number of reasons why you might want to present information to a target audience.

Do you want to attract attention?

If you want people to notice information even though they were not looking for it, you need something that stands out such as a poster or advert.

TALKING POINT 2.3

What makes the NSPCC posters catch people's attention? Do you find pictures attract your attention more than words? Do you find certain colours attract you more than others?

Do you want to inform people?

If details need to be presented clearly and accurately, you may find that a paper-based publication such as a letter or memo is suitable. The letter from Martin the scout leader on page 19 is a good example.

Do you want to collect data?

You will need to think carefully about what information you provide and how you ask the questions so that you get the data you need.

An example is a DVD sales website which asks people for information when making a purchase.

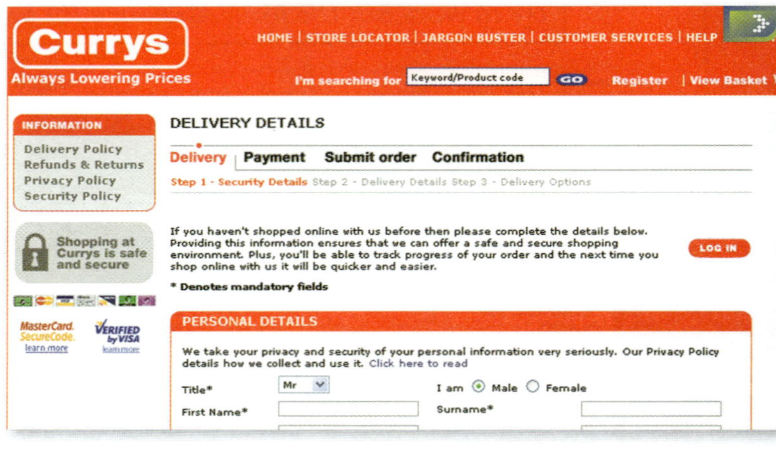

TALKING POINT 2.4

A questionnaire is used to gather data – usually as part of a survey. Look at this questionnaire. Who is the audience? Why do you think it is needed? Why do you think we need to find out people's opinions?

Do you need to tell people something?

If people need to know something, the information must be accurate. The type of publication will depend on where it has to be displayed. The safety rules for the ice rink are an example of this.

Ice Rink Rules

1 Please skate in a clockwise direction around the ice rink. Do not skate across the ice. Do not go back against the flow of skaters.
2 Any medical condition that may be affected by skating must be reported to a steward before skating.
3 Skates must be removed before leaving the rubber mats around the ice rink.
4 Climbing on the barriers around the rink is not permitted.
5 Smoking, alcohol, food and drink are not allowed on or near the rink.
6 Dangerous behaviour should be reported to a steward immediately.

TALKING POINT 2.5

Think of some other publications that are designed to tell people exactly what a situation is or exactly what is required.

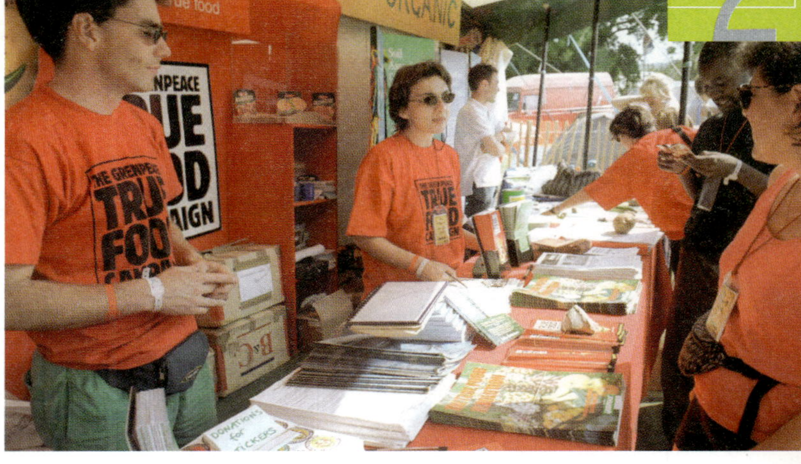

Do you want to persuade people?

Some publications are designed to convince people to take action. For example, a campaign poster may aim to persuade people that they should give money to charity or sign a petition. Others may try to convince people that they should buy a particular product.

TALKING POINT 2.6

Young people who visit an ice rink will be rushing to get on the ice. They are unlikely to take time to read a safety notice. Perhaps the council should produce something that catches their attention. How can this be done?

King's College Hospital NHS
NHS Trust
Arthroscopy of the knee joint
Information for day surgery patients

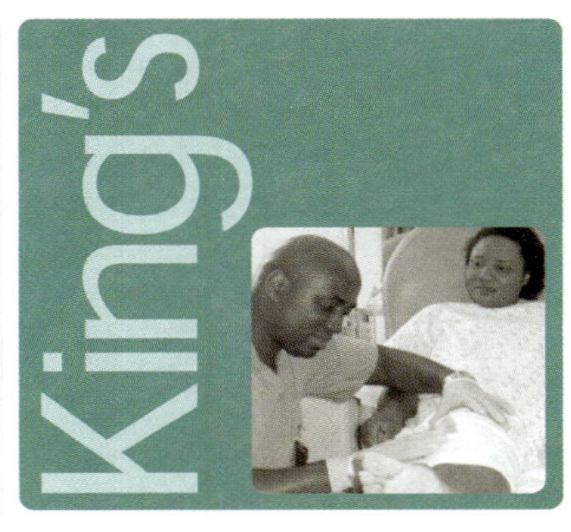

Do you want to explain something?

Where more detail is required to explain something, a publication may require large amounts of text or other components such as charts, tables and images.

Publications such as reports, letters, presentations and information points, are suitable for this.

Do you want to impress someone?

If you are trying to create a good impression of yourself, the type of publication, the content and the presentation are equally important. A job application letter or a CV that is badly presented is unlikely to result in an interview.

Curriculum Vitae

Name:	James Peter Edwards
Address:	19 Lordsbridge Road, Stanegate, NP20 4BD
Telephone:	220 993 428
Email:	james@lordsbridge.wx.yz
Date of Birth:	11 August 1987
Nationality:	British
Marital status:	Single
Driving licence:	Hold full motor vehicle driving licence, no penalty points
Education and Qualifications:	

TALKING POINT 2.7

Try to think of all the things that should be checked before the NSPCC sends a thank you letter to a sponsor.

Often a publication will have more than one purpose. A CV needs to provide information as well as create a good impression. Charity collectors need to attract attention and provide information as well as persuade people to donate.

▸▸ Activity 2.1

Work in groups to collect some examples of publications, both paper-based and on-screen. Identify the audience and purpose for each and highlight good and poor features. See if you can spot any mistakes such as incorrect spellings.

Where and what?

A publication is not much use if it does not reach the target audience! How will you get the information to them?

Where is the audience?

All in one room?

If the audience is gathered in one room, such as for a committee meeting or a training day, they will probably be presented with information as a group. A presentation with a speaker is an obvious choice to target this captive audience. You may want to prepare handouts or reports for people to take away with them.

Passing through?

Often your target audience will be passing through a location such as a reception area, a restaurant, a library, etc. but you do not know exactly who they are.

There are several choices depending on the purpose – for example, posters to attract their attention, an information point to help people find their way around, a leaflet or newsletter for them to take home.

All over the place but you know how to contact them

Letters, reports or emails can be sent if you have contact details. If you decide to set up a website you will still need to contact them to let them know the site address.

Anyone, anywhere?

If you do not know who the audience is, publications can be posted out using mailing lists. There is, though, a danger of this type of publication being seen as junk mail even if you use mail merge to personalise it.

If the information is likely to be of interest to people in a certain area, flyers or leaflets can be delivered through every letterbox in the area.

If you are not bothered that information is restricted to those with internet access then a website might be a good choice. This has the advantage that it can be accessed by far more people than you could ever reach by post.

What must go in it?

Once you know who, why and where you can think about what information is needed. This will affect the type of publication you need to produce. There is much more on this in Chapter 3 where you will think about what the audience needs to know, where you will find information and how to choose what text, images, etc to include. At this stage you need to know enough to be sure that you choose the right type of publication.

How do you go about it?

Choosing between different types of publication and styles of presentation will be much easier if you know exactly what you are trying to achieve. You have seen that you need to think about audience and purpose, where the information is to be made available and what content is needed before you can make a decision on the type of publication.

This diagram sums things up – memorise it, print it out, whatever it takes to remind you not to leap straight in and risk producing a publication that is not the best of the choices available.

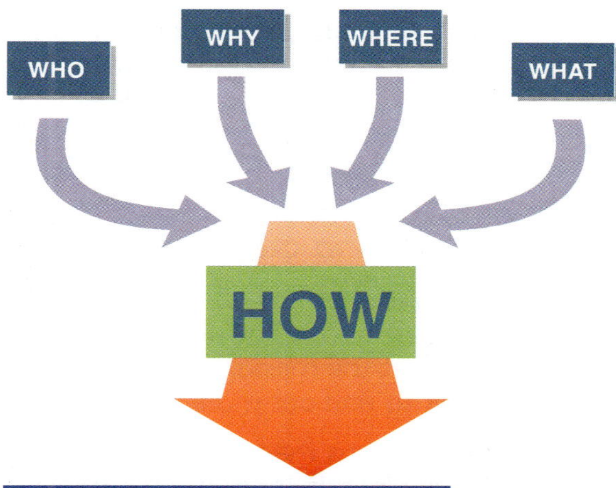

Think carefully before you decide how

Screen vs paper

Should the publication be available on screen or on paper? Sometimes the decision will be made for you – if you need to include multimedia elements such as sound then it will have to be screen-based. Anything that is to be mailed or handed out must be paper-based. Sometimes the audience will expect a certain type of publication.

Suppose you want to conduct a survey by asking people to complete a questionnaire. Should you hand it out locally, post it to people, use email or a web-based form? Unless you are sure that everyone you want to take part is able to complete the questionnaire on screen, you must produce at least some of them on paper.

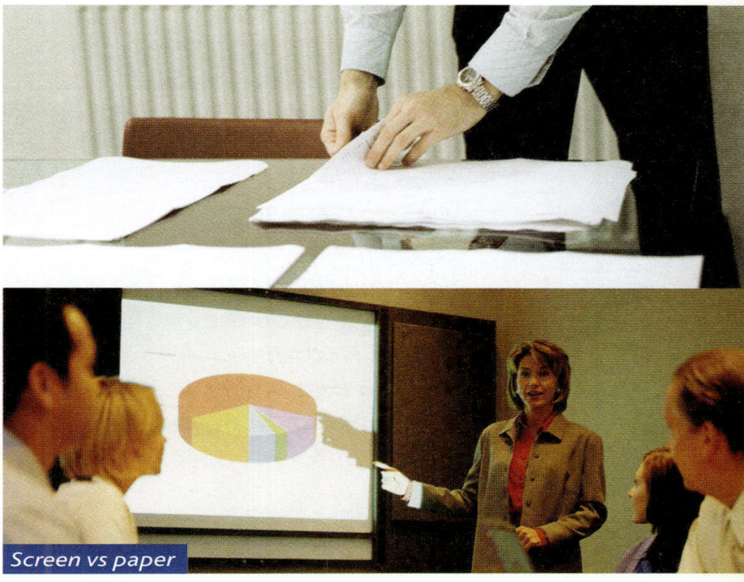

Screen vs paper

If you have a choice, how do you decide which is best? The answer is to focus on your audience.

- **Paper:** If there is a lot of text, people tend to read it more carefully on paper and if it is presented on screen they may want to print it off to read it. Even though DiDA students have chosen a computer-based course, many will choose to read text like this in the printed book. Some people prefer paper because they can read it any time, anywhere and don't need access to a computer. Others are concerned about environmental issues and like to keep the amount of paper they use to a minimum.
- **Screen:** Whilst text designed for the screen should not be too long, use can be made of multimedia features to illustrate what is being said. Presentations allow information to be communicated to groups of people at the same time. The internet makes information available to millions of people.

TALKING POINT 2.8

The Interactive Students' Pack has both printed and digital elements. Why do you think this is? How can you make best use of them?

Choosing the right type of publication

Your aim is to get the message across to the target audience as effectively as possible. There are many different types of publication for screen and print. If you need to choose one, where do you start?

One way is to decide on the type of audience you are dealing with. Publications are generally aimed at one of three types of audience.

Those who are not looking for information

The aim is to attract their attention to information even though they didn't know that they wanted it. The difficulty is that you don't really know who these people are. You will only get the message across if you can first attract their attention and then make them want to find out more. There is more on this in Chapter 6.

Publications that will help you do this include posters, flyers and web adverts. They need to be carefully presented as well as eye-catching. Sometimes publications attract attention for the wrong reasons, for example, because they are badly designed or there are spelling mistakes.

TALKING POINT 2.9

Both these publications stand out and catch your attention. Why? Do they make you want to read them? What impression do they give? Find all the things that need to be changed to make them fit for purpose.

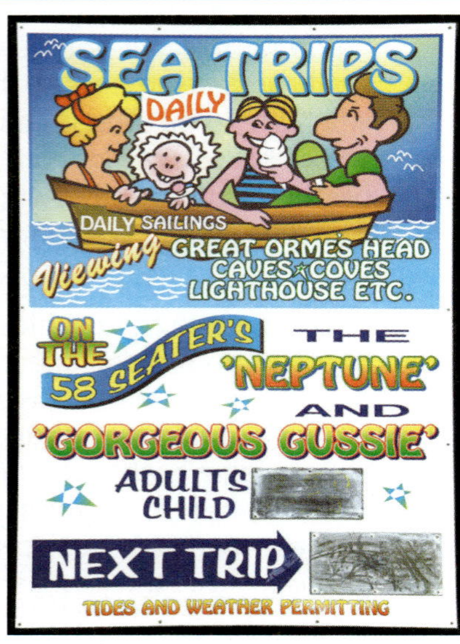

Those who are looking for information

The aim is to make information available to people who might be interested in it. They will find the information for themselves and you do not need to attract their attention. Even though you don't know exactly who these people are, you are likely to include more information than you would in something like a poster. Websites and leaflets are good examples of publications that will allow you to make information available to anyone who wants it – you can learn more about these in Chapter 7.

▸▸ Activity 2.2

Think of something you need to find out for one of your courses or interests. Find some websites about it. Do they give you information that you need? Is it presented in a way that makes it easy to find things? Is the information correct and up to date?

Those who need particular information

The aim is to provide information for people who need it. You know who they are and what they require. You can target individuals and groups using presentations, letters, and reports. Find out more about these types of publication in Chapter 8.

TALKING POINT 2.10

This is an example of a mail merge letter to members of a leisure club. It is targeted at individuals who belong to the club and assumes that they know some information already.

The writer knows who the audience is. What must the audience know already for this letter to make sense to them?

Niraj Patel
35 Sycamore Drive
BENTLEY
BY2 7RF

23 September 2005

Dear Niraj

We are delighted to inform you that you have the chance to upgrade your Silver card membership to a **Gold** card for just £5 extra. This will give you unlimited use of all fitness equipment including peak time sessions. You may also take part in one fitness class per week. If you wish to take advantage of this offer, please return the slip below. Payment can be made at your next visit but please call the membership secretary to register your upgrade as soon as possible.

Name: ....

Address: ....

....

Membership number: ....

I wish to upgrade my membership to a Gold card and will pay £5 at my next visit.

Getting the message across – a summary

Purpose	Examples of publications
To attract attention	Posters
	Flyers
To make information available	Leaflets
	Websites
	Information points
To target individuals or groups	Presentations
	Letters/mail merge
	Reports
	Newsletters

▸▸ Activity 2.3

Match each publication with an appropriate audience and purpose. Complete the last column to show whether the main aim is to attract attention, make information available or target individuals or groups.

Audience and purpose	Publication	Aim
Informing a customer that his central heating is due for a service	Article	
Informing office staff of the date of a Christmas party	Brochure	
Informing your supervisor of the common types of accidents that occur in the office	Fax	
Persuading people to take a holiday in the Caribbean	Letter	
Advertising a party in the College refectory	Memo	
Informing readers about the problems faced by homeless children in a city	Poster	
Providing information to fans of a pop group, giving up-to-date details of their tour dates	Presentation	
Giving information on a company to new employees at an induction	Report	
Sending a copy of some instructions to a technician who needs the information immediately	Web page	

2

How do you choose the style?

You can create a completely different impression by changing the language you use or the way you present information.

Choosing a writing style

The writing style you use will depend on who is going to read the information and what it is for. Should it be formal or informal, written for adults or for children, tell the audience something or try to persuade them? The informal style we use for an email to a friend is very different to the formal style required for a report to a company director. Choose a style that suits the purpose.

Activity 2.4

Don't be tempted to include big or fancy words in an attempt to impress someone. Make sure that the language is appropriate for the audience. Each of the sentences in the table uses a word that is not commonly used and which some people will not understand. Use a dictionary or thesaurus to find more commonly used words to replace the 'fancy' words. They should not change the meaning too much.

Fancy wording	Simple word
Please find attached ***an abridgement*** of my findings.	
Many people in this city live in ***affluent*** areas.	
Thank you for being so ***candid*** with me when describing your part in this incident.	
I feel we must be ***circumspect*** in the way we handle this sensitive issue.	
Please ***disseminate*** the information you learned from the course.	
I am grateful for your ***forbearance*** in this matter. I will deal with your complaint as soon as possible.	
We have had a number of thefts recently. Please be ***vigilant*** at all times.	

Activity 2.5

Visit the website for the BBC. Compare the writing style used for different sections including health, business and children. Is the style formal or informal? Is the language simple? Does the style suit the likely audience?

Choosing a presentation style

The presentation style will also need to be just right. Again you need to decide what impact you are trying to achieve – should the publication attract attention, appeal to children, look professional, impress someone, etc? The type of publication and the writing style will help to set the scene but presentation styles such as fonts, colours, layout, etc will affect the impression you give.

TALKING POINT 2.11

Compare these two versions of Martin's letter. What impression does each give? How do the writing styles and presentation styles differ?

Design and prototyping

It is very tempting to go straight to your computer and create your publication without stopping to think. Even if you are very experienced this will probably show up in your final publication. Before you create any publication you must design it. Keep reminding yourself of the audience and purpose. You will be continually reminded of design principles as you work through these materials.

You should not expect to get it right first time. Produce a prototype – a draft version – test it yourself and ask others for comments.

Test it yourself

Check that your publication matches your design. Check for accuracy and consistency – use the spellchecker and proofread it carefully. Imagine an audience and read aloud what you have written as if they were present. If anything sounds clumsy or too long, or boring, then have another look at the way you have written it. Check that all other content is fit for purpose. This includes images and other components.

Get others to test it

As you develop a publication you should ask suitable people to comment on your prototypes. These people will include:

- test users who are similar to the target audience
- your peers
- your teacher.

You must make sure you get the feedback you need – tell your test users what you want them to comment on. Tell them that you want the truth, it is no help just to be nice! You could help them with their feedback by producing a questionnaire or form to complete.

If the publication is designed to be read by your audience, get someone to read it and tell you what they think of it. If it is designed to be presented to an audience, ask someone to comment on your presentation of it.

If you are asked to test or review work, try to be as helpful as you can. Say what is good about something but *only* if it is good. Test a publication thoroughly and try to 'bust' it. Try to think of everything that a member of the target audience might do!

Activity 2.6

Young people who visit an ice rink will be rushing to get on the ice. They are unlikely to take time to read a safety notice. The manager of the ice rink has asked you to produce a poster that will attract children's attention and persuade them to take notice of the safety rules. Remind yourself of who, why and where this publication is for and then design and create a suitable poster. The rules can be found in this file. Include suitable images.

Produce a questionnaire for your test users, making sure that you are looking for helpful criticism as well as praise! Keep improving and testing until you are sure that your poster is fit for purpose.

The production cycle

Once you and others have tested a prototype, go back to your design to incorporate feedback, make changes to the prototype and then test it again. Repeat this process as many times as necessary – keep going back to the design until you are absolutely sure that it is fit for purpose and you are ready to publish the final version.

This diagram represents the production cycle. Keep it in mind every time you develop a publication.

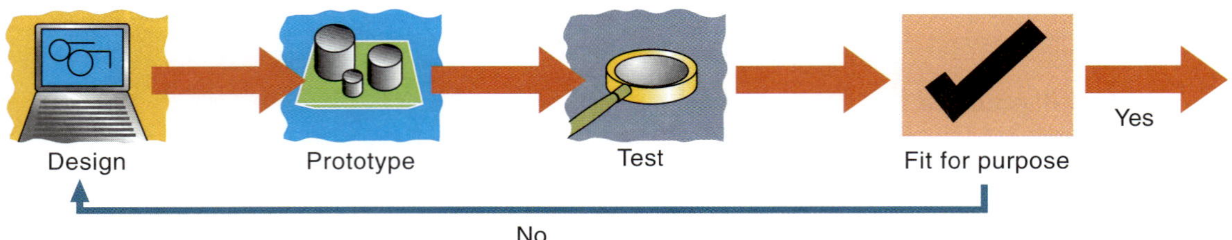

This is the production cycle. Use the loop back as many times as necessary – keep going back to the design until you are absolutely sure that it is fit for purpose.

TALKING POINT 2.12

Look again at Martin's letter on page 19. His target audience were parents/guardians of scouts in the area. He didn't know their names or addresses. He didn't know much about their language skills.

What feedback would you give Martin? Look particularly at the language and style of the letter. Will it all make sense to the target audience? What about the layout and format of the letter? Is it all correct?

Keeping records of feedback

You need to keep careful records of feedback you receive and changes you make as a result. For the SPB, a moderator will want to see evidence of how you made use of feedback. There are several ways you can do this.

Report

The simplest way to record comments from others is by typing up the feedback in a report. For example, Charlotte is a DiDA student who asked her teacher for feedback on a questionnaire. She would need to include her draft questionnaire, this report and the final version in her eportfolio.

Comments on my questionnaire

Mrs Jones is my ICT teacher. I showed her my first attempt at the questionnaire. She liked most of the questions I asked but thought that Question 1 was not needed. She suggested that I make Question 2 simpler and that I should add another answer to Question 4b for saving energy. She said that people would not know what the survey was about so I should write an introduction. She also noticed the word 'warning' should be warming in question 2 and said I should not rely on the spellchecker so much. The rest of her comments were about layout – the boxes and numbers need to be lined up.

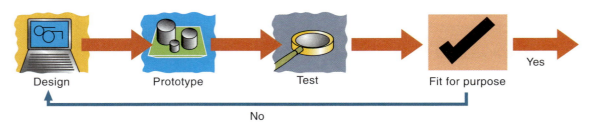

Annotation

Comments can be added using text boxes or comments/notes if your software has these features. Here is the prototype of the questionnaire that Charlotte showed to Mrs Jones, annotated to show her feedback. It is very easy to compare the comments with the revised version alongside.

Alternative energy

Needs an introduction explaining what survey is for.

1a. Are you under the age of 21? YES NO

Don't need questions 1a,b unnecessary.

If answer is no finish here.

Can you make question 2 a bit clearer?

1b. Please state your age ....

2. On a scale of 1-5 how aware are you of the problems with global warning (1 being unaware, 5 being very aware)

1 2 3 4 5

Line the numbers up with the boxes

3. On a scale of 1-5 how concerned are you about these problems?

1 2 3 4 5

Line these boxes up with the ones in question 2

4a. Do you actively do anything to try and help these problems?

YES NO

Do you think Mrs Jones will like the revised version?

Alternative energy survey

This questionnaire is for people aged between 14 and 21. I have designed this questionnaire to find out how much teenagers know about the energy problems in the world today. My aim is also to find out whether you are doing anything to help the energy problem, or if not whether you would be willing to start trying. Thank you for your time!

1. On a scale of 1-5 how aware are you of problems caused by global warming (1 being unaware, 5 being very aware)

1 2 3 4 5

2. On a scale of 1-5 how concerned are you about these problems?

1 2 3 4 5

3a. Do you actively do anything to try and help these problems?

YES NO

3b. If you answered YES to 4a please tick the category that your type of help fits into:

Sound and video

You might consider recording some of the feedback you receive.

Of course, sound and video files are bigger than text files so you will not be able to use them for everything. Use one of these methods if it really is better than text.

Screen activity

Another method is to use special software to record the changes as you make them. You can record a commentary explaining what is happening. This method can be used to show how you do something but in this case it is to show what you did as a result of comments.

All of these methods are perfectly acceptable for Unit 1. You will need to discuss the possibilities with your teacher and find out what equipment and software is available.

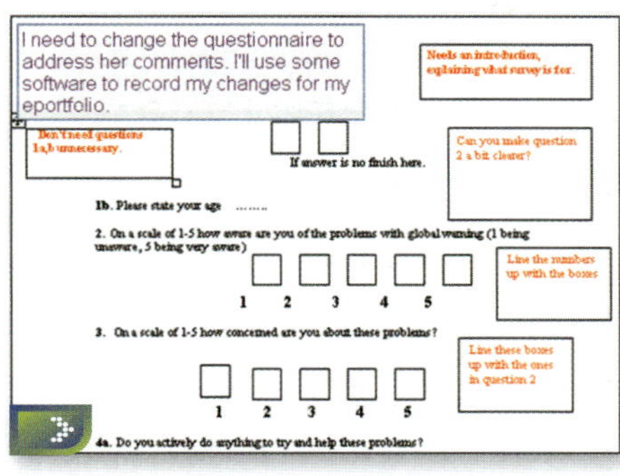

▸▸ Activity 2.7

Imagine that you have to organise work experience for yourself for a period of two weeks next term. Decide where you would like to work and write a formal letter asking for a placement.

Make sure that you use a formal letter layout and that you include enough information about yourself and what you want. Your aim is to persuade the employer to take you on. If you need to be reminded of what a formal letter should include, you will find this information in Chapter 8.

Work in pairs and review each other's letter as if you were the employer. Record your reviewer's comments and changes you made. Try out different methods for recording the feedback. Go through the production cycle as many times as necessary until your letter is fit for purpose.

Tackling **The Project**

Although **The Project** brief has most of the features of a real SPB, you will be asked to tackle sections as you work through the book so some of the planning is done for you!

We have looked at what you need to know if you are going to produce publications that are fit for purpose.

The Project requires you to produce a range of digital publications for screen and print. Read through **The Project** brief so that you have a good idea of what you have to do.

Use ICT to create a table similar to this.

Product	Who	Why	Where	What	How	Style

For each of the publications in **The Project**, enter as much detail as you can by answering these questions:

- **Who** is the target audience? What do I know about them?
- **Why** is it needed?
- **Where** is it for?
- **What** must go in it?
- **How** will you go about it? What type is best? Which medium – screen or paper?

Modify the table structure if you can think of a better way of recording the information.

Add another column called Testing and decide who you will ask to give you feedback on each publication. Try to think of people who are similar to the target audience and who will give you honest comments as you work on the various publications.

You will be able to add more detail to this table as you go along.

You must save the document in one of the folders you created for your work on **The Project**. Select the correct folder and save it as WHICHPUBS.

3 Making use of information sources

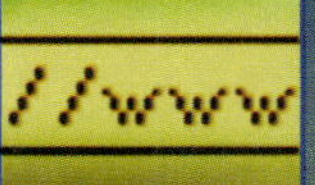

Digimodule

This safety notice is displayed at an ice rink. The notice was created by Max Heathcote, the Health and Safety officer for Bentley council.

Max used the internet to find out about safety issues related to ice skating. Websites are examples of secondary sources – information that has been produced by other people. Secondary sources are not always kept up to date and some are inaccurate. You will learn how to choose good sources and select suitable information.

Max was worried that some of the information was not up to date and might not be correct so he talked to the safety officers at other ice rinks. This is an example of a primary source – Max gathered new information himself by asking people questions.

There are many ways of gathering information and you will need to choose methods that are suitable for the purpose you have in mind. If you decide to reproduce other people's information, you must acknowledge the source in your own publication and you may need to ask permission to use it.

In this chapter you will learn how to make use of information sources by:

- ***deciding what information you need***
- ***finding, selecting and capturing information from secondary sources***
- ***selecting suitable primary sources***
- ***checking that information is accurate and unbiased***
- ***recording and acknowledging sources of information***

3

What content is needed?

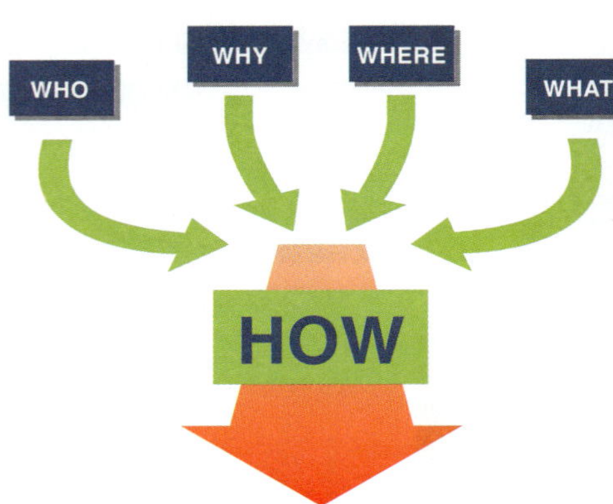
WHO
WHY
WHERE
WHAT
HOW

No apologies for repeating this information from Chapter 2 here! Before you can start looking for content for a publication you must know who it is for, why it is needed and where it is to be used.

Each publication will have two types of content:

- necessary information – what the audience needs to know
- other content to help get the message across effectively.

You will almost certainly include text but perhaps you need other types of content such as images or sound. You can jot your thoughts down in a list or you can use something called a mind map.

Using mind mapping to help you

A mind map is a useful way to bounce ideas around and make sure that you understand what is required. It also allows you to divide the work up into logical sections so that you can plan how you will tackle it.

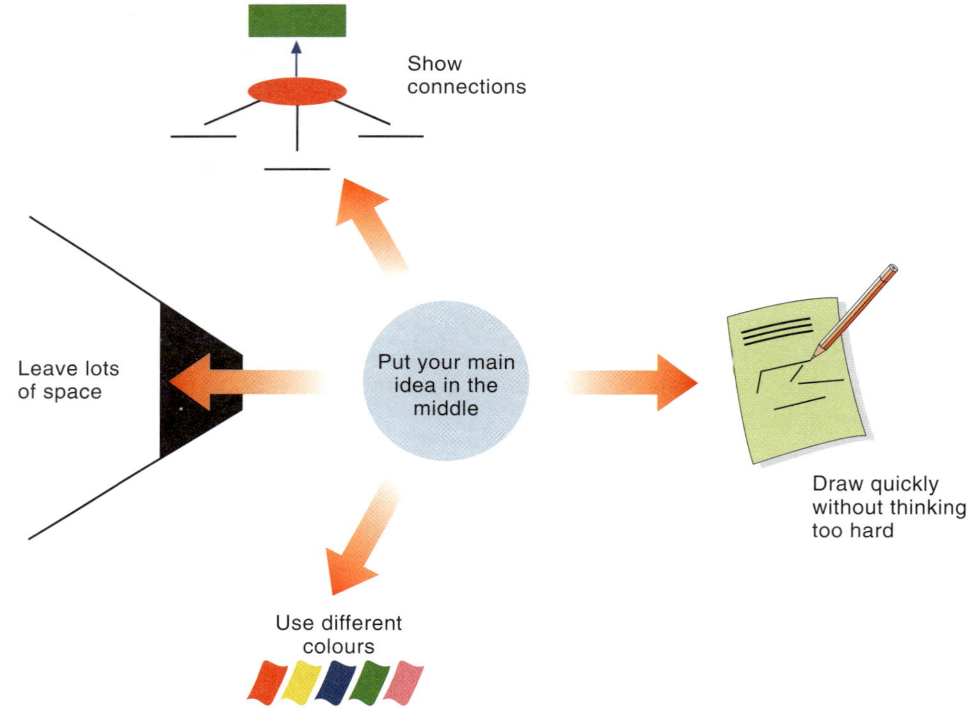
Show connections
Leave lots of space
Put your main idea in the middle
Draw quickly without thinking too hard
Use different colours

How to do a mind map – click on each section to find out more

- **Start by putting your main idea in the middle.** It usually helps to use landscape format with all your ideas coming out from the centre.
- **Draw quickly without thinking too hard.** The idea of mind mapping is to think creatively and to get everything you can think of written down – you can always change it later.
- **Use different colours** to make things stand out or to group different topics.
- **Show connections.** Use lines or arrows to show connections between the ideas.
- **Leave lots of space.** This will allow you to add things as you go along.

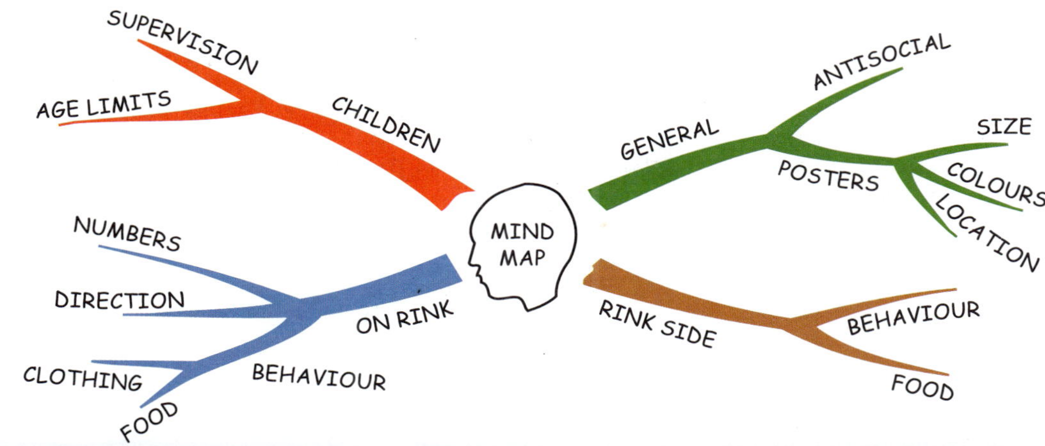

This example shows a simple mind map that Max might have produced to help him with his safety notice

Look at how the mind map is used to sort the various requirements out into logical sections. Mind mapping software is available to help you prepare mind maps but you can use any software that allows you to create diagrams – or you can hand draw them.

▸▸ Activity 3.1

You have to give a 20 minute presentation to new students at your school/ college explaining access to ICT facilities and rules for using them. Produce a mind map outlining the areas you will cover. For example, viruses, misuse of the internet, use of email, etc. Concentrate on one topic at a time and show connections between ideas.

What does the audience need to know?

Think carefully about what information the audience needs. The amount of detail you need to provide will depend on the audience and purpose.

What does the audience know already?

If you are quite sure that everyone in your audience knows something about the subject already, there is no need to include this information in the publication. For example, this book does not include information on how to enter text using a word processor because DiDA students know how to do that already.

The magistrate is likely to impose a detention and training order.

He's in a lot of trouble and may end up in jail.

Watch the video clip. What assumptions does Dan make about the audience in each of his statements?

How much detail is required?

Does all the information have to be included in this publication or are other publications being produced to go with it? If flyers are available to people who read a poster, you may decide to include less information on the poster. If you are producing a slide presentation, perhaps there will be handouts or a report to go with it. Speaker notes also allow the presenter to give extra information without putting it on the slides.

What style of presentation is required?

The way in which the information must be presented will affect what content you need. You must consider the amount of detail required, writing style, the types of image and the amount of space available.

For example, the types of image will need to match the text. A formal style of language is unlikely to be accompanied by comic cartoons. A slide presentation requires short phrases and clear illustrations that will be effective on a big screen.

Using ICT rooms

- No food or drink to be taken into the rooms
- All bags must be placed under chairs
- Any disks brought into school must be checked to see that they are virus-free before being used in any of the ICT rooms

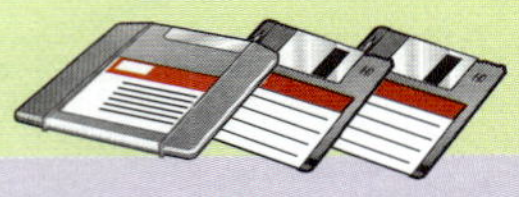

See how the main points are set out clearly leaving the speaker to fill in the details.

What else do you need?

Once you have a clear idea of what must be included, you can think about what else you could include to help get the message across. For example:

- headings and sub-headings
- images
- sound or video
- animation.

Your list will now be complete and include both necessary information and other content.

What information do you have already?

If you look at your list, you may find that you have some of the content already. You may know some of the information. Do you know enough about the subject? Do you need to carry out some research to gather information?

TALKING POINT 3.1

There is a proposal to close down the local cinema. You have been asked to prepare some information for the town council meeting.

There are many issues to look at including:

- *Why do they want to close it?*
- *How many people use it each day?*
- *What films are being shown and at what times?*
- *Where is the nearest cinema if this one closes?*
- *Why do people go to the cinema?*

How should the information be presented? What other questions need to be asked – use mind mapping to help you make sure the list is complete. Where would you get the information?

Making life easier for yourself

Using the same information again

When you are working on a big project like the SPB you will find that the same information can be used more than once because the publications have something in common. For example, if you are planning handouts to go with a presentation, you may find that the same image can be used in both. Not only does this save you time when gathering information, it also links the two publications together in a positive way.

This can also be useful when you have to prepare similar information for different audiences. The notice for the ice rink is very formal and very few children and teenagers will stop to read it. Well, be honest, would you?

Max asked his assistant, Lindsay, to produce this poster. The message is that people can only use the ice rink if they follow the rules. Finding the information was easy for Lindsay. She only needed to use one secondary source – Max's notice. She realised that an image would attract attention and took the photograph herself.

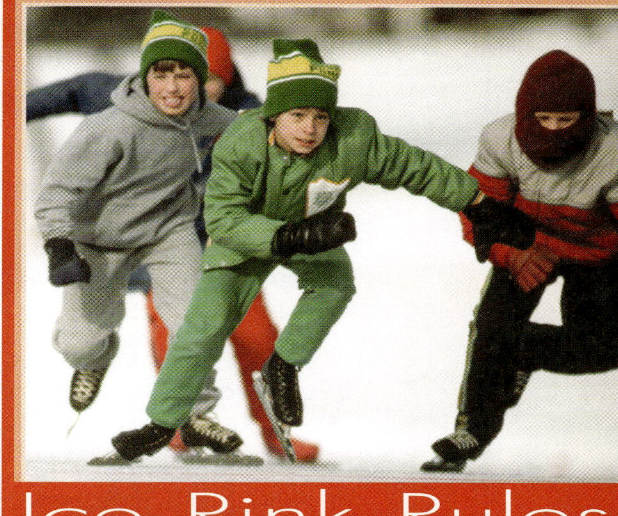

Ice Rink Rules
1 Please skate in a clockwise direction around the ice rink. Do not skate across the ice. Do not go back against the flow of skaters.
2 Any medical condition that may be affected by

Which do you think you would notice – this poster or Max's original one?

TALKING POINT 3.2

Look again at the mind map or list of information you produced for Talking Point 3.1. Think of two other purposes that some of this information could be used for. Who is the audience in each case? What types of publication would be suitable?

Planning your search

You will save a great deal of time if you plan out what information you need to gather before you start looking. If you are going to take the trouble to use the internet, go to the library or capture images at a certain location, it makes sense to do as much as you can in one visit. Using a summary sheet helps you to work out exactly what you will need and to plan your time efficiently.

Keeping the information safe

Keep an accurate record of where you get information from so that you can easily revisit a source when you need to.

If you need to gather a whole range of information – text, images, sound and video – for use in various publications, how do you store it so that you can find items easily?

Chapter 1, page 14, looks at file management. You will need to devise a folder structure to store all the information you gather for a publication or a project. Don't forget to use file and folder names that make sense to you. Sometimes you will store the information itself and sometimes you will decide to store a link to it.

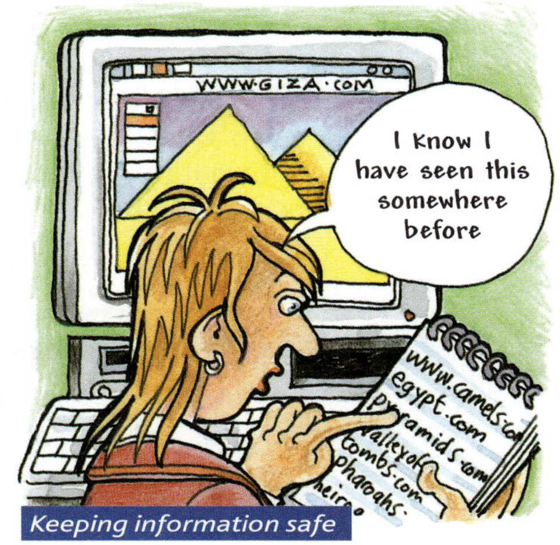

Keeping information safe

Information sources

How will you gather the information you need? Will you use information that is already available or create it yourself?

Secondary sources

Secondary sources

If someone else already has some information you need then it makes sense to consider using it as this will save time. But beware – it may not be as good as it looks!

If you use information that has been produced by someone else then you are using a secondary source. For example, you might:

- analyse data that someone else has collected, perhaps using a spreadsheet or database
- search on the internet
- search in other places – books, magazines, CDs, etc.

Often you will need to use a combination of different secondary sources.

Primary sources

In most projects, you will start by finding out what information is already available from secondary sources and then fill the gaps using primary sources – where you capture information first-hand. For example:

- photographs, drawings or other images that are not already available
- surveys to gather data for analysis
- interviews to find out opinions or to ask for information
- observing a situation to find something out
- using sound recording to capture information.

Using primary sources often means making use of other people's experience and knowledge and can take far more time than using secondary sources.

If you decide to gather information yourself then it is up to you to control what you collect. For example, if you carry out a survey, the way you ask questions and the people you choose to interview will affect the answers you get. It is not acceptable to collect information from other people without them knowing about it. For example, you must ask permission before you take a photo of someone or record what they are saying.

You will learn how to make effective use of primary sources in other parts of this book.

TALKING POINT 3.3

There are many ways of gathering information from primary sources, such as digital cameras, video cameras, interviews, etc. Discuss the methods that Bliss magazine uses and the advantages and disadvantages of each.

Using secondary sources

Paper-based sources

These include:

- newspapers and magazines
- books
- maps and drawings
- printed images
- directories such as Yellow Pages.

You will often find more information than you need – long pieces of text – and you will need to select only those sections that are relevant.

TALKING POINT 3.4

One way to identify main points of information in an article or long piece of text is to highlight the first sentence of each paragraph and then read through these sentences. This should give you the main points or gist of the article. What other methods could you use?

Internet sources

Using a search engine

The internet is not like a library where staff can monitor what is available. Anyone can publish just about anything. Not only does this mean that a lot of the information you find will be unsuitable, it also means that you can easily end up with far too much.

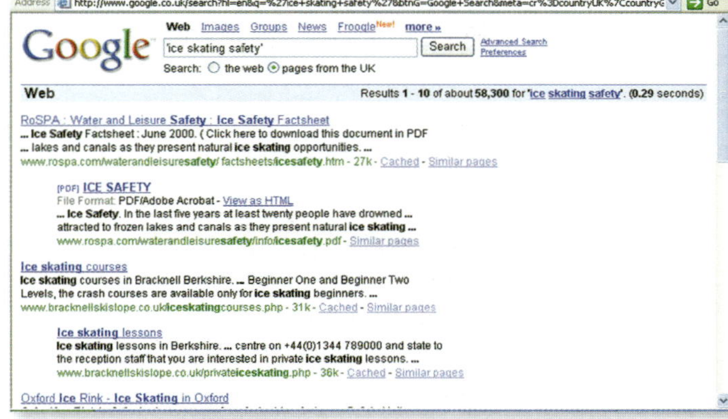

Always think carefully about what you are trying to do and what information you need.

When Max was looking for information for his safety notice, he used an internet search engine called Google and entered the keywords 'ice skating safety' – this came up with over 360,000 results or hits!

By restricting the search to pages from the UK, the number of hits was reduced to 50,000.

Refining the search

If you have too many search results, or results that are not relevant, you will need to refine the search. Think again about what you are looking for.

Max refined his search by adding the keyword 'rules' and this reduced the number of results to about 10,000. Max looked at some of the sites. He found that some were out of date and some did not seem very reliable. He selected some information and made a note of where he got it from.

When you are searching for information on the internet, think carefully about what you actually want so that you can refine your search and avoid information overload. However, be sure to try out a number of sites. Don't rely on the first one you visit.

TALKING POINT 3.5

How could Max have refined his search further?

⏩ Activity 3.2

Try out Max's search using Google, and other search engines. How many hits do you get in each case? Try refining the search using the ideas from Talking Point 3.5.

Entering search criteria

The internet is a very useful tool for finding information but, like any other tool, it is only useful if you use it correctly. You must be careful to type in correct search criteria.

⏩ Activity 3.3

Open the file which contains this table:

Criterion	Result (No of Hits)	Explanation
London Accomodation		
London Accommodation		
Shakespear		
Shakespeare		
Nokia or Samsung		
Nokia OR Samsung		
Nokia AND Samsung		
John Lennon lives on		
"John Lennon lives on"		

Use any search engine and type in each word *exactly* as it is written and record the number of hits. Make sure you understand what happens when you use AND, OR or " ".

You will notice that incorrectly spelled keywords can provide you with some hits. That's because the internet does not leave out sites with poor spelling – which goes to prove that not everything on the internet is reliable!

TALKING POINT 3.6

Compare your results with those of your peers. Which search engines did you use? What difference does it make?

Why use the internet?

Don't assume that the internet is always better than using paper-based sources, even if you prefer looking at a screen. There are advantages and disadvantages to each. Often it is best to use both, compare the results and then select the most useful information. Look out for sources that contradict one another, such as contact details for a business. You will need to explore further to decide which is right.

⏩ Activity 3.4

Yellow Pages is a paper-based business telephone directory. There is an internet version called yell.com. Find out the locations and phone numbers of pet shops in your area using each of these sources. What are the advantages and disadvantages of each source? Which is more up to date?

Using databases

Often you will use a database to find information – finding books and DVDs in the library, shopping on the internet and in many other situations.

If you are using results that someone else has produced, you need to be confident that the information is what it claims to be.

As part of your work for Unit 1 you will learn how to create a database to store a set of data so that you can extract useful information. If you are designing searches yourself, take great care to produce correct information and check that results are as expected.

Never assume that results are correct just because a search appears to work. A common error is to enter the wrong search criterion.

Height over 150cm

ID	Family name	Given name	Title	Height (cm)
5	Almeida	Ana	Ms	155
13	Armstrong-Brown	Kieran	Mr	150
21	Young	Alison	Dr	167
24	Tesfa	Fasil	Mr	180
57	Walls	John	Mr	185
61	Schneider	Emma	Mrs	162

This report should list people in a database who are more than 150 cm tall but if you look carefully you will see that it is not correct. In fact the student entered >=150 as the criterion and included one person whose height was exactly 150cm.

Broadcast media

For up-to-date information on current events, radio and television are useful secondary sources. They have the advantage that access is easier, even when travelling.

Television provides an effective combination of sound and visual effects. The impact of major events such as the 2004 tsunami is far greater on screen than it can be in print or on the radio.

Teletext provides access to a wide range of information, much of which is kept up to date and does not, of course, require internet access.

One of the advantages of broadcast media is that, unlike the internet, most content is independently checked before it is released but you should be aware that many programmes offer personal opinions as well as facts.

Avoiding plagiarism

Plagiarism means presenting someone else's information or ideas without clearly acknowledging the source of the information. There have been cases of well-known people being prosecuted for stealing ideas and information from others. There is some very good software that can detect similarities in students' work – so be warned!

DiDA students are expected to understand that plagiarism is treated very seriously and you should keep these rules in mind at all times:

- You must work independently and produce your own work.
- If you copy from secondary sources, you must show clearly what you have used and acknowledge the source.
- If you summarise information from a source in your own words, you must still acknowledge it.
- You must not, under any circumstances, use another student's work.

3 Capturing information

Getting organised

You may find it helpful to draw up a table including each item of information needed, whether you have it already or, if not, where you will look for it.

What I need	✓	Primary	Secondary	Permission
Information about the influence of league football on children's behaviour		• Capture sound recording of comments by children in local primary school • Interview parents	• Internet search • TV documentary	• Record sources • Ask permission from parents

This table was produced by a student who was working on a project about children and sport, with a focus on football

Activity 3.5

Imagine that you are going to collect all the information for the cinema report. Create a summary of where you would find the information and decide how you would store it.

Finding the information you need is only the first stage in the process. You need to capture this information in a way that is:

- easily stored electronically
- easily found when you want it
- acknowledged correctly.

Capturing images

There are a number of ways of capturing images to use in your work. Some are primary sources and some are secondary. You can:

- draw an image using drawing software
- draw an image by hand and scan in the image
- scan in an image from a paper-based resource, such as an article, a photograph
- use a digital camera to record images and transfer these to your computer
- use the camera on your mobile phone to record images and download these to your computer.

Paper-based images can be captured using a scanner. The quality you need will depend on the way the image will be used – print or screen, image size, etc. You will probably have to compromise between quality and file size but do not use a copy of an image if it is not good enough.

As with text, you must not use other people's images without acknowledgement and you should not edit them in any way without permission.

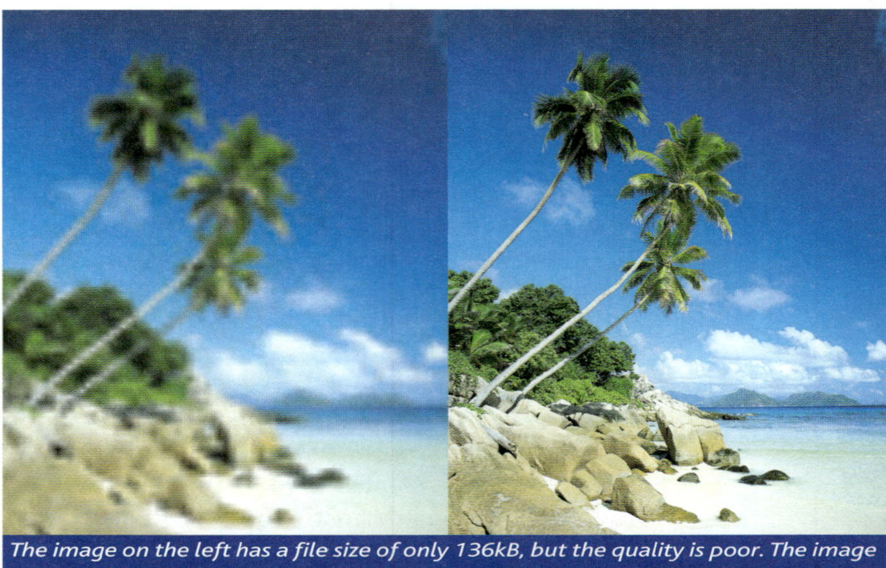

The image on the left has a file size of only 136kB, but the quality is poor. The image on the right is much better, it has a file size of 3.5MB.

Capturing text

- If you only need a short paragraph, you may decide to copy text by typing it into a word processor.
- If the text is quite long, you could capture it using a scanner. This will result in an image of the text which can be pasted into any publication but it cannot be edited.
- Although it is not a requirement for Unit 1, you might want to use special software that can recognise the text in the scanned image and convert it into a form that can be edited.

Whatever you do, remember that the text belongs to someone else. Do not use it without acknowledging the source, even if you rewrite it in your own words. Ask permission if necessary.

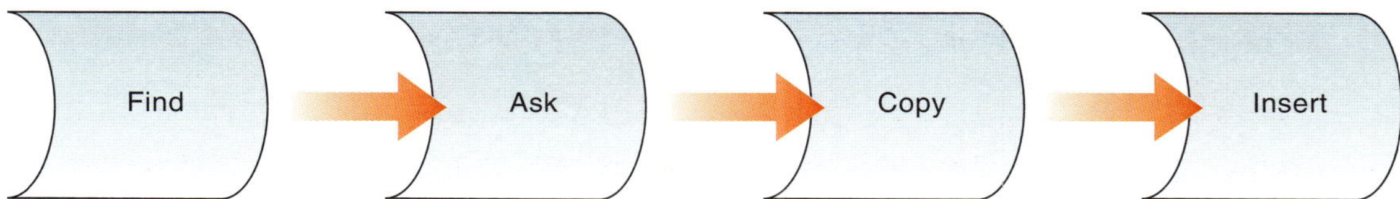

Activity 3.6

Open the file which contains this table:

Method	P/S	Advantages	Disadvantages
Using drawing software		1 2	1 2
Scanning in a drawing		1 2	1 2
Scanning a printed image		1 2	1 2
Scanning a photograph		1 2	1 2
Using a digital camera		1 2	1 2
Using a mobile phone camera		1 2	1 2

Complete the table to show advantages and disadvantages of each method. Show whether the source can be primary (P), secondary (S) or both.

Can I do this?

Using suitable equipment, make sure you can:

Scan an image
Change the settings for a scan
Crop and resize scanned text and images
Use a digital camera

Activity 3.7

Practise capturing printed information and capturing images. Experiment with image size and resolution. Make sure that you can crop and resize material that you have scanned.

Capturing information from the internet

If you are using the internet, you are in danger of information overload as soon as you start. Printing off reams of information from a website is not going to be much help. You need to select material that is relevant. Even if you refine your search carefully and find a particularly useful website, it will probably contain many pages of information that are not really what you want.

Depending on what you want the information for, you can:

- take notes
- extract and store the information
- record the location of information so that you can go back to it later.

You can select, copy and paste the sections you need into another file such as a word processing document.

Can I do this?

To capture information from the internet you need to be able to:

Use an internet browser
Use a search engine
Refine searches using keywords and operators
Bookmark a page
Copy and paste a link
Copy and paste information

Activity 3.8

Go to the Penguin Books website – use it to practise capturing information.

Capture some short paragraphs and images by copying and pasting into a document.

Choose a whole page and store the full address for it in the document – do not copy the page itself.

Using the internet safely

The internet allows you access to almost unlimited information but you should be aware of the dangers.

- Never give out personal information like your name, address, or phone number – some sites encourage you to register your details.
- Use only your log-in name and/or email address when sending email.
- Always delete unknown email attachments without opening them. They can contain destructive viruses.
- Even innocent sounding keywords can sometimes bring up inappropriate information – if this happens, let someone know.
- *When in doubt* – ask for help – and just *log off* if you're not sure! You can always go back online later.

Capturing information from your database

If you have found information using database searches, you can easily capture this information by saving the search results using the database software. You will then be able to use these results in reports and other publications. More of this in Chapter 5.

Capturing information from broadcast media

- **Taking notes:** You may want to jot down notes from a radio or television broadcast or from an interview.
- **Recording sound from radio:** You can capture the sound recording, either directly from the radio or using the internet. Many radio programmes are available over the internet and some offer the opportunity to listen to programmes again at a later date. You might simply include some of the information in text form, but if it is to be included in a screen-based publication you might include a short sound clip.
- **Recording from TV:** As with radio, you can choose to take notes or record the programme using sound or video equipment. If you decide to use video, remember that you could easily end up with some massive files.

Recording sound from radio

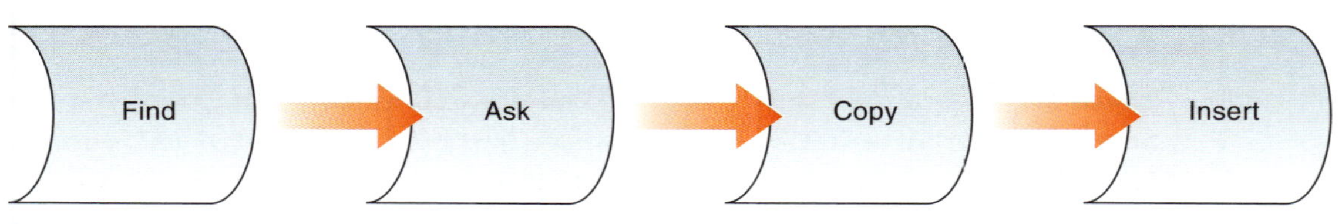

Don't forget!

▸▸ Activity 3.9

Explore the BBC website – look at BBC Online and see what is available. What can you listen to or watch live? What programmes are available after broadcast and for how long? What is available for live streaming? What subject areas are covered? Practise capturing information using different methods.

Checking it out

Never assume that information you find is everything you want it to be. Check it out!

- Websites are often not checked for accuracy.
- Personal opinions can affect what people tell you.
- You can influence what people say by how you ask them questions.
- An incorrect search criterion when using the internet or a database can produce the wrong set of information.
- Look for evidence of bias. For example, if you want accurate information on a football club, would you look at the official website or one set up by a fan?
- Check that the source of the information is clearly stated.
- Different sources do not always agree.

TALKING POINT 3.7

Information can sometimes be made to convey a particular message by the way it is presented. Look at the chart. Do you think it is a fair representation of the information?

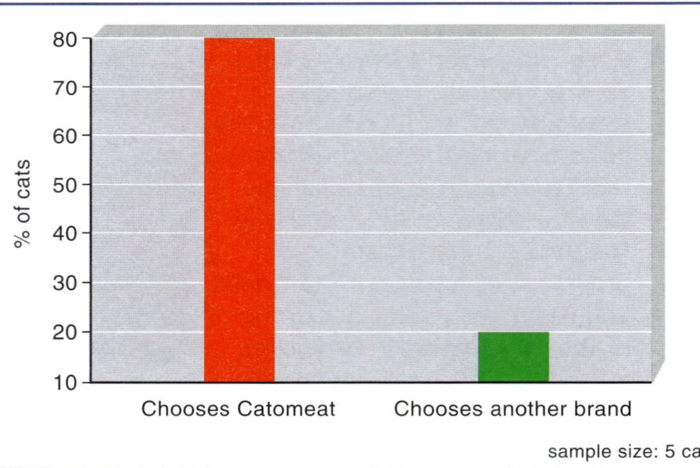

Whatever the source of the information, ask yourself:

- Is it reliable? Who said it, who produced it, where did they get it from?
- Do other sources say the same? If not, which is right?
- Is it up to date?
- Is it unbiased? Why was it produced, what point of view did the producer have?
- Is it fit for purpose?

▸▸ Activity 3.10

There are several websites designed to help you make good use of the internet as a source of information. One example is the Quick website. Ask your tutor for other examples. Look at these websites now and make some notes on how to avoid biased or inaccurate information.

Acknowledging sources

Every time you gather information from a secondary source, you are using material that belongs to someone else. You must not use this information without acknowledging where you got it from. You should get into the habit of recording details of sources as you use them. When you tackle the SPB you will need to do this so that you can include your sources in your eportfolio.

Much of the information will be copyright and you must check that you are not breaking the law when you use copyright sources – the first step towards this is to carefully acknowledge where the information comes from.

Internet sources

What information do you need to keep about each source? You should always include:

- Document title or description
- Author, if possible
- Date of publication
- URL – the full web address for *the page* containing the information (not just the site)
- Permission where necessary
- Date accessed.

For example:

1. Andy Darvill, Solar Power is energy from the Sun <http://www.darvill.clara.net/altenergy/solar.htm> (site accessed 24 May 2005)

Provide a direct link to a web page if possible, rather than to a home page or a menu.

Make sure that the addresses (URLs) you give are correct before you include them. The most common reason URLs fail is that they are transcribed or typed incorrectly. Copy the URL directly from the address window in the browser and paste it into your sources page. That way, you can be sure that there are no errors. Test that it works by clicking on the link in your sources page.

Paper-based sources

You should always include:

- Title of publication, and article if appropriate
- Date of publication
- Publisher
- Permission where necessary.

For example:

Robert Dinwiddle, *Essential Computers: Creating Worksheets* (Dorling Kindersley, 2003)

Primary sources

It is just as important to acknowledge primary sources. For example, if you interview someone, record their name and the date. If you present the results of a survey, record details of the location and date the data was collected.

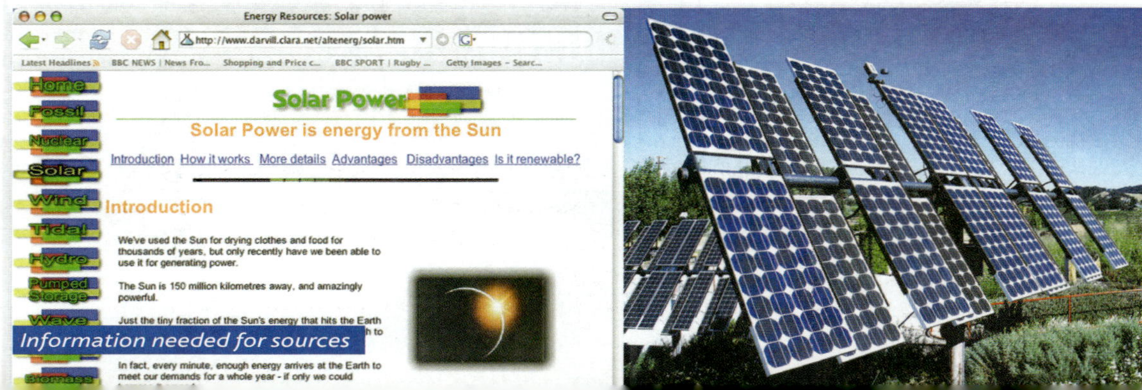

Information needed for sources

Tackling THE PROJECT

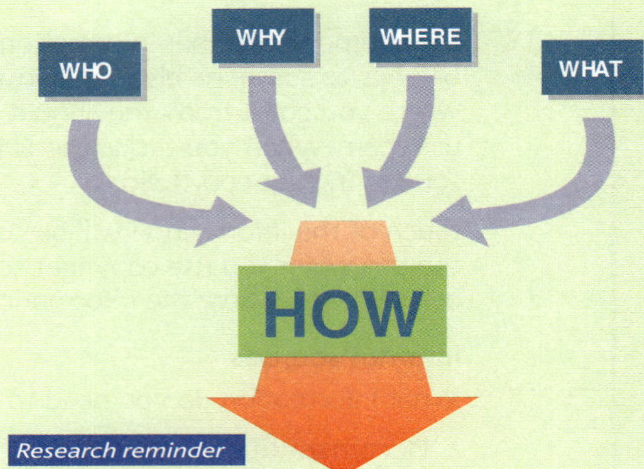

P

Now it's time to tackle 'Gathering information'.

Open your file WHICHPUBS and remind yourself of the publications you need to produce and your answers to these questions.

- **Who** is the target audience?
- **Why** is it needed?
- **Where** is it for?
- **What** must go in it?
- **How** will you go about it? What type is best? Which medium – screen or paper? What style is appropriate?

Ask yourself

What primary and secondary sources shall I use?

Create another table in the document WHICHPUBS, similar to the one on page 40. Include all primary and secondary sources that you will need to use for each publication.

Once you are happy with this, you can begin to gather the information. Don't worry about survey results or information from the data set just yet. You will deal with these in other chapters.

Explore some secondary sources, using the ones you are given to start you off.

You must gather some information from primary sources – interviews, images, sound and so on. Make sure that the information is relevant and that you get permission.

Which information shall I select? How do I know it is reliable?

Select information that you think will be useful. Make sure that it is up to date and reliable.

Make sure you save

- information you have gathered from secondary sources
- links to other information you may need
- information you have gathered yourself from primary sources
- details of all sources you used

Be careful to save things in the correct folders using sensible file names.

4 Making use of surveys

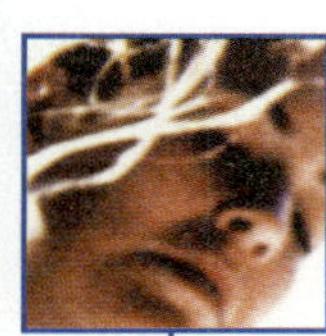

Digimodule

Sometimes you want to gather information from a number of people so that you can compare what they say. You might want to:

- find out what people think – for example, should 17 year olds be allowed to drive?
- gather facts about the way people live – for example, what they do in their spare time, how they spend their money.
- carry out research for a planned business enterprise – for example, how much are people prepared to pay for a product?

If you ask a number of people the same questions so that you can compare their answers, you are conducting a survey. What questions you ask depends on what you want to find out – you will need to make sure that you find out everything you need as you cannot go back and ask everyone more questions. At the same time you must avoid asking questions just for the sake of it.

You will need to make sense of the data you collect – by working out totals, percentages and comparing results from different questions. A spreadsheet is the ideal tool for this. You will learn how to ask questions so that the answers can be analysed in a spreadsheet and how to use spreadsheet tools such as charts to present the findings in a meaningful way.

In this chapter you will learn how to make use of surveys by:

- ***deciding what you want to find out***
- ***deciding who to ask and how to go about it***
- ***designing and testing a questionnaire and spreadsheet***
- ***using a questionnaire to ask a number of people the same questions in the same way***
- ***analysing the results using spreadsheet tools***

Conducting a survey

Who do you ask?

Conducting a survey allows you to ask a number of people the same questions. Surveys might simply involve people in the local area or be carried out nationally to compare responses from different parts of the country. A survey can involve any number of people from a fairly small number to many thousands.

The Census – a national survey

The Census is a survey of everyone living in this country. The last Census took place in 2001 and involved 58,789,194 people. Everyone was asked the same questions at the same time using a questionnaire.

The census provides a detailed and accurate picture of people living in this country on a particular day.

The results took 10 months to analyse! Questions 2 and 3 produced these results:

Males	28,579,869
Females	30,209,325
Aged 0 to 15	11,858,857
Aged 16 to 74	42,525,596
Aged 75 and over	4,404,741
Total number of people	**58,789,194**

Source: http://www.statistics.gov.uk/census2001/profiles/uk.asp

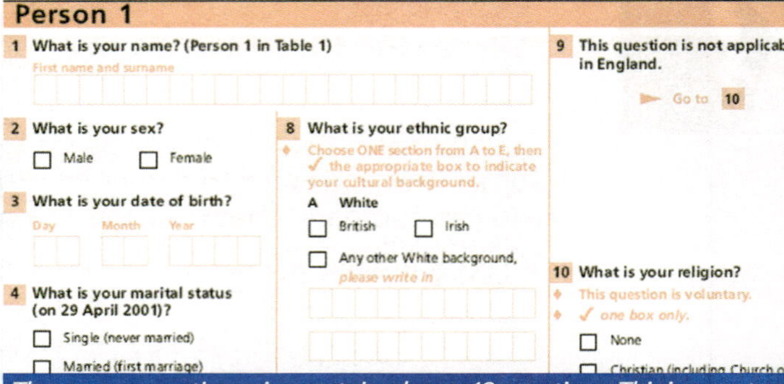

Person 1

1 What is your name? (Person 1 in Table 1)
First name and surname

2 What is your sex?
☐ Male ☐ Female

3 What is your date of birth?
Day Month Year

4 What is your marital status (on 29 April 2001)?
☐ Single (never married)
☐ Married (first marriage)

8 What is your ethnic group?
♦ Choose ONE section from A to E, then ✓ the appropriate box to indicate your cultural background.
A White
☐ British ☐ Irish
☐ Any other White background, *please write in*

9 This question is not applicable in England.
► Go to 10

10 What is your religion?
♦ This question is voluntary.
♦ ✓ *one box only.*
☐ None
☐ Christian (including Church of

The census questionnaire contained over 40 questions. This is an extract

Activity 4.1

Here are the results for one of the transport questions:

Transport (all households in England)	Number	%
Households without car/van	5,488,386	27%
Household with 1 car or van	8,935,718	44%
Household with 2 or more cars/vans	6,027,323	29%

Source: http://neighbourhood.statistics.gov.uk/

Do you think these national percentages reflect the situation in your own community?

Go to the Census 2001 website, Neighbourhood Statistics page. Enter your nearest town or your postcode and have a look at the results. Find out:

1. **What was the total population?**
2. **What percentage of households had no car/van? What percentage had two or more cars/vans? How does this compare with the national figures? Does it surprise you?**
3. **What percentage of the population was under 16 years old?**

Using a sample

Often the number of people you are interested in is too big to manage and it is only possible to involve some of them. This is called a sample – some of the people who live in the town, some of the pupils in a school, etc.

A survey relating to the proposed closure of a school computer club could include all students and parents. However, to carry out a survey about the possible closure of a local train station, you would need to choose a manageable sample.

Who should be in your sample?

If you need to use a sample, how do you make sure that it is fair? If, for example, you need to find out the views of teenagers, does it matter whether they all go to the same school or live in the same town? If you only ask the people you know you may well get a different result than by asking teenagers at random. There is a danger of introducing bias – influencing the results. You need to be sure that your sample will give an accurate picture of the situation.

The chart shows the results of one question in a music survey at Withington School. The question was 'Which type of music do you like best?

This survey uses a small sample and only tells us things about some of the children in year 9. It gives us some idea of what the results from the whole of the year group would be but we cannot be sure that it is representative of year 9 children in general. For example, would a national survey show that 48% of all boys in this age group prefer rock?

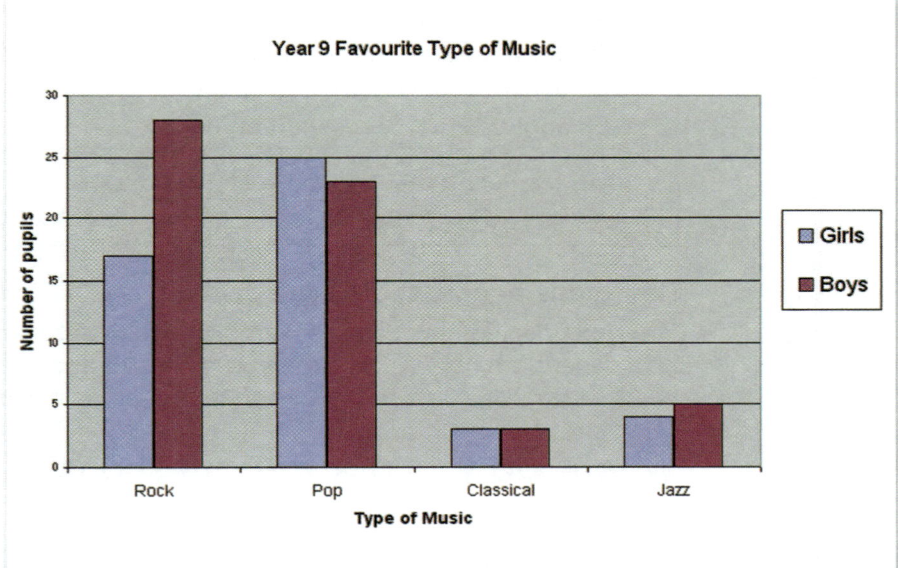

The survey involved about one third of the students in year 9. Students could choose one of the types shown on the chart

TALKING POINT 4.1

Do a quick survey of your class or group – how do the results compare with those from Withington? The survey only offered four different options. Are there other types of music that some of your peers would choose? Should they have been added to the survey?

Activity 4.2

Use the spreadsheet to enter the details for your class or group and create a chart. Make sure the headings and axis labels of the chart are fit for purpose.

Activity 4.3

This table shows some examples of samples that may be biased.

Survey to find out:	Sample	Possible bias	Should also include:
What people think about your art display	Your friends	They are more likely to say what you want them to say	Other teenagers and adults viewing the display
How much exercise people take in a week	Members of a leisure centre		
What people think about the proposed closure of the local cinema	People leaving the cinema		
How much people spend on Christmas presents	People on an email distribution list		
Whether people think university fees should be abolished	Students in a Students' Union Bar		

Complete the blank cells to show possible bias caused by the choice of sample and how the sample should be expanded. Add two more examples of your own.

How many people should you ask?

You must decide how big your sample should be to get accurate enough results. It will also depend on how much time you have and how easy it is to contact the people you want to ask. You must make sure that your sample is big enough to produce useful results.

Where do you ask the questions?

There are many ways of collecting data for surveys and each has advantages and disadvantages.

Surveys can be carried out face to face, by post, email, online or over the phone. What matters is that you gather the data you need from a suitable sample.

The National Census is accurate because there is a legal requirement for people to complete their questionnaires. The problem with surveys generally is that you cannot make people take part. If you use post or email, you do not know how many replies you will get. Companies often offer free gifts or entry into a prize draw to persuade people to answer their questions.

With face-to-face interviews you have the responses there and then but this method is time-consuming.

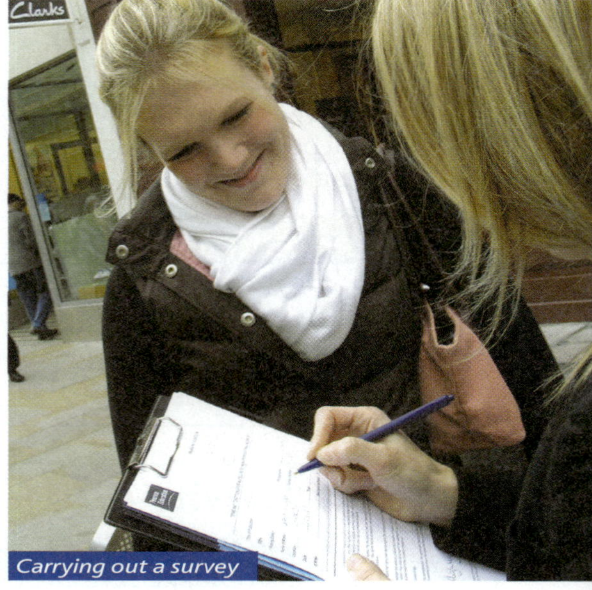

Carrying out a survey

TALKING POINT 4.2

What other advantages and disadvantages can you think of for each method?

Staying safe

You might not be able to conduct a survey in exactly the way you would like. This could be due to lack of time or because it is not safe.

You must take care to conduct any survey safely.

- Never approach people in the street on your own: always work in groups.
- Never send out information to strangers that gives away your personal details.
- Always check the content of your questionnaire and your method of collecting the data with your teacher.

How do you ask the questions?

It is important to ask people the same questions in the same way so that you can compare responses. You will need to decide exactly what you want to know and how you are going to ask it. You will also need to make sure the answers are recorded in the same way. One way to do this is to use a questionnaire.

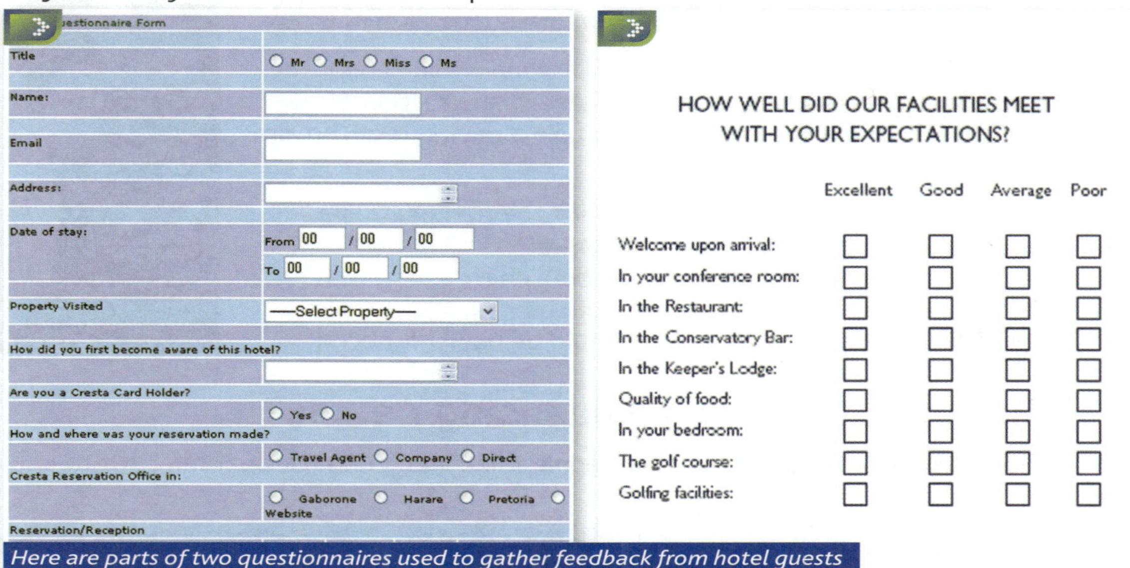

estionnaire Form

Title	○ Mr ○ Mrs ○ Miss ○ Ms
Name:	
Email	
Address:	
Date of stay:	From 00 / 00 / 00 To 00 / 00 / 00
Property Visited	——Select Property——
How did you first become aware of this hotel?	
Are you a Cresta Card Holder?	○ Yes ○ No
How and where was your reservation made?	○ Travel Agent ○ Company ○ Direct
Cresta Reservation Office in:	○ Gaborone ○ Harare ○ Pretoria ○ Website
Reservation/Reception	

HOW WELL DID OUR FACILITIES MEET WITH YOUR EXPECTATIONS?

	Excellent	Good	Average	Poor
Welcome upon arrival:	☐	☐	☐	☐
In your conference room:	☐	☐	☐	☐
In the Restaurant:	☐	☐	☐	☐
In the Conservatory Bar:	☐	☐	☐	☐
In the Keeper's Lodge:	☐	☐	☐	☐
Quality of food:	☐	☐	☐	☐
In your bedroom:	☐	☐	☐	☐
The golf course:	☐	☐	☐	☐
Golfing facilities:	☐	☐	☐	☐

Here are parts of two questionnaires used to gather feedback from hotel guests

Although this chapter will look at questionnaire design and then at spreadsheets, you should remember that the questionnaire and spreadsheet for any survey need to work together. They must be designed and tested at the same time. You will need to make sure that your spreadsheet can cope with all the possible responses in the questionnaire and amend the questions or method of recording responses if necessary.

TALKING POINT 4.3

Have a close look at the hotel questionnaires above. What are they designed to find out? Do you think spreadsheets could be used to analyse the results? How would you present the results?

Activity 4.4

Collect some questionnaires from different sources, both printed and on-screen. What are they for? Have a look at the way questions are worded. Can you find any bias? Compare your findings with others in your group.

4 Creating a questionnaire

Can I do this?

Using word processing tools, make sure that you can:

Align text
Set tabs
Create and use a numbered list
Create tick boxes
Create and use a table
Insert page numbers

What do you want to find out?

Let's suppose that the government is considering changing the rules for learning to drive. We asked a researcher why this might be an issue. Listen to the interview to hear what he had to say.

A survey can be used to find out what people think about the proposals. We are going to concentrate on one section of the survey – how old you have to be to take a driving test. The aim is to find:

- the percentages of people who think the minimum age should be higher, lower, and the same
- why some people think it should be higher
- the age most people think it should be
- whether people think the age should be higher for boys

How can you avoid influencing people?

You really do want to know what people think and you must be careful not to influence their answers.

If you want to know what people think the minimum age for driving should be, there are many ways of asking the question.

- More accidents are caused by drivers under 25 than any other age group. What do you think the minimum age should be?
- What do you think the minimum age for taking a driving test should be?
- Most people think that 17 is too young to drive. Do you agree?
- Some people think that 17 is too young to drive. Do you agree?

TALKING POINT 4.4

Which of these questions might influence people? How would you ask the question?

Activity 4.5

You can make a question even more biased by the way you ask it. Listen to this recording. Is it better if the interviewer asks the question or the person reads it? Who should record the response?

Recording and analysing the data

Keep it simple!

Spreadsheets need numbers for calculations, not lots of text. For Question 1 in our driving survey, people have to choose one of three different answers. The totals will be entered in a spreadsheet.

1) The minimum age for taking a driving test is 17 years. Do you think it should be:

17 ☐ **go to question 2**

higher ☐

lower ☐ **go to question 2**

Limit the number of possible answers

If you ask the question 'What do you think the minimum age for driving should be?' you may get many different answers because it is open-ended. Some people may think the age should be 17, others may think the age should be 30 or even higher!

You need to limit the number of possible answers and ask each person to select the one they prefer. You will then know before you start how many different answers you can get.

What do you think the minimum age for driving should be?

18 ☐ *19* ☐ *20* ☐ *21* ☐ *higher* ☐

You will be able to count up how many people gave each answer.

Avoid information overload

Things get much more complicated when you want to ask people for reasons. 'Why do you think the minimum age should be higher?'

The number of different answers to this question is endless and each one will be text – not so good for calculations in a spreadsheet!

Again, you need to limit the number of different options. The trick is to include a good range of different answers, for example:

- traffic is much faster now
- traffic is much busier now
- 17 is too young to be sensible.

When you test the questionnaire you may want to ask people to give any other reasons they have. You can add more options to the final version if necessary.

TALKING POINT 4.5

Working in groups, have a look at the questionnaires you collected. Is it clear what they are for? Who will complete them? Can you find questions that will result in many different answers? How could this be avoided? Are there any ambiguous questions? Can you make them clearer?

Setting the scene

A questionnaire needs a heading and a simple explanation of what the survey is about. The layout needs to be clear and easy to use.

TALKING POINT 4.6

Have another look at the questionnaires you collected. Look for effective use of writing style, format and layout. Apart from the questions, what other information is included? How would you improve the content or presentation?

Developing the questionnaire

Here is the first draft of the questionnaire, ready for testing.

Safe to Drive?

We are conducting a survey to find out what local people think about the government's plans.

1a) The minnimum age for taking a driving test is 17 years. Do you think it should be:

17

higher

lower

If you answered higher, answer 1b) and 1c)

1b) What is your main reason?

17 is too young to be sensible ☐

There are to many drivers already ☐

Learners should practise for at least a year before taking a test ☐

Other, please specify... ☐

1c) What do you think the minimum age for driving should be?

17	☐	*18*	☐
19	☐	*20*	☐
21	☐	*higher*	☐

2) Do you think the minimum age should be higher for boys than for girls?

Yes *No* *Don't know*

The first draft of the questionnaire

At this stage, some initial testing can be carried out by asking people for feedback. You cannot be sure that a questionnaire is exactly right until you test it with the spreadsheet but you can make sure that:

- there are no spelling or grammar errors
- it is clear what the questionnaire is for
- the questions are clear and unambiguous
- there is enough space for the answers.

Safe to Drive?

We are conducting a survey to find out what local people think about the government's plans.

I don't understand the introduction

1a) The minnimum age for taking a driving test is 17 years. Do you think it

There is a spelling mistake in 1a)

17

higher

lower

If you answered higher, answer 1b) and 1c)

Question 1 is really confusing

1b) What is your main reason?

Tick boxes are not in line

17 is too young to be sensible ☐

There are to many drivers already ☐

It's the wrong spelling of 'to' in 1b, second answer

Learners should practise for at least a year before taking a test ☐

Other, please specify... ☐

There shouldn't be a tick box for the last answer in 1b) and there should be more space to write a reason

1c) What do you think the minimum age for driving should be?

17	☐	*18*	☐
19	☐	*20*	☐
21	☐	*higher*	☐

What's the point in having 17 as an option if I have said it should be higher?

2) Do you think the minimum age should be higher for boys than for girls?

Yes *No* *Don't know*

Use tick boxes throughout

Here is a summary of the feedback received

Activity 4.6

Open the draft questionnaire, and make changes to take account of the feedback. Save it as DRIVING QUESTIONNAIRE. Ask several people to try out your new version and make any necessary changes to ensure that it is fit for purpose.

Building spreadsheets to analyse results

Can I do this?

Using spreadsheet tools, make sure you can:

Use formulae
Use SUM and AVERAGE functions
Use the IF function
Use absolute references
Create charts
Switch to and from formula view
Select areas for printing or charts

Building a spreadsheet

Why choose spreadsheet software to analyse the survey results?

For a simple analysis that only involves calculations, a spreadsheet is very effective and allows you to present results using charts and graphs.

How do you transfer the data from the questionnaires to the spreadsheet?

You may not need to record each person's responses separately – it depends what you want to find out.

If you only want to analyse the number of people who gave each possible response, you can use a tally chart to manually count up the totals.

This tally chart shows the type of heating in some people's homes		
Oil	~~IIII~~ ~~IIII~~ ~~IIII~~ III	18
Gas	~~IIII~~ ~~IIII~~ ~~IIII~~ ~~IIII~~ ~~IIII~~ II	27
Electricity	~~IIII~~ ~~IIII~~ II	12
Solid fuel	~~IIII~~ IIII	9

Now we are going to build a summary spreadsheet to store the data we will collect using our **Safe to Drive**? questionnaire. In order to check that our formulae are correct, we need to enter some fictitious data.

	A	B	C	D
1	The **Safe to Drive?** Survey Results			
2				
3	Total of number of completed questionnaires	15		
4				
5	1a) The minimum age for taking a driving test is 17 years. Do you think it should be 17, higher or lower?		% of those surveyed	
6	17	5	33.3%	
7	higher	6	40.0%	
8	lower	4	26.7%	
9				
10	Total	15	100.0%	
11				
12	1b) If higher, what is your main reason			
13				
14			% of those surveyed	% of those who said 'Higher'
15	a) 17 is too young to be sensible	2	13.3%	33.3%
16	b) there are too many drivers already	0	0.0%	0.0%
17	c) Learners should practise for at least a year	2	13.3%	33.3%
18	d) Other, please specify	2	13.3%	33.3%
19				
20		6	0.4	

Which formulae should you use?

Open the spreadsheet in formula view.

B10 - Adds up the cells in the range B6 to B8 (the number who gave each possible answer for question 1). This should equal the number of completed questionnaires stored in B3

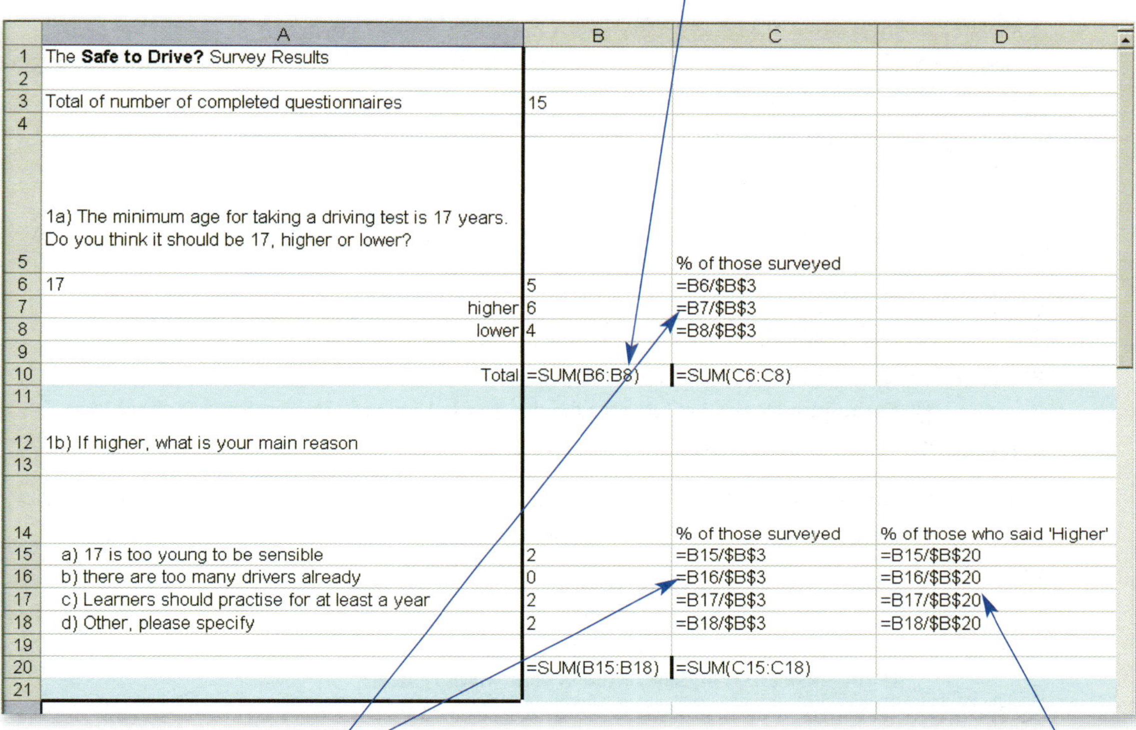

	A	B	C	D
1	The **Safe to Drive?** Survey Results			
2				
3	Total of number of completed questionnaires	15		
4				
5	1a) The minimum age for taking a driving test is 17 years. Do you think it should be 17, higher or lower?		% of those surveyed	
6	17	5	=B6/$B$3	
7	higher	6	=B7/$B$3	
8	lower	4	=B8/$B$3	
9				
10	Total	=SUM(B6:B8)	=SUM(C6:C8)	
11				
12	1b) If higher, what is your main reason			
13				
14			% of those surveyed	% of those who said 'Higher'
15	a) 17 is too young to be sensible	2	=B15/$B$3	=B15/$B$20
16	b) there are too many drivers already	0	=B16/$B$3	=B16/$B$20
17	c) Learners should practise for at least a year	2	=B17/$B$3	=B17/$B$20
18	d) Other, please specify	2	=B18/$B$3	=B18/$B$20
19				
20		=SUM(B15:B18)	=SUM(C15:C18)	
21				

These formulae calculate the percentage of people surveyed who selected each answer. The formula divides the number of people by the total number who took part. This total is stored in B3 and it will change when the full survey is carried out. The absolute cell reference ($ signs) makes sure that every number is divided by the correct total in cell B3.

These formulae will only display as percentages if the cells are formatted to percentage. Otherwise, each formulae would have to multiply by 100. eg =B15/$B$20*100

Activity 4.7

What does the formula in cell B20 do? This should equal the value in another cell. Which one?

What do the formulae in cells D15 to D18 calculate? Why is the absolute cell reference not B3 this time?

Look at the rest of the formulae in the complete spreadsheet and make sure you understand what they all do.

Testing a spreadsheet

You must check that all formulae are correct by manually carrying out the calculations using the same test data. All your results should be the same as those in the spreadsheet.

Make sure that you test everything.

Testing the questionnaire and spreadsheet together

Before you use a questionnaire and spreadsheet for a survey you must check that they are fit for purpose by testing that they work together.

Final questionnaire

Using the data we collected from test users, we found that our spreadsheet and questionnaire didn't work together for one of the questions. Several people thought that the age should be higher because roads are so busy. We have added this to the questionnaire and removed the option 'Other' as it generated too many different answers.

Safe to Drive?

The government is considering changing the rules for learning to drive. We are conducting a survey to find out what local people think.

Section A: Minimum age for taking the driving test

1) The minimum age for taking a driving test is 17 years. Do you think it should be:

17 ☐ **go to question 2**

higher ☐

lower ☐ **go to question 2**

If you answered 'higher', what is your main reason?

Roads are much busier now ☐

17 is too young to be sensible ☐

There are too many drivers already ☐

Learners should practise for at least a year before taking a test ☐

What do you think the minimum age for driving should be?

18 ☐ *19* ☐ *20* ☐ *21* ☐ *higher* ☐

2) Some people think that the minimum age should be higher for boys than for girls. Do you agree?

Yes ☐ No ☐ Don't know ☐

This is the final version of the questionnaire

TALKING POINT 4.7

Compare the draft and final versions – What changes have been made? Is the final questionnaire fit for purpose? How does it compare with your version (DRIVING QUESTIONNAIRE)?

Final spreadsheet

We updated the spreadsheet to match the final questionnaire and used it to carry out a street survey. We interviewed 120 people.

	A	B	C	D	E	F	G	H	I	J
1	The **Safe to Drive?** Survey Results									
2										
3	Total of number of completed questionnaires	120								
4										
5	The minimum age for taking a driving test is 17 years. Do you think it should be		% of those surveyed							
6	17	50	41.7%							
7	higher	54	45.0%							
8	lower	16	13.3%							
9										
10	Total	120	100.0%							
11										
12	If higher, what is your main reason									
13										
14			% of those surveyed	% of those who said 'Higher'						
15	a) Roads are much busier now	7	5.8%	13.0%						
16	b) 17 is too young to be sensible	20	16.7%	37.0%						
17	c) There are too many drivers already	13	10.8%	24.1%						
18	d) Learners should practise for at least a year	14	11.7%	25.9%						
19										
20		54	45.0%	100.0%						
21										
22	If higher, what age do you think it should be?		% of those surveyed	% of those who said 'Higher'						
23	18	14	11.7%	25.9%						
24	19	20	16.7%	37.0%						
25	20	7	5.8%	13.0%						
26	21	10	8.3%	18.5%						
27	higher	3	2.5%	5.6%						
28										
29	Total	54	45.0%	100.0%						
30										
31	Do you think the minimum age should be higher for boys than for girls?		% of those surveyed							
32	Yes	53	44.2%							
33	No	49	40.8%							
34	Don't know	18	15.0%							

The final version of the spreadsheet with the results of the 120 interviews

Presenting findings

Good charts are often the best way to get a message across. They can show at a glance how things change over a period of time or can compare different sets of data.

TALKING POINT 4.8

Look at this chart which shows the responses to question 2 of our survey – would it be clear to someone who has not seen the spreadsheet or the questionnaire? How would you improve it?

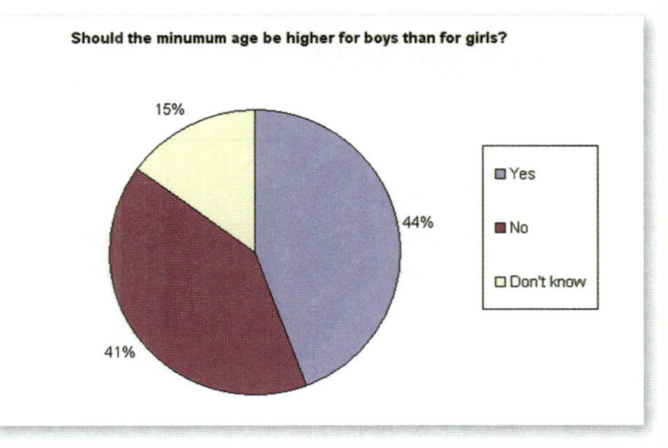

If a chart is included in a publication then extra details can be included in the text rather than by adding more information to the chart itself.

Which type of chart should you use?

Pie charts, column/bar charts and line graphs are the most common types. The type you choose will depend on the purpose – what information you want to present, who it is for and how it will be presented.

Column and bar charts

Use column and bar charts to compare different values such as sales each month, or different answers to a survey question.

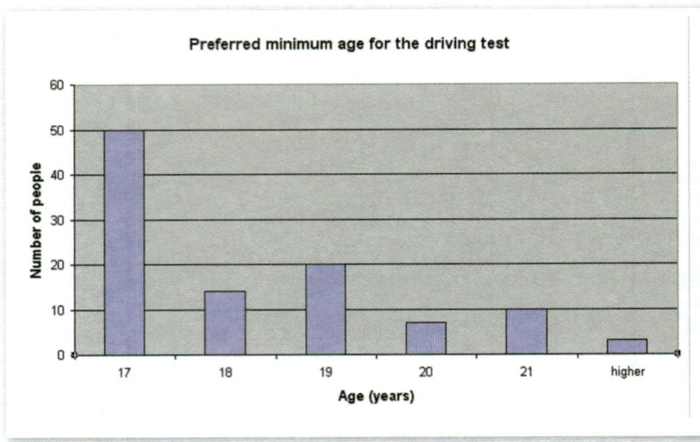

Pie charts

Pie charts are good for showing proportions or percentages for each item. The sectors need to be clear, so if you have too many items avoid using a pie chart.

Although it is possible to read the information shown in this chart from the spreadsheet, the chart shows at a glance how opinions were divided. It is easy to make comparisons.

Legends are useful if you don't want to put all the labels on a chart.

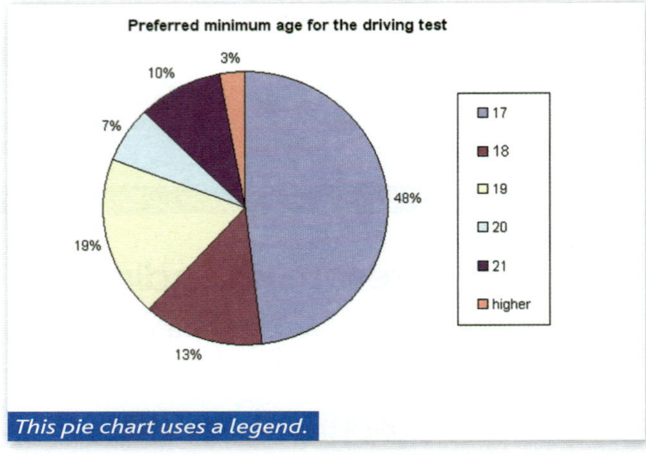

This pie chart uses a legend.

TALKING POINT 4.9

What would you do to improve the charts above?

Line graphs

Line graphs should only be used for values that are continuously changing such as daily temperatures.

Do not use them for survey responses!

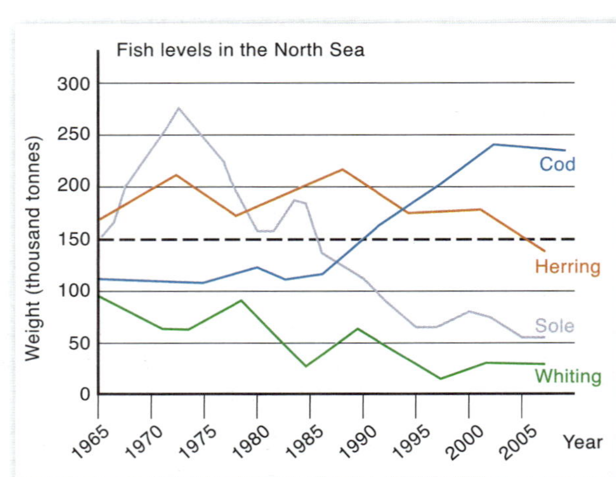

What will the chart be used for?

You must make sure that your chart is clear before it is included in a final publication such as a web page, presentation or report.

Charts in slide presentations

If the chart is included in a presentation and will be projected onto a screen, remember that some paler colours are difficult to distinguish on screen. Stick to bold colours as much as possible.

Members of the audience can't usually control the time that each slide is on the screen. They won't be free to study a chart for as long as they like so you should make sure that it is clear and simple.

Charts in printed reports

If the chart is to be printed in a report, you can include more detail and explanation because readers will have time to take it all in.

Colour vs black and white

If a chart is going to be printed in black and white, all the columns or sectors will be in shades of grey. Be careful that what you see on screen in colour can be read in black and white or use patterns.

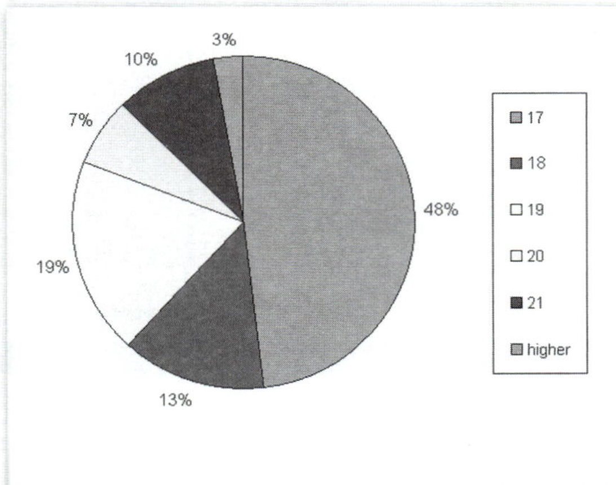

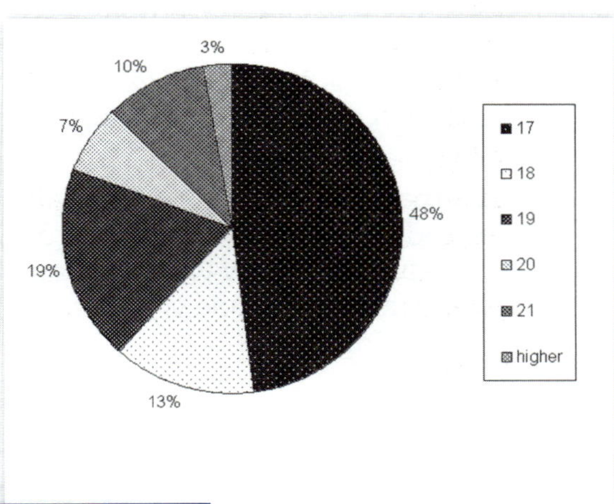

These charts were created using the same data as the chart on page 60.

▸▸ Activity 4.8

Open the spreadsheet and experiment with different colours (including black and white) and patterns for pie and column charts. There is no need to print – use print preview to check them.

Creating a chart

Good charts take time to produce. You need to select the most appropriate type of chart, a sensible scale, colours and format. You must also use headings and labels that make the contents of the chart clear to the audience. Most importantly, you must be careful to select the correct data to include in your chart. Poor charts can mislead readers because the information is unclear.

You can use a chart wizard but remember that wizards are not magic! It is up to you to customise them to make them fit for purpose.

Careful selection of the data to be included

People sometimes include extra columns or rows when selecting the data. This results in charts that do not make sense.

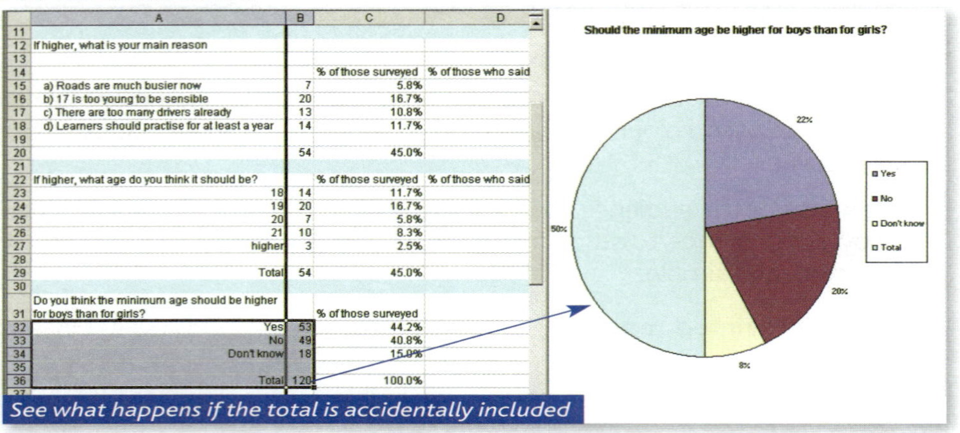

See what happens if the total is accidentally included

A meaningful title

How else will others know what the chart is for? Don't assume that it is clear from the chart itself. Many students – and professionals – let themselves down by not giving enough thought to the title.

As a DiDA student you will know by now that you need to think about what information is being presented, who it is for and where it will appear. You only have space for a few words so you must make sure you include vital information and nothing else.

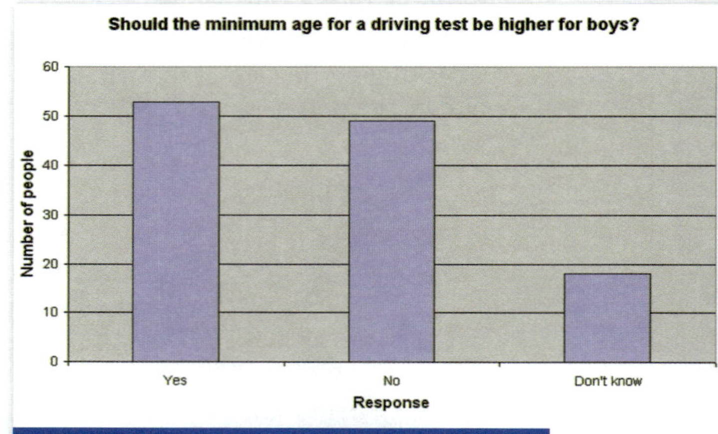

Compare this with the title of the pie chart above

Sensible axis labels

Decide on these at the same time as the title. Between them, the title and labels should give enough information to make the chart clear.

Gridlines and values

There is no point in having a chart if it is impossible to read off the values. The chart above is difficult to read – exactly how many said yes, no or don't know?

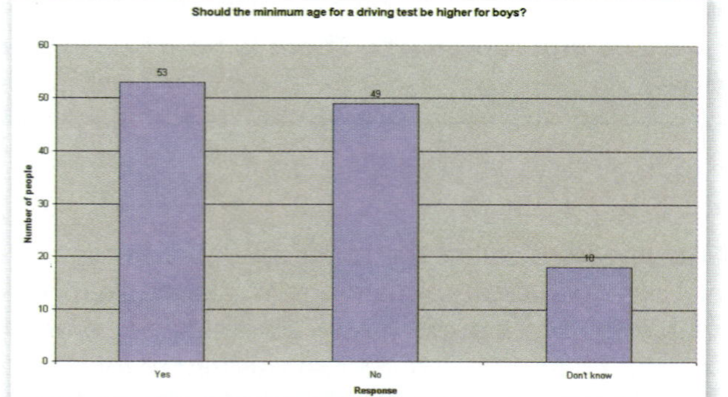

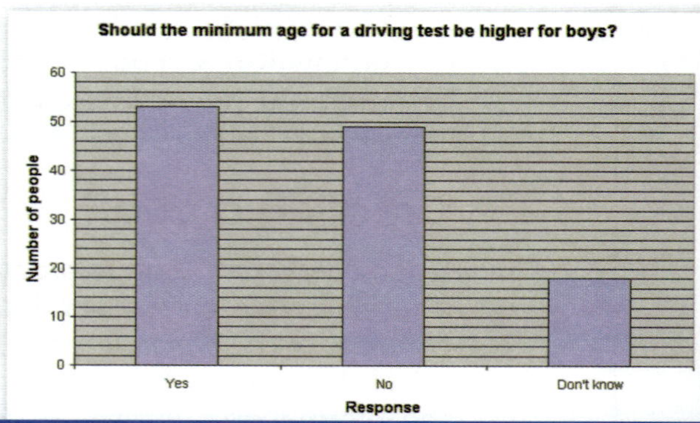

Here are two possible methods of showing the user more precise values. In the example on the left, the number of people in each category is shown above the column. In the example on the right extra grid lines make it easier to see the number of people.

Legend or data labels

Your chart will include the row and column headings you use in your spreadsheet. You may find that they are too long to use as horizontal data labels. Sometimes changing the angle of the labels works. Alternatively, legends can be used to identify the data.

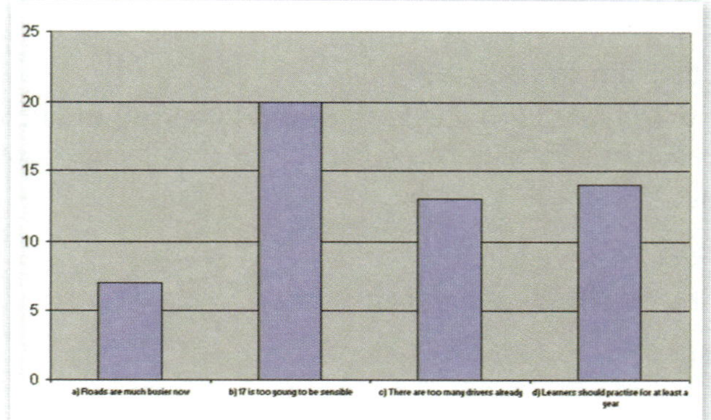

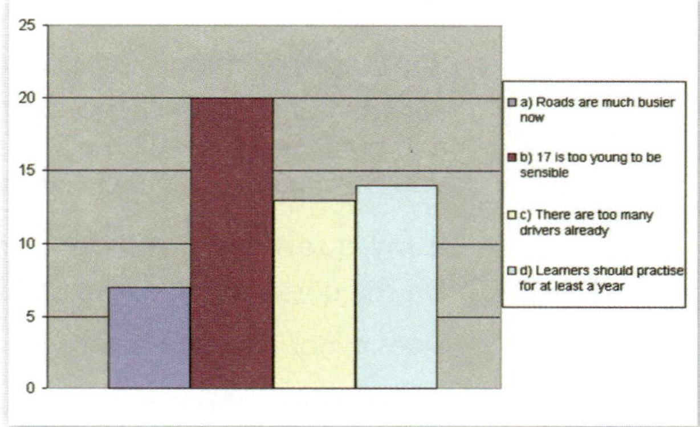

TALKING POINT 4.10

Look at the spreadsheet on page 59 again. What other charts could be produced using this information? Who would find them useful? How would you present them?

▸▸ Activity 4.9

Open the final version of the spreadsheet. Produce some useful charts. Try out different types, colours, legends, data, labels.

More complex analysis

Our summary spreadsheet example is very straightforward. If you wanted to look at the combined responses from two or more questions, then you would need to enter each person's responses into the spreadsheet separately. For example, if you wanted to answer the question 'Of those who think that the age should be higher, how many also think that the age should be higher for boys than girls?', our spreadsheet could not be used because it does not store individual responses.

For THE PROJECT or the SPB, you may need to use your results in more than one publication. The message here is to think carefully about what information you want to extract *before* you design the spreadsheet.

▸▸ Activity 4.10

We have entered the data from each questionnaire into another spreadsheet. Open this and use it to find all those who said 'higher' for question 1 AND 'yes' for question 2. Carry out some other useful complex analysis of the data. Save the edited spreadsheet as ALL RESPONSES.

4 Tackling THE PROJECT

Now it's time to tackle 'Conducting a survey'. Don't forget to check what you will be doing with the results later on. This might affect what you ask or how you design your spreadsheet.

Ask yourself

Which publications will use results from the survey?

For each of these publications, use your file WHICHPUBS to remind yourself of audience and purpose. How will the survey results be used in the publication? What questions will you need to ask to get this information?

Is my questionnaire fit for purpose?

Do the questions make sense? Try them out by asking test users.

Does every question have a purpose?

Is my spreadsheet fit for purpose?

Is a summary of the totals enough or do you need individual responses so that you can carry out complex analysis?

Don't try to use complicated formulae just for the sake of it but make sure that your analysis will produce all the information you need for each publication.

How will I carry out the survey?

It might be difficult for you to find 50 people willing to complete your questionnaire. Ask your teacher about working in groups.

Don't forget you must work in pairs or groups if you want to survey people you don't know, e.g. asking people in a shopping centre.

Make sure you save

- a draft of your questionnaire, annotated with comments from test users
- the final version of your questionnaire
- evidence of any changes made to your spreadsheet as a result of testing
- the final version of your spreadsheet including charts/graphs

5 Making use of databases

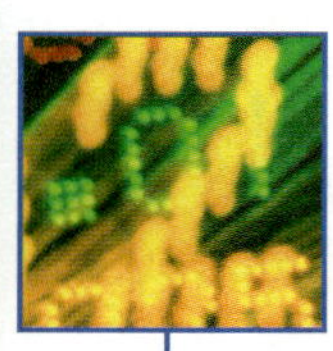

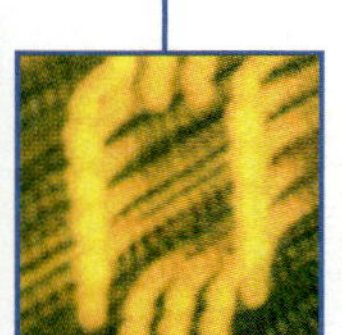

What are the names and addresses of club members who are over 60 with a birthday between 1 January and 31 March? Which DVDs can be rented by under 18s in the comedy category? Who is organising parties in March and wants a clown? These are questions that can easily be answered if data is organised in a database.

Why not use a spreadsheet? Spreadsheets are good for number crunching – adding up totals, finding averages, comparing results and producing charts. That's why they are so useful for analysing survey results. Databases are much better for organising a range of data including text, numbers, dates, times and images.

Databases are designed to hold exactly the same data items for each person, object or action – a record for each club member, rental DVD, party booking, etc. Database tools can be used to check that data is as accurate as possible and to create forms that are easy to use for entering new data.

As a DiDA student you are expected to make use of database software to organise a large data set so that you can extract and present useful information for specified audiences and purposes.

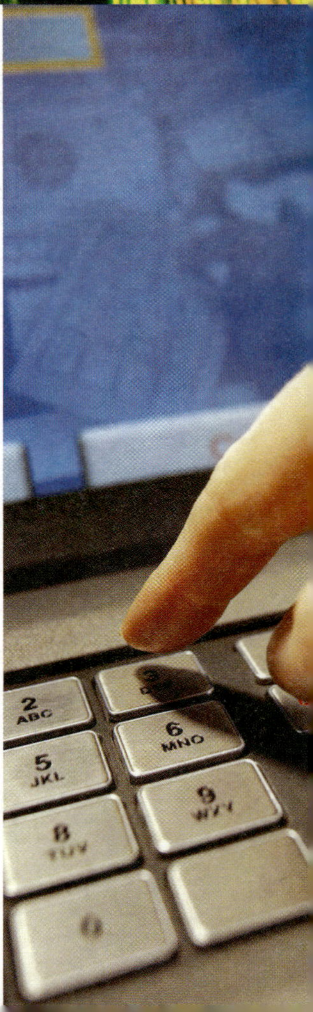

In this chapter you will learn to how to make use of databases by:

- ***creating a database to hold a given data set***
- ***designing and using validation rules***
- ***importing data into a database***
- ***creating data entry forms that are easy to use***
- ***sorting data in a database to make information clearer***
- ***searching a database to find useful information***

Why use a database

More and more data is generated all the time. Organisations need to be able to store, search and sort the data to produce valid and useful information.

Case study: The Boots Advantage Card

Many high street stores offer customers some kind of loyalty card and need to store information about cardholders.

For example, Boots customers can use the Advantage Card. Every time the customer makes a purchase, the card is scanned and points are added. These points can be used at any time to buy products in the store. When the card is scanned, the till displays the current value of points on the card.

Boots has over 1400 stores and about 400 of these have an Advantage Point – this is an information point where a customer can insert the card and find out how many points they have to spend.

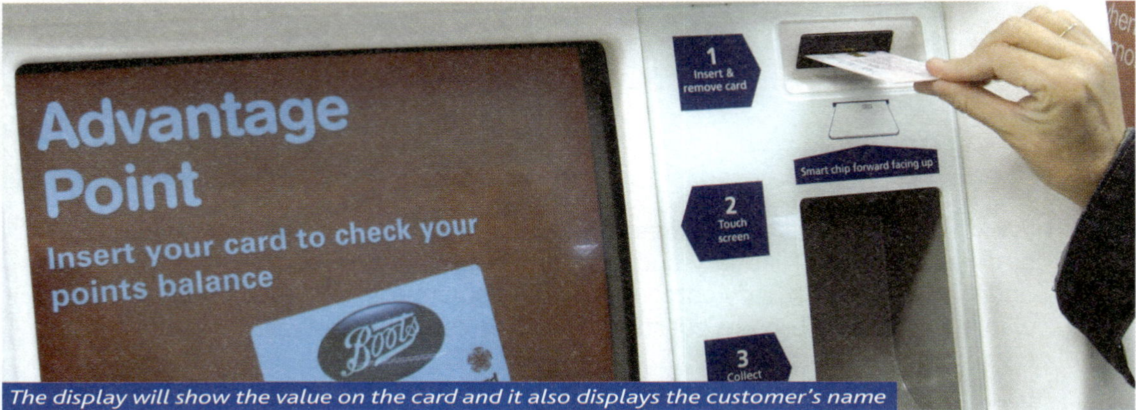

The display will show the value on the card and it also displays the customer's name

⏩ Activity 5.1

Every time a customer applies for an Advantage Card, a form is completed. Look at the online application form for a Boots Advantage Card to find out what data is collected from each customer.

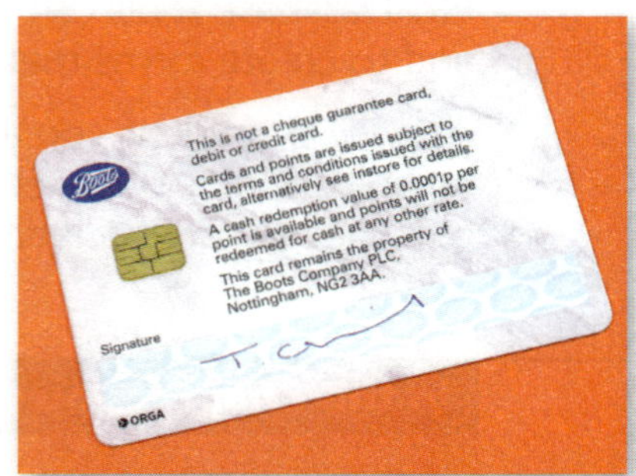

The same details are collected from each Advantage Card holder and the same data is stored for each of them. This data is stored on a computer along with the card number issued and a points total of zero.

The Advantage Card is not a swipe card with a magnetic strip – it is a smart chip card. This means that some data is stored on the card as well as in the database. When a customer makes a purchase, the chip is read to identify the customer and this speeds things up.

TALKING POINT 5.1

Think about different things you and your family do in a typical week and when and where data is being collected. What might it be used for?

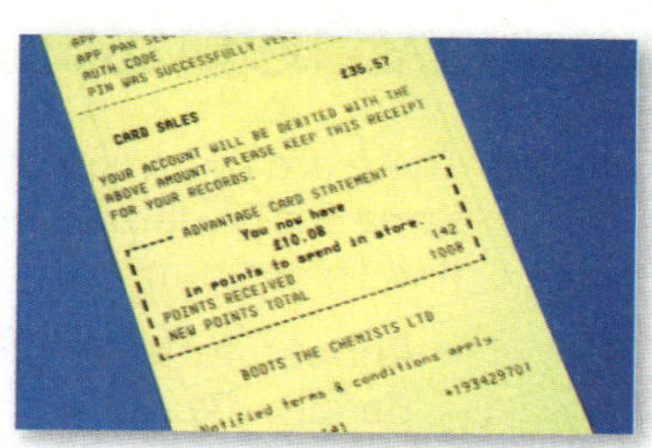

Most of the stored data stays the same but the points total is updated and printed on the till receipt.

This allows Boots to keep a record of the number of points each customer has but what else can they do with the data that is stored?

Apart from making Boots more attractive to customers, using an Advantage Card can generate lots of useful information about customers. The computer can record data about what they buy, when and where they buy it. All this data can be stored in the database and used to work out customer demand for different products, which stores are more popular, which customers buy certain types of products and much more.

Searching for information

Suppose Boots want to find all cardholders with more than 500 points. If there were just a small number of people, it would be easy to look down a list and identify them. Boots actually has 18 million cardholders so the information is not so easy to find manually – unless you fancy scrolling through millions of records!

Making it easier

Here is some data that might be stored for five Advantage cardholders:

James, Byron, 42 Little Road, Nottingham, NE34 8JH, 489, 13, 4/11/04, 7653
Anna, Svensson, 45 Thornhill, Southampton, SO99 4JD, 48, 2, 29/4/05, 7159
Emma, Stomp, 17 Portsway, Northampton, NO7 7QT, 79, 14, 12/3/05, 7587
Alex, Finch, 34 Ashurst Road, Lyndhurst, SO91 6GH, 1345, 4, 25/4/05, 7123
Chris, Boil, 78 Oak Road, Harlow, CM49 6JD, 426, 6, 28/5/04, 7135,

It is not immediately clear what some of this data means so let's put some labels on it.

Name 1	Name 2	Address	Town	Postcode	Points	Last points	Last used	Branch
James	Byron	42 Little Road	Nottingham	NE34 8JH	489	13	4/11/04	7653
Anna	Svensson	45 Thornhill	Southampton	SO99 4JD	48	2	29/4/05	7159
Emma	Stomp	17 Portsway	Northampton	NO7 7QT	79	14	12/3/05	7587
Alex	Finch	34 Ashurst Road	Lyndhurst	SO91 6GH	1345	4	25/4/05	7123
Chris	Boil	78 Oak Road	Harlow	CM49 6JD	426	6	28/5/04	7135

Field names

Record in database

Now the data makes sense – and this, in a nutshell, is what a database is for – storing data in an organised way so that information can be found at the touch of a button. Every customer has a record with the same data items stored in fields. The column headers are the field names and tell us what each field contains. It is easy to sort the records and to search on the different fields.

TALKING POINT 5.2

How would the database be used to find this information? What other fields are likely to be in the database? Think about what information the company would find useful. How would they extract it from the database?

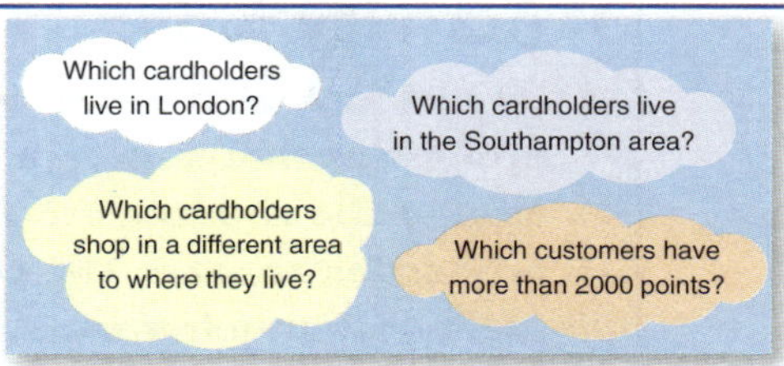

Which cardholders live in London?
Which cardholders live in the Southampton area?
Which cardholders shop in a different area to where they live?
Which customers have more than 2000 points?

5

When should you use a database?

There are many situations where a database is useful – any time you want to store the same set of data items for a number of different people, objects or actions and use it to find things out:

- **People:** for example, credit card customers – card number, full name, address, contact details, date of birth, credit limit etc.
- **Objects:** for example, DVDs in a rental store – item number, title, description, type, number available, rental category, certification, etc.
- **Actions:** for example, bookings at a theatre – customer ID, date of booking, performance code, number of adults, number of children, etc.

TALKING POINT 5.3

Often we do not even notice when a database is being used. The Boots Advantage card system is one example but there are many more. Think of as many situations as you can where it is likely that a database is being used. Try to think of examples involving people, objects and actions.

Many websites are supported by a database. If you are able to carry out searches on one or more items, the chances are that you are using a database without realising it!

Activity 5.2

Try out the National Rail website and the Trainline website by searching for trains from Chester to London next Friday that arrive between 4 and 5 pm. These sites are designed differently but they both use a database of information that is searched using the criteria you enter. Try some other journeys in both sites and compare the results.

Hideaways is a holiday cottage letting agency run by Nick and Annie Pash. You can use the company website to search for suitable properties and you can book online. This is possible because the company uses a database with a record for each property.

Activity 5.3

Have a look at the Hideaways website and you will see that you can search for properties that suit your requirements. Try entering the number of people, the area of the country, etc. As soon as you click to continue, a list of suitable properties appears. The computer is searching the database for cottages that meet your requirements. What fields do you think are stored for each property?

Designing a database structure

Choosing the software

The SPB for Unit 1 will require you to work with a large data set using database software.

Database software can recognise different types of data. When you design a database you must make sure that each field can accept the correct type of data.

Data types and formats

It is very important to use the correct data types for fields as this helps to reduce errors by restricting what can be entered. You should make sure that you understand exactly what can and cannot be entered in fields with different data types.

For each type, you can also specify the format. This table shows the common data types with examples of formats:

Type	Description	Examples of formats
Alphanumeric (Text)	Text including numbers	Upper case, lower case
Numeric	Numbers	Decimal places, currency, percentages
Date/Time	Date and time Date only Time only	05/06/87 15:45 Various date formats such as: 05/06/87, 5 June 1987, Various time formats such as: 15:45, 15:45:05, 03:34PM
Currency	Money	Symbol £, €, etc. Decimal places
Yes/No	Where input is limited to two values	

Can I do this?

Using database tools, make sure you can:

Create a new database table
Create new fields in a table
Enter sensible field names
Select suitable data types
Change data types
Select field sizes and formats
Change field sizes and formats
Enter simple validation rules

You can specify how data must be displayed even if it is entered in a different format.

▸▸ Activity 5.4

Create a database table and enter a field called BIRTHDAY. Select the correct data type and format it to dd/mm/yyyy. Try entering 4/5/05, 4 May 05, 04/05/2005, etc – you should see 04/05/2005 in every row of the table.

What is validation?

Validation is used to check data as it is entered to help prevent errors finding their way into the database. There are several different ways of validating data.

Type check

Setting the data type is one way of reducing the number of data entry errors. For example, a numeric field will not allow you to enter text by mistake.

Format check

Input masks allow you to limit the format of data being entered. Check the software you are using to find out what input masks are possible.

Range check

Validation rules can be used to restrict the values that can be entered. If there is a small number of possible entries these can be listed. For example, ***1, 2, 3*** will only accept these values.

In the example there is a field for the maximum number of people who can book for an activity. This field has the data type numeric with 0 decimal places. The field has a validation rule that only accepts numbers in the range 10 to 20. If it did not have a validation rule, then the user could accidentally enter any number, even 300 or more, for one session on the squash courts!

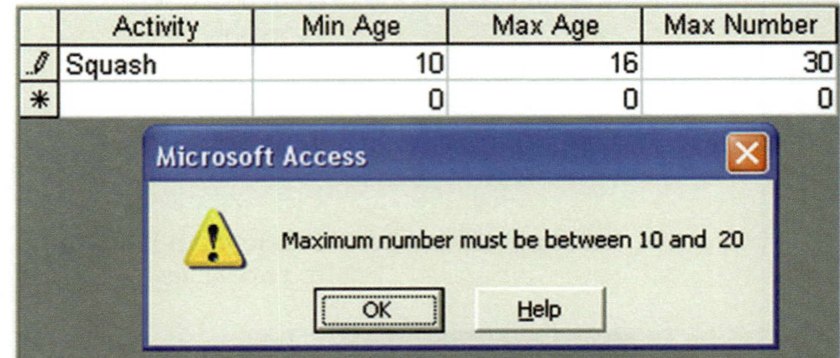

Every record that is entered is checked to see whether the data for the number of people is valid. If it isn't, the user must correct the error before continuing.

Using operators

All the usual operators can be used in validation rules including:

Operator	Example	Means
=	=X	X is the only acceptable input
<	<10	Must be less than 10
<=	<=10	Must be less than 10 or exactly equal to 10
>	>£50	Must be greater than £50
>=	>=£50	Must be greater than £50 or exactly £50
<>	<>X	Must not be X
NOT	NOT 100	Must not be 100
OR	Cat OR Dog	Can only be Cat or Dog
AND	>0 AND <10	Must be greater than 0 and less than 10.

For example, if the entry in a field called Age must not be more than 18, the validation rule would be ***<=18***.

If the age must be between 5 and 18, the rule could be ***>=5 AND <=18***. Some software, such as Access, allows you to type ***between 5 and 18*** instead.

TALKING POINT 5.4

What should the data types, formats and validation rules be for each of these fields in a car rental database?

a) TYPE must be VAN or CAR
b) SIZE must be one of these: S, M, L
c) SEATS must not be more than 7
d) FEE must be from £23 to £50

Find at least two ways of entering the validation rules for c) and d).

Validation messages

What happens when you try to enter invalid data? If you don't create your own validation message, the software will probably display a default message.

Database software allows you to enter validation messages so that when invalid data is entered a sensible message comes up telling the user what is wrong. Of course, you need to make sure that the message matches the validation rule!

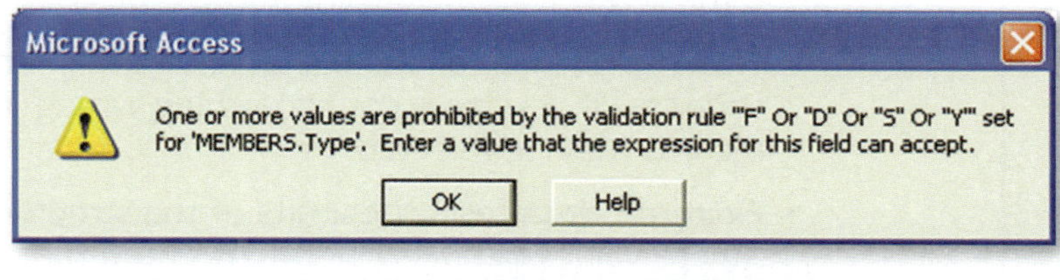

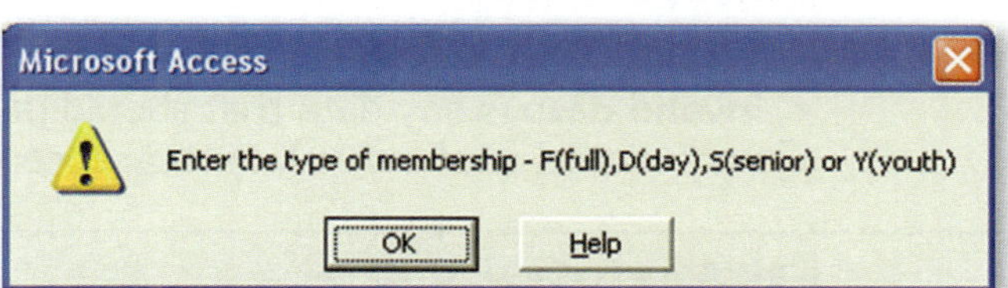

The top message is not very friendly, is it? The bottom one is more helpful

When should you use a validation rule?

It's very tempting to validate everything in sight in the hope that this will make your database error-free. If you look at a list of data and the entry for a particular field is always A, B or C you might think that a validation rule can be used. This is not necessarily the case! If you were told that the field must contain one of A, B or C only then it would be fine.

You can only include a validation rule for a field if you are absolutely sure that you know what is acceptable and what is not. Of course there are some fields where validation is obvious. There are only seven different days, 12 different months, etc.

If you can check that there can be no other values in the field then you can go ahead and enter a validation rule. If you are not sure, you must not make assumptions.

TALKING POINT 5.5

You are going to create a database table for films available in a rental shop. It must include FORMAT (DVD or video only), TYPE (includes Cartoon, Drama, Family, Humour) coded using the initial letter of each type, AGE (U, PG, 12 and 15 only), COST (£3 to £5). Think about what other fields should be included. What should the data types and formats be? What can be validated?

⏩ Activity 5.5

Open a new database and create a structure for the FILM RENTAL table. Use the field names from Talking Point 5.5 plus others that make it clear what each field is for. Use suitable data types and formats and enter validation rules and messages where appropriate. Save the database as FILMS.

Testing a database structure

Before you enter data into a table, you must be confident that all data types, field lengths and validation rules are correct and that the database:

- has all the required fields and no unnecessary fields
- rejects all invalid data
- accepts all valid data
- displays data in the formats you want.

You must test each field using three types of data:

- **Normal data** is valid and should be accepted by the database. This is not as daft as it sounds – if you have got something wrong in the structure or the validation rules, the records may be rejected.
- **Extreme data** tests the limits of the structure and validation. If a field should only accept values between 5 and 18, check that it allows both 5 and 18. If you have entered ***>5*** in place of ***>=5***, records will be rejected.
- **Invalid data** is any data that should definitely not be accepted. Try entering text in a numeric field, values well outside acceptable ranges, etc.

⏩ Activity 5.6

Open your database FILMS. Test the structure of the FILM RENTAL table thoroughly using normal, extreme and invalid data. Does it all work as it should? Are the validation error messages helpful? Make changes if necessary.

Test users

Once you are satisfied that the database is correct, ask test users to see whether they can 'bust' it – find something that doesn't work as it should.

You must keep a record of the feedback and results of your testing and of changes you make. You can use a word processed document but you may want to record interviews with test users and capture screen shots of problems you found.

⏩ Activity 5.7

Work in pairs and test your partner's FILMS database. If you can bust it, help your partner to sort it out. What is wrong – fields, data types, formats or validation rules? Do the error messages make sense to you?

Once you are happy that your database is working correctly, add 15 records of your choice. You can use the internet to get accurate information about current films.

Working with a large data set

One of the features of Unit 1 is that you create databases to hold real data and you get to work with a large number of records – probably between 150 and 200 people, objects or actions. Your task will be to create a database to hold these records.

So if you have to create the database, where do you get the data from? You will be given a text file that contains raw data – all the data for each record in a list.

```
1,Mr,A,Heathcote,heath@sunit23.co.uk,L39,D
2,Mrs,F,Bolton,bolton@sunit23.co.uk,B74,D
3,Mrs,D,Brookes,brookes@oldschool.ac.uk,N
4,Mrs,E,Jones,elliej@web5890.com,MK4,D
5,Mrs,C,Jones,jonesy@24gold3.co.uk,SS15,
6,Mrs,C,Burgess,burgess@sunit23.co.uk,L37
7,Mrs,B,Smith,b.smith.2@sunit23.co.uk,II3
8,Mr,A,Wilson,wilson@sunit23.co.uk,PR26,L
9,Mrs,D,Caine,caine@web5890.com,LS12,S
10,Miss,F,Hussain,hussain@24gold.co.uk,C
11,Mrs,E,Chell,chell@web5890.com,OX16,S
12,Mrs,F,Jones,jonesfred@sunit23.co.uk,ST
13,Mrs,C,Jones,carlij@24gold3.co.uk,LE11,
14,Mrs,D,Coghlan,coghlan@blakingschool.ac
```

Part of the data set for the specimen SPB

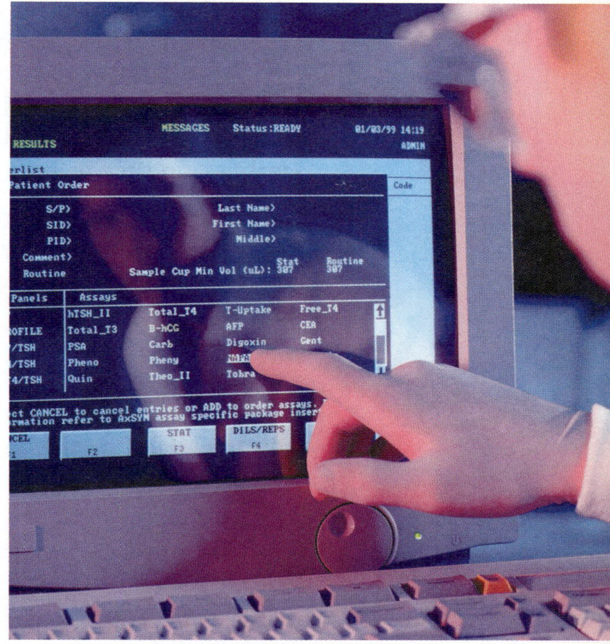

In this example, items of data are separated by commas.

Don't let this put you off – you will also be given a list of what the data means. The list for this section of the data set is:

1 Questionnaire number
2 Title of householder
3 Initial
4 Surname
5 Email address
6 Postcode (first half only)
7 Type of home (coded):
- D – Detached house
- S – Semi-detached house
- T – Terraced house
- B – Bungalow
- F – Flat

By looking at both the raw data and the items list, you can work out what fields you need and what validation rules can be added.

What can be validated?

You need to be able to import a data set from a text file into a database structure. The data set may contain invalid data – your validation rules should ensure that only valid data is imported. However, as we said before, you can only validate fields where you are sure that you know exactly what is acceptable data and what is not.

Importing raw data into a database

You have a database structure and you have a text file containing the data. How do you import the data into the database? No worries, the database software should do this for you – exactly how will depend on the software you are using. You MUST create the database structure *before* you import the data otherwise you will risk importing invalid data and you will not give enough thought to the design of the database.

You will need to open the database and tell the software to import a file. Then you must specify the file name and what method is used to separate the data items – commas, tabs, etc. The software will attempt to import the data into your database structure. If it finds a data item that does not match the field, an error will occur. In this case, you must identify the problem and decide to do one of two things.

- **Reject the record:** If you are sure that your database is correct and that there is invalid data in the record, you must remove the record. NEVER alter the data that is given to you – it's not your data and you have no right to change it.
- **Amend the database:** If you are sure that the data is valid and there is an error in the field type, length or validation, you should not import any data. You should amend the database and try to import the data set again.

Sometimes this process can be time-consuming but if you have designed and thoroughly tested your database and included sensible validation, this should not be the case.

Oasis Leisure Centre

Oasis is owned by Bentley Town Council. The manager is Alistair Larsson. There are various facilities at the centre including a swimming pool with diving area, squash and badminton courts, a gym, etc.

Oasis Leisure Centre wants to store details of members in a database. Members details are stored in a text file – this is a list of the data items in this file.

Membership number – X and 3 digits only **Title** **Family name** **Given name** **Gender** – M or F **Telephone number** **Address**	**Town** **Postcode** **Date of birth** **Membership type** – F, S, D, Y only (Full, Senior, Day, Youth) **Areas paid for** – S, C, G, SC, SG, A only (Swimming, Courts, Gym, Swimming and Courts, Swimming and Gym, All) **Renewal month** – any month, first three letters e.g. Jan, Feb **Assistance** – Y or N (Y if the member requires assistance)

Data list for MEMBER data set

TALKING POINT 5.6

Open the data set. Using the list above, make sure that you understand what each item of data is. You should only need to look at the first few rows in the data set. Now look at the database structure. Why is the telephone number a text field? Are you happy with the validation rules?

Activity 5.8

Create a database and call it OASIS. Create a table called MEMBER using the given structure. Check the validation rules.

Save the data set in your user area. Import the data set into the database. The data set contains just one error – your software may remove the record for you or simply tell you that there is an error. This record cannot be included in the database. If your software finds more errors, you should look again at the structure and validation rules.

Managing the database

Up until now we have talked about designing a database. Now we need to look at using one. This is an entirely different matter. You need to think about the needs of the user or audience – it might not be you!

Records can be added by typing straight into a database table but it is not very user-friendly, is it? Other people will not be familiar with the field names you have used and may not have experience of using the software. A data entry form solves the problem – it provides a user-friendly interface and can remind users, including you, of what is acceptable and what is not.

Creating a data entry form

Your forms need to be clearly laid out, easy to read and easy to use.

If you are feeling brave, you might like to try creating a form from scratch! If not, you can use a wizard.

Wizards are not magic!

Wizards can help you create data entry forms but you will still have some work to do to make them fit for purpose.

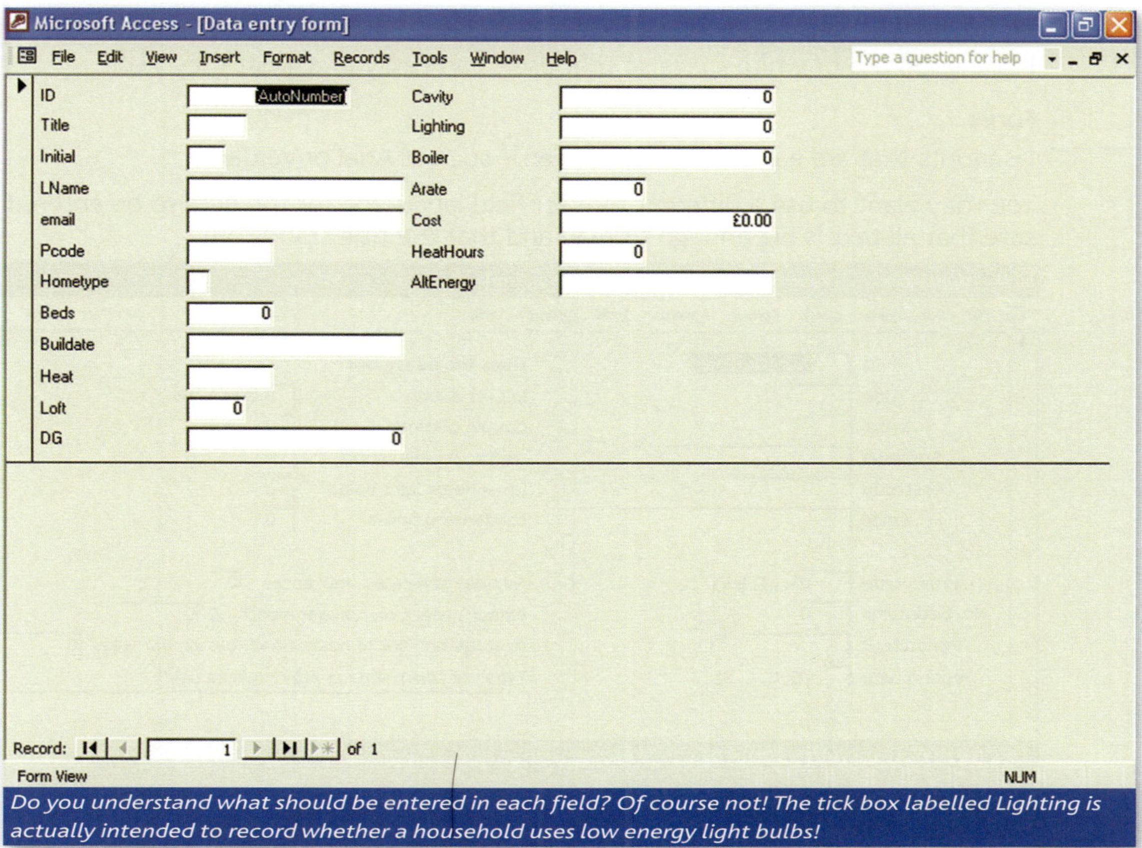

Do you understand what should be entered in each field? Of course not! The tick box labelled Lighting is actually intended to record whether a household uses low energy light bulbs!

TALKING POINT 5.7

What needs to be done to the form above before it is ready to use? Make a note of all the questions you need to ask before you can be sure what it is all about. Look at the layout – what could be done to improve it?

Customising a data entry form

Heading

This should make it quite clear what the form is for. Don't let a wizard do it for you without checking that the heading it selects makes sense.

Labels

Each data entry field needs a label to tell the user what it is. The wizard will try to use the field names from the database. These may not make sense – look at the example on page 75! Field names are usually short and only make sense to the person who created the database. Labels need to be clear to others.

The input field labelled Lighting in the example is using the field name 'Lighting' from the database. On the form, a label such as 'Low energy bulbs?' would be far more helpful but could still mean 'Does the person use them?' or 'Does the person approve of them?' etc.

Order of fields

Organise the fields in a logical order and group related fields, for example, all the lines of an address.

White space

Make good use of white space so that users can easily find what they want.

Fonts

Use fonts that are easy to read on screen – such as Arial or Verdana.

You may want to use a different font for field labels and for the data to be entered. Make sure that all text is big enough to read and that the title stands out.

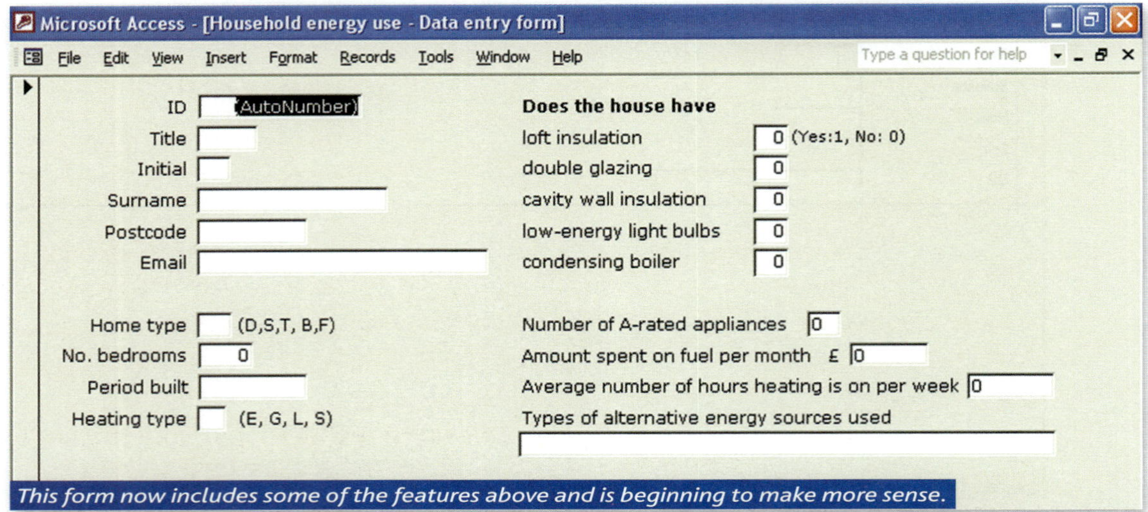

This form now includes some of the features above and is beginning to make more sense.

TALKING POINT 5.8

Look at the data entry form that Boots customers use to apply for an Advantage card. Pick out all the features that make it fit for purpose. Can you suggest any improvements?

Choose effective colours

Make sure that there is good contrast between text and background. Check that the colour combinations are accessible to people who are colour blind.

Tab order

As you enter data you can move from field to field using the tab key. Make sure that the tab moves through the fields in a logical order. It can be very frustrating to type the first line of an address only to find that the tab key takes you to the date of birth field before the next line of the address. This increases the risk of entering data into the wrong field. The tab order can usually be changed in the design or layout menu.

Help messages

You can make data entry even easier by providing help messages. These can be entered in text boxes on the form – for the type of Heating in the example, you could add the message 'Enter G (gas), S (solid fuel), O (oil), E (electric) or A (Other)'. If you are feeling adventurous, explore features in your software such as pop-up tips.

Drop-down lists

When a field has a limited number of options, you can make data entry much faster by providing a dropdown box with the list of possible choices.

Can I do this?

Using database tools, make sure you can:

Create a data entry form
Select fields for the form
Enter a suitable title
Enter labels
Enter help messages
Change colours and formatting
Change layout
Use features such as dropdown lists

Activity 5.9

Create a form for the MEMBER table using the wizard and then customise it. Add as many features as you can to make it easy for others to use. Use it to add two new records, one for yourself and one for a friend.

Testing, testing!

You must test a data entry form with sample records and, since the form is to be used by other people, it is essential that you ask for feedback from test users.

Activity 5.10

Ask one of your peers to test your data entry form by entering new records. Ask them for comments on ease of use, choice of title and labels, layout and use of white space, choice of fonts, styles and sizes, choice of colours, other features you have included. Make any necessary changes.

Find a way of recording what your test users said. For example, you could annotate a screen shot or record yourself making the changes.

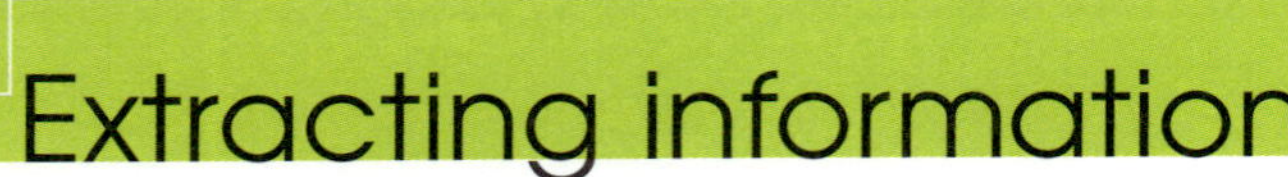

Extracting information

This is what databases are really about – finding things out. It depends on what you need to know and who the information is for or to put it another way, you need to consider audience and purpose.

What do you need to find out?

The database software will, like all computer programs, do exactly as it is told. If you want to get something out of a database you must be careful to tell it what you want using the correct language. Imagine the consequences if you get it wrong – a club manager needs a list of those over 18 who can drink alcohol and you enter ***<=18*** when you meant ***>=18***. One manager in serious trouble!

Searching on one field

<=18 is an example of a search criterion. Any field in a database structure can be searched. The way in which you enter search criteria will depend on the software you are using.

If you are using text criteria, be careful to match the text in the table. If, for example, you are searching for 'February' and there are no results, it may be because the months are stored as Jan, Feb, Mar, etc.

Relational operators

Any of the operators you can use in a validation rule can also be used in a search. Don't forget that you can use them for text as well as numbers.

- A particular value
  = *D* entered for Type in the MEMBER table would only find those who are day members
  = *Mahmood* entered for FamilyName would only find those with this family name
- A range of values
  < *1/7/76* in DoB will find all those born before 1st July 1976
  > = *Mahmood* will find all those in the alphabet from Mahmood onwards

Think carefully about what you need to know. For example, do you need a list of those born before 1/7/76 or do you actually want to include those born on this day, in which case you would need to enter ***<=1/7/76***.

TALKING POINT 5.9

Open your FILMS database. What would the search criteria be for a) films costing less than £4.00 and b) cartoon films?

Logical operators

You can also use the logical operators AND, OR and NOT with more than one criterion. Make sure that you understand the difference between AND and OR!

- **OR** finds more records where either criterion is true.
  - One value or another
    Jan or Feb in the renewal field would find all those whose membership renewal is due in January or February
    S OR Y in the Type field will find all senior members and all youth members
  - More than one value and less than another
    <1/1/48 OR >=1/1/89 will find all those with dates of birth that are **either** before 1948 **or** from 1989 onwards.
- **AND** finds records where all criteria are true.
  - Between two values
    >=Jones AND <=Peters will find all names from Jones to Peters

TALKING POINT 5.10

In your FILMS database, what would the search criterion be for cartoon and drama films only?

Searching on more than one field

You can enter complex search criteria for as many fields as you like. Concentrate on one field at a time and then make sure that the complete search is what you want.

So what if you want to find full and day members who only pay for the courts and the swimming pool? You need to search on two fields. This is no problem if you are clear what you want.

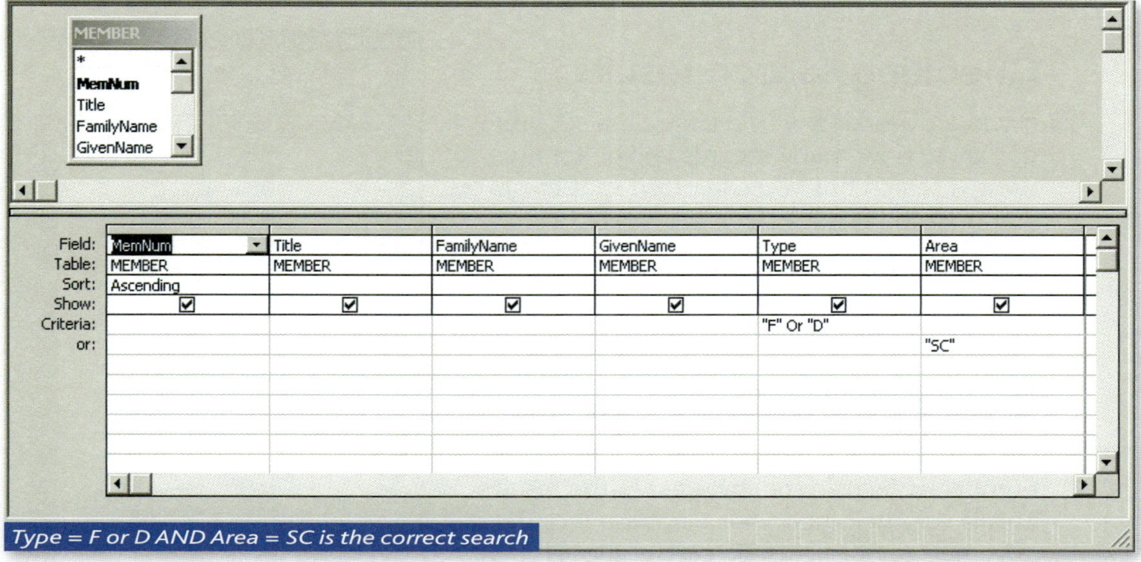

Type = F or D AND Area = SC is the correct search

Type = F **OR** D **OR** Area = SC (will find all those with full or day membership and all those who pay for swimming and courts). Make sure you understand the difference and that you enter the correct search criteria!

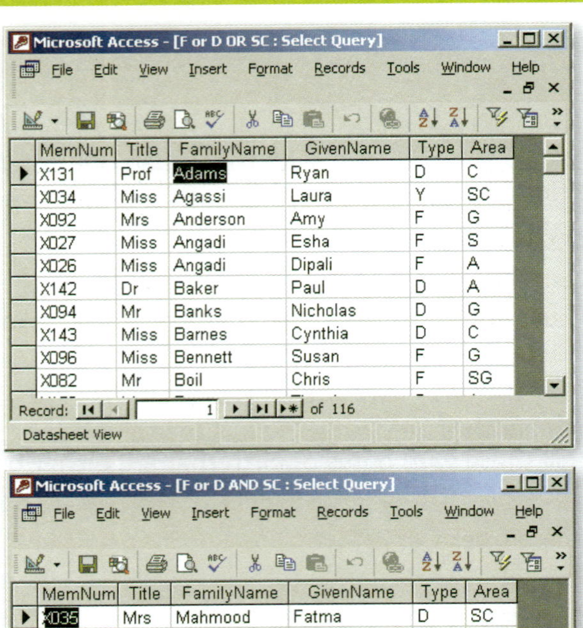

Microsoft Access - [F or D OR SC : Select Query]

MemNum	Title	FamilyName	GivenName	Type	Area
X131	Prof	Adams	Ryan	D	C
X034	Miss	Agassi	Laura	Y	SC
X092	Mrs	Anderson	Amy	F	G
X027	Miss	Angadi	Esha	F	S
X026	Miss	Angadi	Dipali	F	A
X142	Dr	Baker	Paul	D	A
X094	Mr	Banks	Nicholas	D	G
X143	Miss	Barnes	Cynthia	D	C
X096	Miss	Bennett	Susan	F	G
X082	Mr	Boil	Chris	F	SG

Record: 1 of 116

Datasheet View

Microsoft Access - [F or D AND SC : Select Query]

MemNum	Title	FamilyName	GivenName	Type	Area
X035	Mrs	Mahmood	Fatma	D	SC
X036	Mr	Mahmood	Faruq	F	SC
X042	Mr	Nelson	Gregory	F	SC

Record: 1 of 3

Results using OR and AND

Make sure that you check the results – don't assume that your search is correct just because some records are found!

TALKING POINT 5.11

Are you sure that you understand the difference between these two searches? Why is there a youth member in the first set of results?

Using your FILMS database, what would the search criterion be to find a) cartoons costing up to £3.50 and b) drama or humour films on DVD?

Checking search results

If you are working with a large data set you will not know how many records will be found using a search but you can often spot errors by scanning the results.

When looking at the results, remind yourself of what you were trying to find out. Have you found what you need?

Choosing the fields you need

When you design a search, you can limit the number of fields to be included in the results. This is very helpful if your database includes a large number of fields. Be careful though if you want to use search results in a report as reports can only include the fields you allowed in the search. If in doubt, leave a field in; you can always take it out when you design the report.

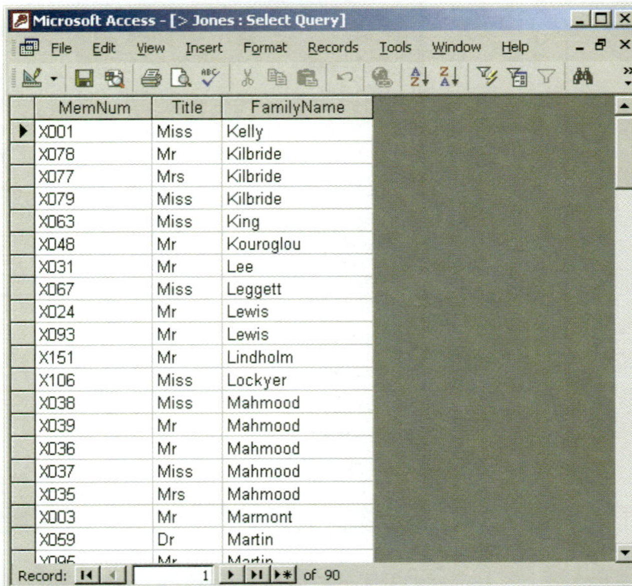

Microsoft Access - [> Jones : Select Query]

MemNum	Title	FamilyName
X001	Miss	Kelly
X078	Mr	Kilbride
X077	Mrs	Kilbride
X079	Miss	Kilbride
X063	Miss	King
X048	Mr	Kouroglou
X031	Mr	Lee
X067	Miss	Leggett
X024	Mr	Lewis
X093	Mr	Lewis
X151	Mr	Lindholm
X106	Miss	Lockyer
X038	Miss	Mahmood
X039	Mr	Mahmood
X036	Mr	Mahmood
X037	Miss	Mahmood
X035	Mrs	Mahmood
X003	Mr	Marmont
X059	Dr	Martin

Record: 1 of 90

If you intend to search for family names of Jones and beyond, and you type >Jones when it should be >=Jones in you may not notice your mistake in the design but hopefully you will spot that there is no one with the surname Jones in the results.

Why save searches?

If you update a database by adding, amending or deleting records, your search results may be incorrect. You will need to run the search again to get up-to-date results. If you don't save it, you will have to start from scratch each time.

If you have created useful searches, then you will want to use them again. How will you find them? Save your searches using sensible names. Don't call them Search1 or Query1, etc.

Can I do this?

Using database tools, make sure you can:

Search on a single field
Search on more than one field
Use relational operators
Use logical operators
Select fields to include in results
Sort on one field
Use a secondary sort

Activity 5.11

Check your skills by creating searches to extract this information from the MEMBER table. Save the searches with meaningful names.

a) All those who are over 60. Show all fields.

b) All youth members who have use of the swimming pool (be careful here!). Show name, telephone number and type of membership only.

c) All those aged 11 to 16 who live in Threepines, showing name and address only.

d) All those who use the gym and require assistance. Show membership number, full name and telephone number only.

Check the results and compare them with others in your group.

Sorting a database table

One method of making information easier to read is to sort it into a particular order. This will depend on the purpose of the information. Think about the MEMBER table. If you run a search to find people who use the gym, you might want to list them in alphabetical order of family name. Alternatively, a list in order of date of birth might be helpful if you are interested in the ages of these people. Or perhaps you want to know which other facilities they use, in which case you could sort on the Area field.

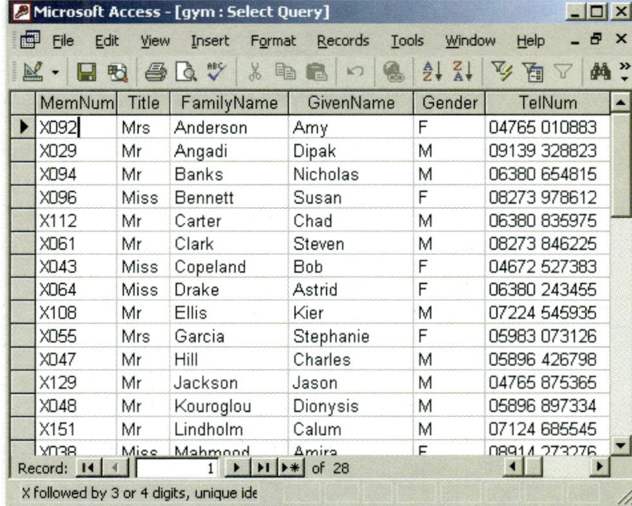

MemNum	Title	FamilyName	GivenName	Gender	TelNum
X092	Mrs	Anderson	Amy	F	04765 010883
X029	Mr	Angadi	Dipak	M	09139 328823
X094	Mr	Banks	Nicholas	M	06380 654815
X096	Miss	Bennett	Susan	F	08273 978612
X112	Mr	Carter	Chad	M	06380 835975
X061	Mr	Clark	Steven	M	08273 846225
X043	Miss	Copeland	Bob	F	04672 527383
X064	Miss	Drake	Astrid	F	06380 243455
X108	Mr	Ellis	Kier	M	07224 545935
X055	Mrs	Garcia	Stephanie	F	05983 073126
X047	Mr	Hill	Charles	M	05896 426798
X129	Mr	Jackson	Jason	M	04765 875365
X048	Mr	Kouroglou	Dionysis	M	05896 897334
X151	Mr	Lindholm	Calum	M	07124 685545
X038	Miss	Mahmood	Amira	F	08914 273276

Record: 1 of 28

X followed by 3 or 4 digits, unique ide

Secondary sorts

It is also possible to sort on two fields at the same time.

You will need to check how to sort on two fields with the software you are using. You need to be clear which is the main sort field and which is the secondary sort field. The main field is sorted from top to bottom of the table in ascending or descending order. For each different value in this main field, the second field is sorted into order.

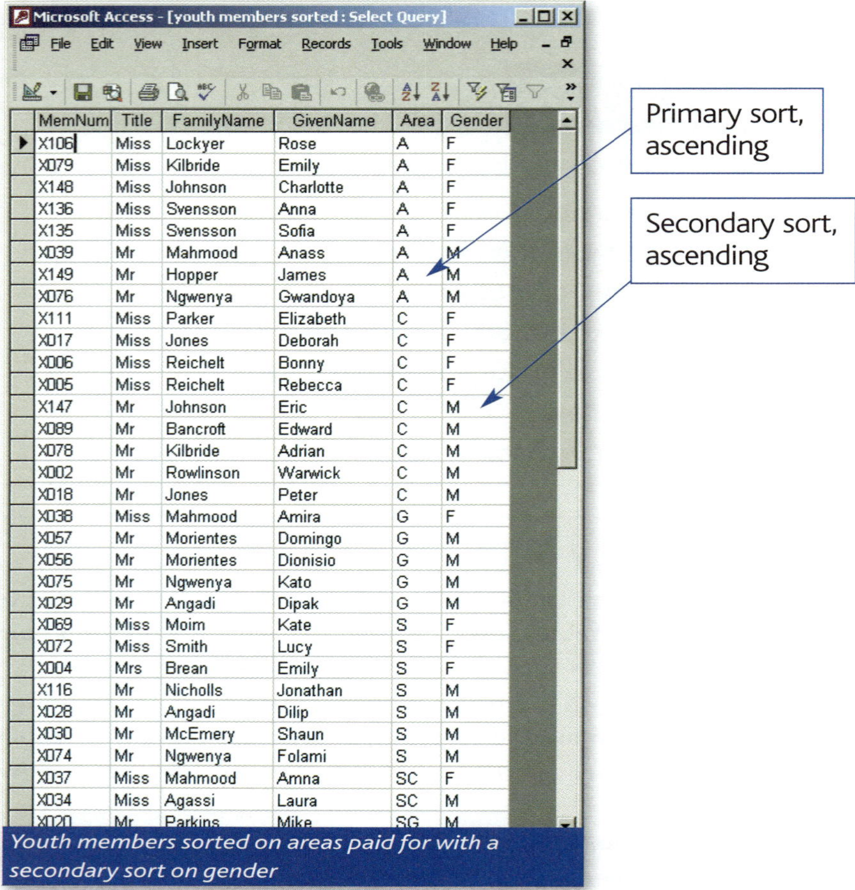

MemNum	Title	FamilyName	GivenName	Area	Gender
X106	Miss	Lockyer	Rose	A	F
X079	Miss	Kilbride	Emily	A	F
X148	Miss	Johnson	Charlotte	A	F
X136	Miss	Svensson	Anna	A	F
X135	Miss	Svensson	Sofia	A	F
X039	Mr	Mahmood	Anass	A	M
X149	Mr	Hopper	James	A	M
X076	Mr	Ngwenya	Gwandoya	A	M
X111	Miss	Parker	Elizabeth	C	F
X017	Miss	Jones	Deborah	C	F
X006	Miss	Reichelt	Bonny	C	F
X005	Miss	Reichelt	Rebecca	C	F
X147	Mr	Johnson	Eric	C	M
X089	Mr	Bancroft	Edward	C	M
X078	Mr	Kilbride	Adrian	C	M
X002	Mr	Rowlinson	Warwick	C	M
X018	Mr	Jones	Peter	C	M
X038	Miss	Mahmood	Amira	G	F
X057	Mr	Morientes	Domingo	G	M
X056	Mr	Morientes	Dionisio	G	M
X075	Mr	Ngwenya	Kato	G	M
X029	Mr	Angadi	Dipak	G	M
X069	Miss	Moim	Kate	S	F
X072	Miss	Smith	Lucy	S	F
X004	Mrs	Brean	Emily	S	F
X116	Mr	Nicholls	Jonathan	S	M
X028	Mr	Angadi	Dilip	S	M
X030	Mr	McEmery	Shaun	S	M
X074	Mr	Ngwenya	Folami	S	M
X037	Miss	Mahmood	Amna	SC	F
X034	Miss	Agassi	Laura	SC	M
X020	Mr	Parkins	Mike	SG	M

Youth members sorted on areas paid for with a secondary sort on gender

▶▶ Activity 5.12

Sort the MEMBER table in the following ways – save each sorted table with a suitable name.

a) Type of membership in alphabetical order.

b) Type of membership in alphabetical order with a secondary sort on date of birth, descending.

You can also sort and search at the same time. How you do this will depend on your software.

▶▶ Activity 5.13

Using the MEMBER table, find all youth members who are under 14 today. Sort the results in descending order of date of birth. Save the search.

Database reports

Since the only real purpose of a database is to provide information, you need to make sure that you present that information in the most effective way.

There is more on database reports on page 124 in terms of presenting the information effectively to a specified audience.

Extracting information for use in other applications

There are many reasons why you might want to extract information from a database and in many cases a database report will not be what is required. One example is mail merge.

a great big
4 points in the £

Dear Mrs Rice

£12 worth of offers just for you

After the exciting makeover of No7 cosmetics, we've now re-launched No7 Bodycare with some wonderfully indulgent pampering products all wrapped up in beautiful new packaging. There are lotions and potions to moisturise, firm, smooth and contour. Now summer's on its way you'll find everything under the sun to protect and care for your skin; including tan enhancers, shimmer and firming lotions plus a fabulous new range of advanced, easy to use self tanning formulas.

You have 2,688 Advantage Card points* which means you have the equivalent of £26.88 to spend on over 55,000 products in larger Boots stores. So go on, treat yourself to a fabulous No7 bodycare product. You deserve it.

Head straight down to your local Boots store in Wokingham to make the most of the enclosed coupons and check out the latest great offers.

We look forward to seeing you very soon.

Yours sincerely

Rebecca Pearson

Rebecca Pearson
Advantage Card Manager

P.S. We hope you like all our latest offers. And don't forget to use the coupons we've sent you, we'll be sending lots more very soon.
*As at 27/02/2005.

01/02704635/79126Av1

collect a generous 8 points for every £1 you spend in store. Take this double points coupon, on two shopping trips, and collect points doubly fast.

double points just for you
Mrs Rice 05912818 1
VALID FOR TWO USES on your total spend in a single transaction, on all products on which points are available, on two different days. Your coupon will be retained by store staff after its second use. Normal Advantage Card terms and conditions apply. Only you can use this coupon and it can't be used with any other discount or offer. We can't accept this coupon on infant formula milk (up to six months), products on prescription, Giftcard or gift vouchers, postage stamps or at Boots Opticians, David Ormerod Hearing Centres at Boots, on Bootsdirect orders or on Boots.com. Boots reserves the right to cancel or vary this offer without prior notice.
Offer ends: 30/04/05
To Boots store staff: please retain this coupon after the second use. advantage card

1000's of offers every week on your favourite things
here's some you might like...

Free No7 Moisture Drench Lipstick when you spend £15 or more on the New No7 Range
Offer ends 26/04/05

1000 Advantage Card points when you buy any 2 Clarins products - one to be skincare.
Offer starts 23/04/05 and ends 22/05/05

Buy a combination of 3 and **the cheapest is free** on all vitamins and herbal products

Save £1 with every purchase of new Rimmel Volume Flash Mascara, Full Volume Lipstick and Duo Eyeshadow.
Offer starts 13/04/05 and ends 10/05/05

Boots photo CD only £1
Each CD holds up to 200 images
Offer starts 13/04/05

FREE Valentino V 200ml Body Lotion when you buy Valentino V 50ml Eau De Parfum.
Offer starts 13/04/05 and ends 10/05/05

Buy 1 get 1 free on all Soltan Sun Protection and Aftersun
Subject to availability

Buy any 2 Sunsilk shampoos and conditioners and **receive the cheapest free.**
Offer ends 27/04/05

Date and size restrictions may apply and all offers are subject to availability. See in store for details.

1000's of prices lowered this year
Lower prices you'll love here to stay

Personalised

Mail merge is designed to produce personalised copies of a letter or other document. The software combines a standard letter with a list of contact information so that each copy includes the details for a different person. There is more on this on page 117.

Where does this personal information come from? Usually a database table! This might be a complete table or it might be the results of a search for particular people. When you run a mail merge you specify the table or search results that you want to use.

If you need to produce a contacts table for a mail merge, you will need to make sure that you include all the required fields from the database.

When you produce a mail merge letter, make sure that you include the required fields.

Always check the output – don't assume that it is correct just because a number of letters are produced. Check that the fields you included have generated the correct information.

TALKING POINT 5.12

What fields would you definitely need to include in a contacts list for a mail merge letter to Advantage Card holders?

Tackling THE PROJECT

Now it's time to tackle 'Creating a database' and 'Using a database'. Make sure you know what information you need to extract by reading the project brief again.

Ask yourself

What database structure do I need?

Use the meals data set list and take a good look at a few of the rows in the dataset. Make that you use meaningful field names and sensible data types and formats.

What can I validate?

If the list clearly states what can be input into a particular field, then you can validate it.

When you import the data set you may find that some records are rejected. Is the data invalid or is there something wrong with your database structure?

Which publications will use information from the database?

For each of these publications, use your file WHICHPUBS to remind yourself of audience and purpose. How will the results from the database be used in the publications?

What information do I need from the database?

Your searches should be designed to find exactly what you need and you will almost certainly need to include some complex searches to make the best use of the database. Do the results need sorting?

You MUST check the output to see if it is what you want. Go back and change your search designs if necessary.

Make sure you save

- the complete database
- evidence of testing

6 Getting the message across – attracting attention

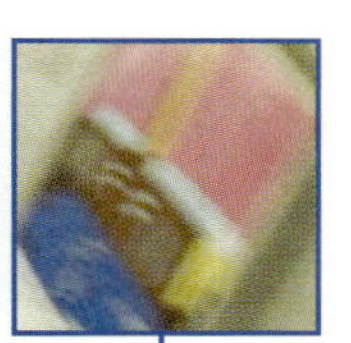

Digimodule

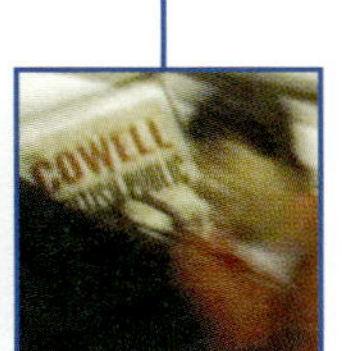

How do you get a message across to busy people on the move? They don't have time to stop and read lots of information. You need to attract their attention and get your message across to them in seconds. You've guessed it, you need a poster!

Posters can be used to announce an event such as a disco or a sale, promote a service or new product or to campaign for something.

However good your poster, the audience will be limited to those who see it. What if you want to get the information to more people? This is where flyers come in. They can be delivered through doors or left in public places. Although flyers are smaller, they can contain more information. Each person gets their own copy so they can take their time to read the content.

A good poster or flyer takes time to design and produce. Space is limited, so what you choose to include and where you put it is very important. Everything must have a purpose.

In this chapter you will learn how to attract attention by:

- *designing posters and flyers for specific audiences and purposes*
- *selecting appropriate images and text*
- *combining components to produce effective posters and flyers*
- *using prototyping and feedback to ensure that you get the message across*

Posters

What do posters aim to do?

Posters aim to do three things:

- attract the attention of people who are passing
- persuade them to read all the content
- get a message across.

Stop them in their tracks!

You cannot be sure who will see a poster or who will read it. You can try to select the audience by choosing where to display it but it must be eye-catching so that people stop to look.

Let your poster do the talking!

You will not be around when people read your poster. They will not be able to ask questions if it doesn't make sense. Not only must your poster attract attention, it must convey the message in a style that is appropriate.

Poor design will be displayed for all to see and people won't bother to read it. Before you rush off to create a poster, stop and think. What is it that you want to say and how should you present it?

TALKING POINT 6.1

Look at the poster above. What is its purpose? What message does it communicate? Who is the intended audience – is it selected people or random? Will these people stop and look? Is the poster effective? What else do they need to know?

Don't waffle!

Assuming you know who and what the poster is for, you can think about what the content should be. The amount you can say is limited by the size of the poster – it's not like a leaflet or a website where you can have as many pages as you like. Use plain English that most people will understand.

You will often find that you have too much information and you will need to decide what is important and what is unnecessary.

Don't be tempted to fill every space by adding more text or images – a poster is NOT an essay or a photograph album!

Get the size right

A poster can, of course, be any size but that does not mean that any size will do!

Paper size may be limited by the sizes that your printer will cope with. If many copies are going to be produced by a commercial printing firm then you have far more choice. Either way, you may be restricted by the cost.

Display space will also affect the sizes you can choose. Where will it be displayed? If you only need a small number and you know exactly where they will go, then you will know what space is available and you might choose A3 or bigger. If a large number are to be distributed around a town then you must allow for limited space in shop windows and the like. In this case, A4 is probably more suitable. Every situation will be different.

Flyers

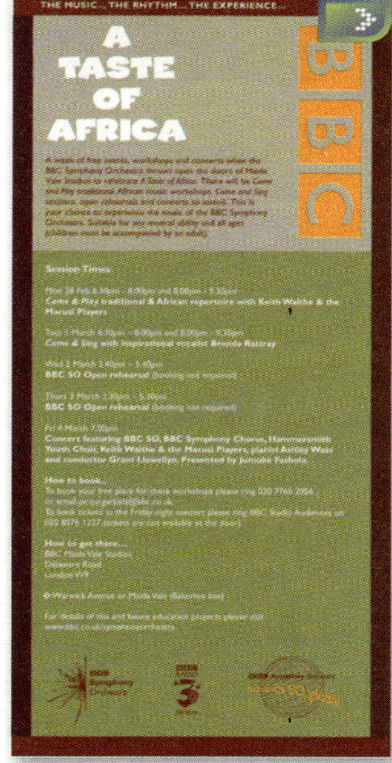

TALKING POINT 6.2

What is the difference between a flyer and a poster? Think about audience and purpose as well as format and style.

Many of the design principles for flyers and posters are the same. So what is the difference with a flyer?

Target your audience

- Flyers are intended for individual people. Sometimes they are delivered so you know exactly who has received them.
- Flyers are for people to have their own copy of the information.

Get the size right

- Flyers are generally smaller than posters. A5 is popular because it fits through letterboxes without folding. Also, piles of them can be left in public places without taking up too much space.

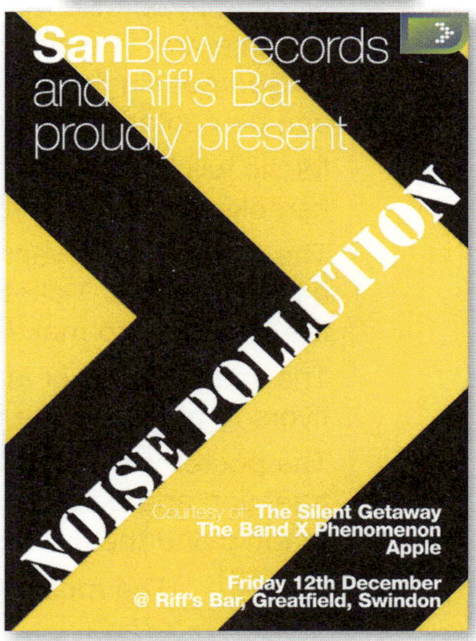

Make good use of the space

- Flyers often contain more information than a poster. Designers frequently use one side for a poster-like introduction and the other for the details.
- Text and images are smaller on a flyer and the quality needs to be good enough for all the information to be clear and easy to read.

Make it stand out from the crowd

- Flyers are often placed in holders or on tables with others. You need to make sure that yours gets noticed.

Activity 6.1

Collect examples of flyers and posters. Look at how the designers have combined text and images. Try to identify the audience and purpose. Select some that you think are effective and some that are not.

TALKING POINT 6.3

What is going to persuade someone to read a poster or flyer rather than ignore it or throw it in the bin? Look at each of the examples you collected and the NSPCC posters.

How effective is it? Do images help get the message across? Does it have too much text or too many images? Is it confusing? What does the designer hope the reader will do? Talk about the colours used in the background; images and text; letters; pictures, and message.

Where do you think it was displayed or available? How might you improve it?

Bentley Charity Ball

To help us through the rest of this chapter we will use a scenario. This gives us a purpose and a target audience for what we are doing.

Scenario

Bentley Town Council is planning a charity ball for 16-19 year olds. It will be held on 14th February from 8pm until midnight. The venue is the Town Hall which is situated in the Market Place. Free parking is available in the Central Car Park.

Tickets cost £20. Dress is black tie.

QuickCabs taxi firm is offering a limo pickup for groups of 6 or more within a three mile radius of the town centre. The cost is £5 per person per single trip. The manager can be contacted on 03432 845874.

Music will be provided by local bands throughout the evening and there will be a karaoke competition from 10pm to 11pm with prizes for the best entrants.

The costs of the event are high because there will be live music and lasers as well as a buffet supper. Tickets are limited to 500 but it is vital that at least 300 are sold if the council is to make a donation to Children in Need.

The event organiser is Jamie Hendrix and he needs help to produce posters and flyers to advertise the ball. The publications must meet the council's requirements.

The poster will be displayed around the town. It must be A4 size. It should attract attention and persuade people to buy tickets. It must include at least one suitable graphic and these lines:

The most eagerly awaited event of the year will soon be here!

Probably the best ball in the world!

The council will print 10,000 A5 flyers. A copy will be enclosed with the free local newspaper delivered to every household. The leaflets will also be left in public places including the library, theatre and leisure centre for people to take away. The flyer must include all the necessary information and at least one image.

Jamie can be contacted on 03432 847844 or emailed at charityball@bentley.gov.uk.

TALKING POINT 6.4

Who is the audience? Does Jamie need to attract their attention?

Why is Jamie's advertising material needed?

Where will the publications be displayed or read?

Activity 6.2

Think 'who, why, where?' and use a list or mind map to decide what the flyer and the poster should include. What style of language is appropriate?

Designing posters and flyers

There is nothing worse than a boring poster! It takes up space that could be used for something else, it does not look good and it certainly does not attract attention. Posters should shout out to people and make them say 'I want that' or 'That sounds good'. A poor quality poster might even put people off completely.

Activity 6.3

Choose a poster from those you have collected. Try to 'get into the designer's mind' and draw the design that you think would have resulted in the poster. Make sure that all components are indicated and that the layout is clear. Would someone else be able to look at your design and describe a poster that is something like the one you chose?

Choosing colours

- **How many?** Don't use too many colours – it can look messy and put the reader off.
- **What shades?** Light pastel shades give a very different effect to bright or dark colours.
- **Contrast?** Choose background and foreground colours that complement each other and make sure that the foreground stands out.
- **Headings** can be highlighted by using different colour combinations to the rest of the page.

Choosing fonts

- **How many?** As few as possible! Too many font types look messy.
- **Which fonts?** Choose ones that are easy to read.

Would you like to read a poster in this font? Or perhaps you prefer this

Would a poster be easier to read in this font? How about this?

- **What sizes?** Choose the size according to the importance of the text but be consistent. Bear in mind that it is the size combined with the colour that makes the impact.

- **Which case?** Do not use all UPPER CASE type in your posters. It can make the text look cramped and difficult to read.

THIS IS WHAT IT LOOKS LIKE WHEN ALL THE CHARACTERS ARE IN UPPER CASE

This is what it looks like when only the first character is in upper case

Death by word art!

If some of the posters we see around are anything to go by, many people think that word art, any word art, and as much as possible, is essential for any poster!

Use word art by all means but only if it improves your design and you can justify it. It must serve a purpose. If in doubt, leave it out!

A picture is worth a thousand words

Or so they say! Photographs and other images can be very effective if you make sure that they are:

- appropriate
- positioned sensibly on the page
- good enough quality and not blurred
- not distorted.

Remember that you must have permission to use images if they belong to someone else.

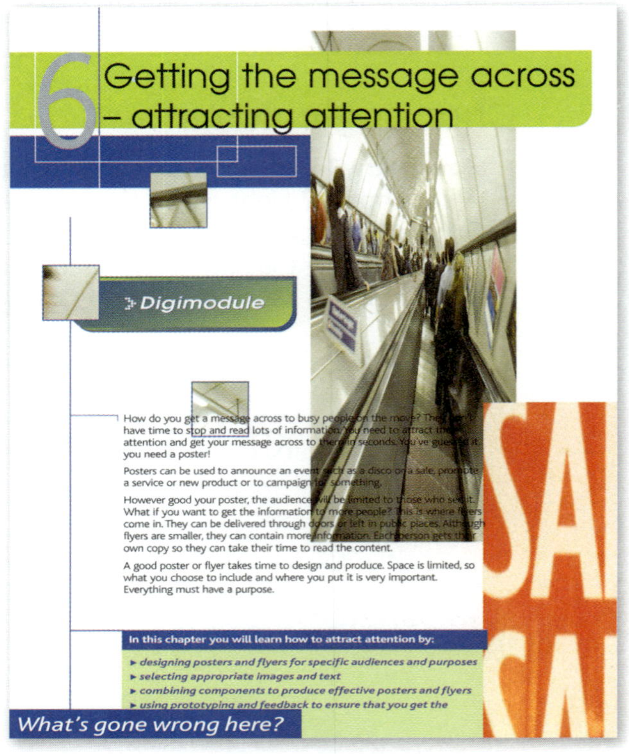

6 Getting the message across – attracting attention

Digimodule

How do you get a message across to busy people on the move? They [illegible] have time to stop and read lots of information. You need to attract [illegible] attention and get your message across to them in seconds. You've guessed it: you need a poster!

Posters can be used to announce an event such as a disco or a sale, promote a service or new product or to campaign for something.

However good your poster, the audience will be limited to those who see it. What if you want to get the information to more people? This is where flyers come in. They can be delivered through doors or left in public places. Although flyers are smaller, they can contain more information. Each person gets their own copy so they can take their time to read the content.

A good poster or flyer takes time to design and produce. Space is limited, so what you choose to include and where you put it is very important. Everything must have a purpose.

In this chapter you will learn how to attract attention by:

- *designing posters and flyers for specific audiences and purposes*
- *selecting appropriate images and text*
- *combining components to produce effective posters and flyers*
- *using prototyping and feedback to ensure that you get the*

What's gone wrong here?

TALKING POINT 6.5

Compare the two versions of the poster on page 89. Try to identify everything that could be done to improve them.

Death by clip art

Clip art seems to pop up everywhere. Sometimes it adds interest but it can just as easily distract attention from the rest of the poster. Use it sparingly and only if it serves a purpose.

Looking through clip art files can be fun. Don't be tempted to spend more time fiddling about choosing cartoons than concentrating on the content.

Borders

Page borders can sometimes look effective, especially if there isn't very much information on the page but use them with care. The page itself can be the frame provided that you allow some white space around the edge.

Borders, boxes, and lines can also be used within the page to set off a particular block of information. Look at how this is done for the Bentley Charity Ball scenario on page 88.

Layout

Once you have decided on all the items that must appear on your poster, you can concentrate on the layout. Spend time thinking about the layout. Make full use of the space, but don't be tempted to squash in as much as possible. Think about how you will emphasise key items.

Don't add things to your design in random places. Each item should be aligned to something else otherwise it will look random.

Organise your information into small, manageable chunks. Items scattered all over the place are confusing. The reader doesn't know what order to look at things in. For example, if there are contact details on the page, put them in a tight little block and put some white space between that block and other elements.

White space

White space is any empty space on a page (if the background is a different colour, then it may actually be blue space or pink space but it's the same idea).

Don't be afraid to have plenty of it on a poster – it helps the reader move from one area to another. A cluttered poster is hard work and is unlikely to get that important message across.

White space is just as important on a flyer, even though there is often far less space than on most posters. Use it to separate different parts of your flyer so that the reader can take in one section at a time.

Alignment

Try right and left alignment as well as centring each group of information to see what looks best.

TALKING POINT 6.6

How could this menu be improved?

▸▸ Activity 6.4

Produce a design for a poster and a flyer for the Bentley Charity Ball. Use the scenario and the notes you made earlier to make sure you include all the necessary content. Keep an eye on file and image sizes as well.

Creating posters and flyers

Choosing your software

Once you have decided exactly what you want to produce and you have a design to work with you need to choose which software you will use to create it.

What are the options?

Word processing tools has enough features to enable you to create excellent posters and flyers. However, you may prefer to use specialist desktop publishing tools.

The choice is yours!

Can I do this?

Using word processing or desktop publishing tools, make sure you can:

Format text
Align text
Use text boxes
Wrap text
Import and position images
Crop and resize images
Use lines and borders
Change colours
Use spelling and grammar checkers
Proofread for other errors

Review, review and review

Keep checking your work as you go along.

Produce prototypes and check them for:

- mistakes in spelling or grammar
- readability
- consistency of style
- layout and use of white space.

Be critical of your work and make changes if necessary. Ask others to check your prototypes and make use of their feedback.

Proofreading

Although the spellchecker is very good at finding mis-spelt words, it is not always right!

It can be annoying when it questions you about surnames and other words that it does not have in its dictionary. But you can choose to ignore it!

It can be disastrous if you think that all you have to do is get rid of all those red squiggly lines (or whatever your software uses to highlight mis-spelt words).

The real problem comes when you have typed in the wrong word – if it is spelt correctly the poor spellchecker can do nothing to help. You must proofread all the text in every publication you produce and look carefully for this type of error.

⏩ Activity 6.5

Type the two sets of sentences into a word processing document and spell check.

Sentence One	Sentence Two	Which is the correct sentence? Did spell check tell you?
Many young people get pocket money from their parents.	Many young people get pocket money from there parents.	
The student sitting at the back of the lecture theatre could not here the lecturer.	The student sitting at the back of the lecture theatre could not hear the lecturer.	
I use my PC all the time. I use it for the internet as well as for typing up work.	I use my pea sea all the time. I use it for the internet as well as for typing up work.	
I love to write short stories.	I love to right short stories.	
I don't like reading bucks. I much prefer to play sports.	I don't like reading books. I much prefer to play sports.	
I am going to ask my Mum to give me a cheque for the school trip.	I am going to ask my Mum to give me a check for the school trip.	
When should we meet up to discuss the project?	When should we meat up to discuss the project?	

Test users and feedback

No matter how pleased you are with your poster, the real test is what other people think.

When you have the final version, try to find people who are part of your target audience or have similar interests. Ask them what they think.

- Does the poster attract attention because it is well designed?
- Is it accurate?
- Does it communicate clearly and effectively with the reader?
- And finally, does it convey the right message?

⏩ Activity 6.6

Use your designs to produce a poster and a flyer for the Bentley Charity Ball. Read the scenario again and check back through the pages in this chapter to make sure that you end up with products that get the message across.

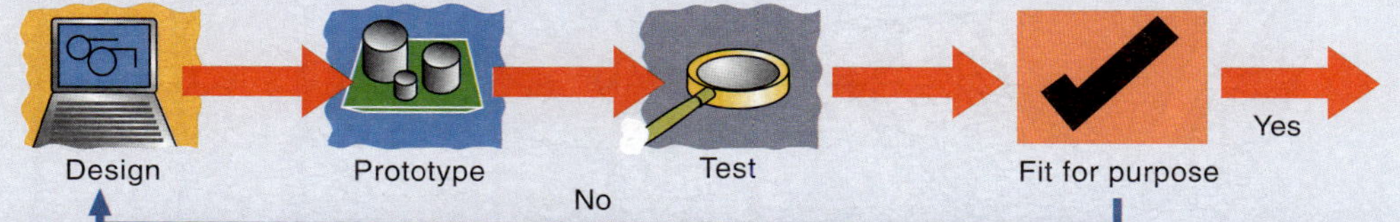

Here is a reminder of the production cycle. Use the loop back as many times as necessary – keep going back to the design until you are absolutely sure that the publication is fit for purpose.

Keep a record of the feedback you receive from reviewers and the changes you made.

Tackling THE PROJECT

Now it is time to tackle 'Attracting attention'. This aim of this section of THE PROJECT is to produce two publications that attract attention and persuade people to read the content.

Open your file WHICHPUBS and check that you are still happy with your plans for the poster and flyer.

Ask yourself

Have I got all the information I need?

Review the information you have gathered for use in these publications and carry out further research if you are not happy with your collection.

Have I included appropriate content?

Start by designing the layout and working out where you will place components in each publication. You should have found suitable images and text but it is not too late to add more or change these now.

Does each publication get the message across?

Create prototypes and ask for feedback from suitable test users. Remind yourself of the audience and select test users who will give you the most useful feedback. Make any necessary changes and review the publications again.

Make sure you save

- prototypes with user feedback
- final versions

7 Getting the message across – making information available

Where do you look when you need information for that dreaded coursework? Or when you want to check train times or what's on at the cinema? A few years ago, people would have taken a trip to the library, reached for Yellow Pages or bought a newspaper – but things are changing fast! More and more people are turning to the internet for information.

If you have information, whether it's something you want to sell, latest news for parents, or anything else that you think people out there may be looking for, you might consider creating a website or adding pages to an existing site.

Some members of your target audience may not have access to the internet but if they are looking in a specific location, such as a leisure centre or an exhibition, then an information point may be suitable – this is similar to a website but only available in the location. If you want to make information available to people to read in their own time, leaflets are a possibility – you will need to leave them where people will find them.

If you want people to read what you have to say, your publications must stand out from the crowd.

In this chapter you will learn how to make information available by:

- ***identifying the type of audience and where they might look***
- ***designing web pages, information points and leaflets***
- ***combining components to produce effective publications***
- ***using prototyping and feedback to ensure that you get your message across***

7 Websites

A website is a collection of web pages that aims to make information available to a widespread audience.

There are a number of reasons why you might choose to make information available via a website:

- it is possible to reach a world wide audience
- it is easy to keep the information up to date
- the audience can be of unlimited size at no extra cost
- there is no limit to the amount of information you can include.

Making people stop and look

Anyone who has access to the internet may choose to visit a website. What will persuade them to explore the site?

TALKING POINT 7.1

Look at this website for youth information. What is its purpose? What message does it communicate? Who is likely to find it? Will they stop and look at everything? Consider download time for each page, layout, colours, images, style, navigation.

Helping visitors find what they want

Nowadays, it is not just computer experts who use the internet to search for information. It must be easy for visitors to a website to find their way around. Planning is crucial to the success of any website.

Getting the message across

Visitors need to be able to access all the information on a website easily. The information must be well organised and clear.

There is no limit to the number of pages or the amount of information you can include but beware of information overload. Say what you need to say and leave it there.

Activity 7.1

Explore the BBC website and look at ways in which features are used to make the site easy to use and to get different messages across.

Designing web pages

Paper-based publications such as posters and leaflets restrict you to text and images but web pages can include other components such as sound, animation and video. However, don't get carried away! No amount of multimedia wizardry will make up for poor design.

All information about a particular topic or item should be on the same page. Some pages will need more content than others but this is not a problem on a website because there is no fixed page length. However, people don't like scrolling down too often.

Using text

Reading large amounts of text on a screen is tiring on the eyes and it is easy to lose your place. Unnecessary text should be avoided. Although web authoring tools do not allow as many formatting options as word processing tools, there are enough features to allow you to present your text effectively.

Fonts

- **How many?** As few as possible! Too many font types look messy.
- **Which fonts?** Choose ones that are easy to read such as Verdana or Georgia which were designed specifically for web pages. Experiment and ask other people what they think.
- **What sizes?** Choose the size according to the importance of the text.

Alignment

Selected text can be centred or right, left or fully aligned (justified). Think carefully about the overall look of the page when you are aligning sections of text. It is very easy to make a page look messy and confusing.

This text is *left aligned*

This text is *centred*

This text is *right aligned*

This text is *fully aligned*. Be careful if you use it in narrow columns. This can result in large gaps between words.

Headings

Use headings and subheadings to help people find information they want to read.

Bullets

Bullets can be used on web pages for lists. Take care that the bullets are consistent in style and size and that the line spacing between the bullets is the same.

As with alignment, bullets are a feature designed to improve the layout of a page but they can easily have the opposite effect if used inappropriately.

Activity 7.2

Open the file using the tools you use for producing web pages. Format the text to make it easier to read. Preview the page in your browser and ask others for comments. Save your file as OASISSWIM.

Oasis Swimming
Classes
Run by our qualified instructors. Application forms from reception.
Early birds aqua aerobics
6:30-7 a.m. Monday, Wednesday and Friday
This session will get you off to a flying start
Aqua tots
2-3 p.m. Tuesday, Saturday
Help your child grow in confidence in the water.
Aqua fit
10-11 a.m. Tuesday and Thursday
You don't need to be able to swim to enjoy this session of gentle exercises. Designed for those who want to avoid anything too strenuous
High jumps
7-8 p.m. Thursday
Introductory diving course. Over 14s only.
Swimming lessons
7-8 p.m.
Beginners: Monday
Intermediate: Wednesday
Special sessions
Just turn up
Adults only swim
8-9 p.m. Monday-Friday
This session is free from hustle and bustle. Soothing music to help you relax and re-energise.
Chart swim
7-8 p.m. Tuesday
Swim along to the latest chart hits
Private pool hire
Hire the pool for private functions
Clubs
Several clubs are based at the pool. Details of their sessions are available from reception

Using images

Almost every web page you view has at least one image such as a photograph, cartoon, map or drawing. An image can convey a surprising amount of information if chosen with care.

Gathering images

Only include images that help to convey the message. Use ready-made images if they are suitable but remember that you must have permission to use them if they belong to someone else.

If you can't find something suitable, think about creating your own. Never include an image just for the sake of it. See Chapter 3 for information on capturing images.

Deciding where to put images

If an image relates to a section of text on the page, make sure that this is obvious by its position. You can left align an image so that the text appears to the right, right align it with the text on the left or centre it. You can also create white space around an image so that the text is not too close to it.

Making sure images are not distorted

Be careful to keep the same proportions when resizing. When you resize an image, always drag a corner handle so that the proportions are kept. Otherwise you will end up with some interesting effects. We will leave you to work out which one of the images below has the correct proportions!

Making sure images are not too big

Images can dramatically increase the file size and the download times. You have almost certainly had to sit and wait while a web page downloads onto your computer. You may need to reduce the quality of the image to make the file smaller. You can do this by lowering the resolution and/or by changing the file format.

You should remember that simply resizing an image once you have put it on the web page does not alter its file size.

Optimising images

Resolution is a measure of the quality of an image. Images for display on screen can be of a lower quality than for print. However, you must preview images in browser tools to make sure that they look good enough.

The process of achieving a sensible file size for an image but making sure that it is good enough quality is called optimisation. You may want to use graphics tools to optimise images as it will tell you the current file size and estimated download time.

Optimising images

Selecting a file format

Images can be stored in a number of different file formats, such as:

- GIF (.gif) for images with blocks of colour such as drawings
- JPEG (.jpg) for photos and other images that have changing colours.

You should check your DiDA SPB when the time comes as this will list which file formats you are allowed to use.

Accessibility

You should make sure that your web pages can be read by as many people as possible even if they cannot view the images. For example, people who are visually impaired use special tools that can read the text on web pages to them but the tools cannot tell what is displayed in an image. Every image should have what is called alternative text entered to describe what the image shows.

A surprising number of people are colour-blind and can't tell the difference between red and green so you should be extra careful with these colours.

Adding sound

Sound can enhance a web page – a simple piece of music can create a particular mood whereas a voice recording can provide additional information.

However, not all computer systems have sound cards fitted and many people prefer to work with the speakers switched off, so don't rely on sound for essential information.

Of course, when it comes to tackling the SPB you must ensure that any sound files used are in the list of acceptable formats.

Now I know what it was like to watch silent movies.

Choosing colours

- **Which colours?** For websites you need to be careful as some computer screens may not display the full range of colours. Web-safe colours are the colours that will display correctly on any machine. If you are using web authoring tools there will be an option to select from the Web-Safe Palette which will have 212 or 216 colours.
- **How many?** Don't use too many colours – it can look messy and put the reader off.
- **What shades?** Light pastel shades give a very different effect from bright or dark colours.
- **Contrast?** Choose background and text colours that complement each other. Try to use combinations that look good and are easy to read. The safest option is to stick to these rules:
  - Use dark text on light backgrounds.
  - Use light text on dark backgrounds.
  - Don't rely on differences in colour to emphasise information.

DiDA Designed to develop real-world practical skills	DiDA Designed to develop real-world practical skills	DiDA Designed to develop real-world practical skills	DiDA Designed to develop real-world practical skills
DiDA Designed to develop real-world practical skills	DiDA Designed to develop real-world practical skills	DiDA Designed to develop real-world practical skills	DiDA Designed to develop real-world practical skills
DiDA Designed to develop real-world practical skills	DiDA Designed to develop real-world practical skills	DiDA Designed to develop real-world practical skills	DiDA Designed to develop real-world practical skills

Some good and bad colour combinations

▸▸ Activity 7.3

Using web tools, open the file OASISSWIM you created for Activity 7.2 and experiment with different combinations of web-safe colours.

Using links

Users need to know where they are in a site, where they can go next and how to get back again. Although you are not required to develop a complete website at this stage, you need to add links to your web pages so that users can move around easily.

Different types of link

There are four main types of link that can be used in a web page:

- Internal link – goes to another page on the same website There must be at least one of these on every page so that the user can move on easily.
- Anchor (or bookmark) – goes to a specific position on the same page. This is useful if the page is very long. 'Back to top' is a common example.
- External link – goes to a different website.
- Email link – opens a blank email message rather than another page.

Entering a path

Whenever you create a link to another page or website, you need to enter its path or address so that the browser will take the user to the correct location. You can learn more about this on pages 150 and 151. The most important thing to remember is that links between pages must use relative paths.

Identifying links

You need to make links obvious to the user. You can use text or an image.

A text link is the most common. A word or phrase can be used so that the user clicks the text to move to a new page. The text is often underlined but it can be a different colour, bold or italic.

Alternatively, a user can click on an image or a button to activate a link.

Activity 7.4

Look through THE PROJECT. The menu is actually a series of text links to other pages. Identify other examples of internal links using text and images. Look for any external links.

Storyboarding

You won't be surprised to hear that web pages are only as good as the designs allow them to be. Each page should have a distinct purpose and message. Not only do you have to think about individual pages, you also have to plan how the pages will work together. They need to have the same 'look' and 'feel'.

You will find a storyboard is a useful planning tool. This helps you to plan:

- how many pages you need
- what components will appear on every page
- the position of components on each page
- the links between pages and what they will look like
- colours and combinations
- font styles and formatting.

Page/Screen Title:	Oasis Swimming	File name:	Swim.htm
Comments	When page is opened, manager starts to speaker after 1 second delay.		

Navigation bar
Home
Indoor activities
Outdoor activities
How to find us

Photo of pool in use

List of activities

Back

Colours
Background: Pale blue
Text: Dark blue
Buttons – white text on dark blue

Font:
Verdana
Titles – 16pt, centred
Body text – 12pt

Rich media
Audio
30 second recording of manager welcoming pool users plays once
Video
None

Files:
Pool_ in_use.jpg
Welcome.wav

Example of a student's storyboard for web page

Paper vs screen

Should you create your storyboard on paper or on screen? Electronic storyboards can be shared with more people so feedback is richer, you can easily make changes and you can keep copies – but there is still something to be said for good old-fashioned pencil and paper! You can sit and scribble your ideas any time, anywhere and there is no limit to the size.

You might start by creating an outline on paper and then refine your ideas on screen or you might want to create a template on the computer, print it out and fill in the slides on paper. There are special storyboarding programs around but you have all you need in basic tools applications such as word processing.

You don't need to put everything that's going to be a part of your finished presentation into your storyboard – use it to map out your ideas.

Consistency

Pages on a site need to be consistent.

Activity 7.5

Look at these pages in your browser. You can tell from the images that they are probably from the same site, but they don't look or feel as if they belong together, do they? What could be done to improve them?

Activity 7.6

Read the brief for Bentley Charity Ball on page 88. Design a storyboard for four or five web pages for the ball. These will be published on the council website with a link from the home page. Include as much detail as possible, including alternative text. Make sure the pages are consistent. Ask other people to comment on your storyboard. Make changes based on this feedback.

Designing an information point

An information point has much in common with a website. It is screen-based, has multimedia components and is interactive. The user can select which pages to view and in which order. Almost all the design issues we have looked at for websites can be applied to an information point. It can even be created using web tools. The main difference is that an information point is local – it is not uploaded to the web. Most commercial information points include a touch sensitive screen where users press links to move around but any PC can be set up as an information point using the mouse to navigate.

An information point is most useful when you have some idea of the audience but do not know exactly who will choose to read your information. For example, an open day at a country park attracts many different types of visitor but they have all chosen to be in the same place on the same day. Some will have visited before and will know some of the information; others will be first-time visitors.

An interactive map offers many different items of information. Visitors can select information by clicking on an area of the map. Different people will find different things useful and some will ignore it all together. The information point makes information available to those who want it.

Persuade people to use it

If people are milling around at an open day and come across your information point, it will have to be good if they are going to make use of it. All they will see at first is a computer monitor so what they see displayed is going to make all the difference. How will you make it stand out and persuade people to use it?

Make it easy to use

When people visit a website they have chosen to use a computer to access information. If an information point is available for use by anyone, it will have to be very straightforward. The presentation and navigation will need careful planning.

Design clear and consistent menus for navigation, using images as well as text. Avoid confusion by keeping the number of options on each page to no more than six.

Activity 7.7

Your school or college is planning an Open Day for students who might want to enrol for next year. There will be an information point in the reception area. This must include a map with links to a summary of what can be found in each area. Use a storyboard to design this information point. Include as much detail as possible.

7

Creating web pages and information points

Choosing your tools

Once you have decided exactly what you want to produce and you have a design to work with you need to choose which tools you will use to create it.

What are the options for web pages?

For Unit 1, you need to be able to create and link web pages but you are not expected to produce a complete website. Although you may use specialist web authoring tools such as Dreamweaver or FrontPage, you can meet the requirements of Unit 1 by using the web authoring features of word processing or desktop publishing tools. Specialist tools will be essential if you move on to Unit 2 which is all about using multimedia tools.

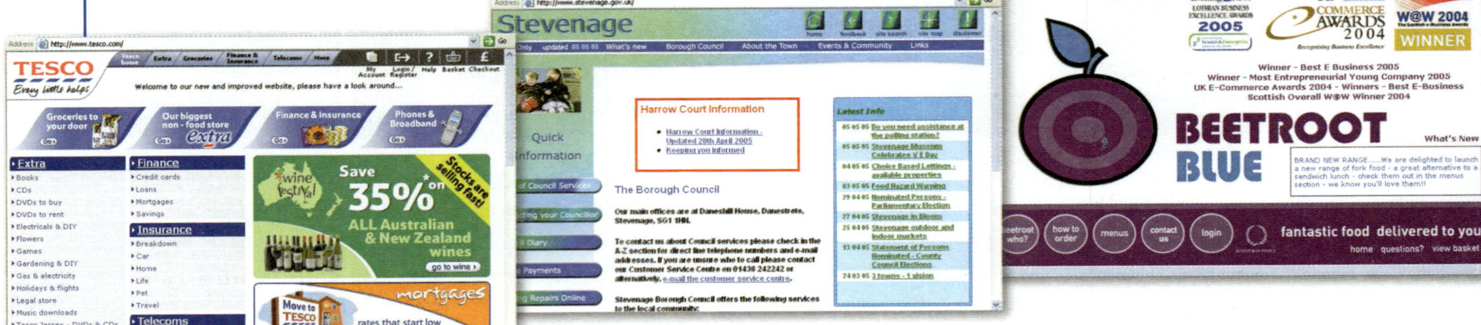

What are the options for information points?

An information point can be created using the same tools that you use for your web pages. Presentation tools is also a possibility. The tools must allow you to create a series of interactive multimedia pages with a flexible navigation route.

Can I do this?

Using web authoring tools, make sure you can:

Format text
Align text
Use bullets
Use lines and borders
Change colours
Import and position images
Align text and images
Crop and resize images
Optimise images
Insert links
Use text and images for links
Use a table for page layout

⏩ Activity 7.8

Use your storyboard from Activity 7.6 to produce some web pages for the Bentley Charity Ball.

Read the scenario again and check back through the pages in this chapter to make sure that you end up with a publication that is fit for purpose.

Keep on checking!

Keep checking your work as you go along.

Create prototypes of your pages and check them for:

- accuracy
- readability and consistency of style
- layout and use of white space
- usability.

Be critical of your work and make changes if necessary. Ask others to check your prototypes and make use of their feedback.

No matter how pleased you are with your finished web pages, the real test is what other people think.

When you think you have the final version, try to find people who might be part of your target audience or have similar interests. Ask them what they think. Do the pages:

- offer information that will be useful to others?
- persuade people to read all the content?
- communicate clearly and effectively with the user and convey the right message?

Remember the production cycle!

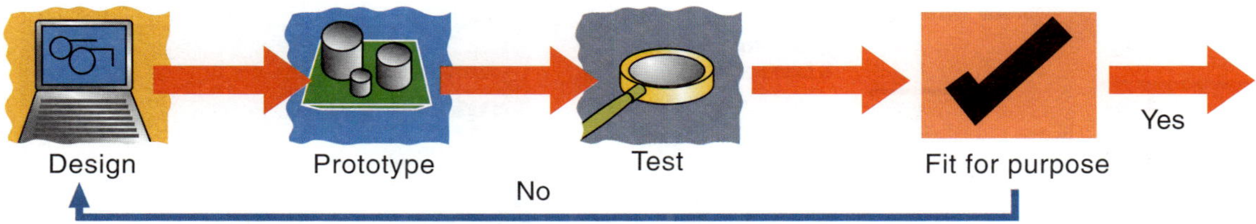

Preview your pages in at least one browser. If you can, check them with other browsers. The most common are Internet Explorer and Netscape Navigator although others such as Mozilla Firefox are becoming popular.

⏩ Activity 7.9

Use your storyboard from Activity 7.7 to create an information point for the Open Day at your school or college. If possible, ask students of an appropriate age to act as test users and give you feedback.

7 Information leaflets

Not everyone who is looking for information has access to the internet and many people still prefer printed publications.

Leaflets can be sent out to anyone who requests a copy, handed out to people or left in public places for people to pick up if they are interested. Many organisations make information available in this way.

Sometimes an organisation will use a poster or flyer to attract attention and make further information available in a leaflet.

This leaflet has a poster to go with it, *see page 86.*

TALKING POINT 7.2

These days, anyone with a computer can create and print a leaflet but some are better than others. Look at each of these leaflets and discuss the features listed:

- *Audience and purpose*
- *Size of paper*
- *Orientation*
- *Colours (full colour/2 colour/b&w)*
- *Number of folds*
- *Balance of text and images*
- *Use of white space*

Planning

You will find that some of the leaflets you collected are better than others and it will come as no surprise to hear yet again that it is the design that makes the most difference. Any leaflets you produce need to be attractive, clear and interesting if they are to avoid the rubbish bin. Start by deciding:

- **who** the target audience is and **why** the leaflet is needed
- **where** it will be distributed
- **what** content must go in it
- **how** you will go about it.

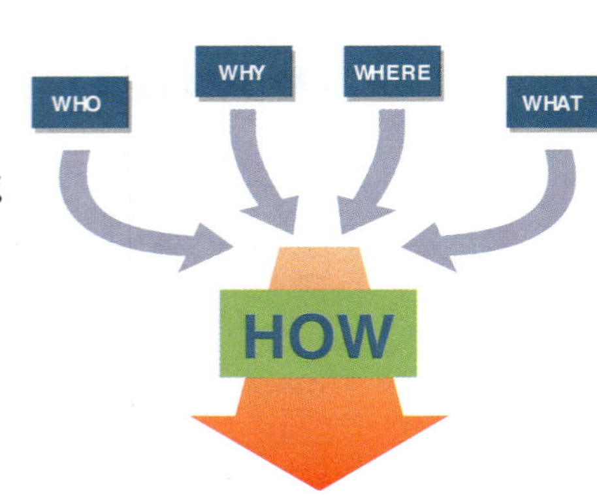

Designing a leaflet

Many of the general design principles that you have learned for posters, flyers, web pages and information points also apply to leaflets.

Before you can start work on the design of a leaflet you must decide what paper you will use and how it will be folded.

A4 can be folded once to make A5 leaflets like this

A4 can be folded twice to produce a leaflet like this

What paper size?

Most leaflets are printed on A4 paper and then folded.

How will it be folded?

You need to decide how you will fold the paper once it is printed because this will affect which way up you place blocks of text and images.

Sketch your design on paper and fold it to make sure that it works.

Choosing colours

Which colours? Stick to simple colour combinations. Try to relate the colours to the content or to the mood of the leaflet

Contrast? Choose your background and foreground colours carefully. Make sure that all content is easy to read when printed, particularly blocks of text. What you see on screen won't always look the same in print.

Greens and earthy colours will suit a leaflet about a country park but would not be so effective for a leaflet about children's toys

Using text

Fonts

- **Which styles?** Choose ones that are easy to read when printed. Generally all the text should be the same font except possibly the headings.
- **What sizes?** Choose the size according to the importance of the text but make sure that all the sizes are legible when printed.
- **What formatting?** Use bold, underline or italics for emphasis.

Alignment

As you know text can be right, left, centre or fully aligned. Think carefully about the overall look of the leaflet when you are aligning sections of text. Don't be tempted to use different alignments unless you can justify it.

Think about how the alignment will work when the leaflet is folded.

Bullets

Bullets are very useful for making lists easier to read. Make sure that all the bullets in a list are consistent. Generally, bulleted lists should be left aligned so that the bullets themselves are in line.

Using images

Images are an essential part of most leaflets and can make all the difference, especially on the front cover.

Finding suitable images

Images printed on a leaflet will often be quite small and you should bear this in mind when you are selecting or creating them on-screen.

Don't forget that you must have permission to use images if they belong to someone else.

Deciding where to put them

Each image must have a purpose and must be positioned so that it relates to other content. If the paper is to be folded, make sure that the whole image remains complete on the finished leaflet. Make sure that there is space around the image. Text that is too close will be very difficult to read. Text wrapping features allow you to place an image next to or in the middle of text. Make sure that there are not too many hyphens and that the page or column looks balanced.

Making sure they are good enough quality

If you look at a variety of leaflets you will notice that the quality of the images varies. Images that display clearly on screen won't necessarily look so good when printed. This is particularly true for photographs. Use images that have good resolution. If you are capturing images using a digital camera, set it to at least medium resolution – you can always reduce it using computer tools if you need to. Check that you have got it right by printing the image the same size as it will appear in the leaflet.

TALKING POINT 7.3

Look at the leaflets collected and comment on the use of text styles, formatting, and images.

Using tables

Insert a table into a leaflet whenever a grid of rows and columns will make the information clearer. Make sure that the table does not get folded when the leaflet is produced.

Headings and sub-headings

Use headings and sub-headings to introduce each section of text.

Make sure that the format and style of headings is consistent.

A leaflet with two folds.

Layout

To some extent the layout will be determined by the way you decide to fold the paper. Organise your information into manageable chunks so that the reader can take in one section at a time. Try to space things out evenly and think about how you will emphasise more important items.

White space

Don't be tempted to cram as much information as you can into a leaflet. Make good use of white space to separate different sections.

Margins and columns

Set page margins that allow space around the edge but don't make them too big. Default settings often work for an A4 page but may need to be reduced if you use smaller pages.

If each page of the leaflet is A5 or bigger, you could divide the text into columns. Check carefully that this results in a sensible layout of the text that is easy to read.

Activity 7.10

In Activity 7.9 you created an information point for an Open Day at your school or college. This gives a summary of what is on offer. Design a leaflet that will provide further information.

Creating a leaflet

Can I do this?

Using word processing or desktop publishing tools, make sure you can:

- **Use columns**
- **Format text**
- **Align text**
- **Wrap text**
- **Capture images**
- **Import and position images**
- **Align text and images**
- **Crop and resize images**
- **Use bullets**
- **Change margins**
- **Change colours**
- **Use text boxes**
- **Use lines and borders**
- **Create a table**
- **Insert page numbers**

Activity 7.11

Use your design to create an information leaflet for the Open Day. Make sure that it is suitable for the intended audience and purpose – don't forget the production cycle on page 105!

Tackling The Project

Now you are ready to tackle 'Making information available'.

This aim of this section of **The Project** is to produce publications that make information available to people who might be interested but are not necessarily looking for it.

Ask yourself

Have I got all the information I need?

You will need information from your survey and database as well as other components. Open WHICHPUBS and check that you have everything you need. If necessary, carry out further research. Make sure you include original components that you have created yourself as well as ready-made items.

Which publications should I produce?

You have a choice of an information point or a series of web pages. Decide which option will be more suitable for the audience and purpose – which are parents more likely to see? It is up to you to make sure that you get the message across in the most effective way.

Have I included appropriate content?

You should start by designing each of the publications. Keep reminding yourself of audience and purpose.

Will users be able to find their way around?

Have you included features that make your publication easy to use? Remember that you will not be around to explain things. Navigation bars, menus, headings and other features all help users to find what they want.

Will people find the information useful? Does it make sense?

This can be difficult when you don't know exactly who will be looking at your publications but you should have some idea of the target audience. Create prototypes and ask for feedback from suitable test users. Make any necessary changes and review your publications again.

Make sure you save

- prototypes with user feedback
- final versions of the web pages/information point and leaflet

Well I followed the instructions on the information point.

8 Getting the message across – targeting a known audience

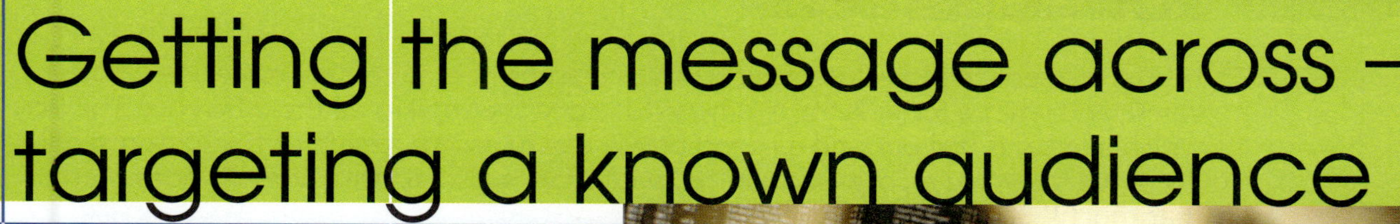

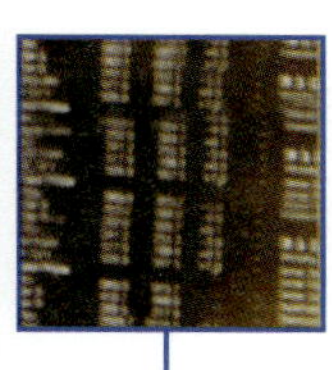

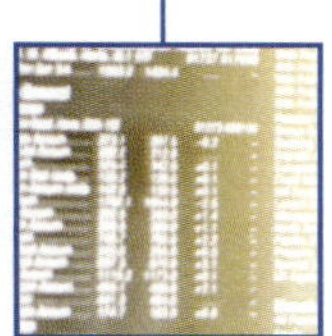

Sometimes you know exactly who will read your publication. Whether it's a letter to an employer, a presentation to parents or a report to club members, you have the great advantage of knowing exactly who your message is aimed at.

If you know who the audience is, you are also likely to know why the publication is needed – to apply for a job, to promote a new course, to report to members on fundraising events held this year. It will probably be quite clear where the information must be presented – by post, in the school hall, at a meeting.

What content do you need? How will you present the information? For some purposes, the type of publication will be clear – such as a formal letter for a job application. If you are presenting information to a group of people, you will have a choice – a printed report, a slide presentation, or a newsletter, for example. Don't assume that an on-screen publication will always be the best option.

In this chapter you will learn how to target individuals and groups by:

- ***designing publications including formal letters, presentations, newsletters and reports***
- ***creating prototypes for testing and feedback***
- ***ensuring that final publications are effective and fit for purpose***

Formal letters

Letters are sent to individuals for particular reasons. It is quite easy to decide who, why, where and what a letter is for. It is how it is done that makes all the difference. The way in which a letter is laid out and its content will create an impression of the person sending it. If it is a letter from an organisation, its reputation is also at stake. It really does matter that much!

A job application letter is an opportunity to impress a potential employer. To make a positive impression you must produce a good letter. If your letter is poorly written or misses out important information, you will appear disorganised and forgetful.

Standard components of a formal letter

You must make sure that a formal letter includes all standard components. An example is shown below. Notice that all text, except the sender's address, is left aligned – it is best not to indent paragraphs. If all your letters follow this format you can't go far wrong.

Letterhead

If you are sending a personal letter, you should include your address and contact details at the top, either on the right or centred. You should not include your name.

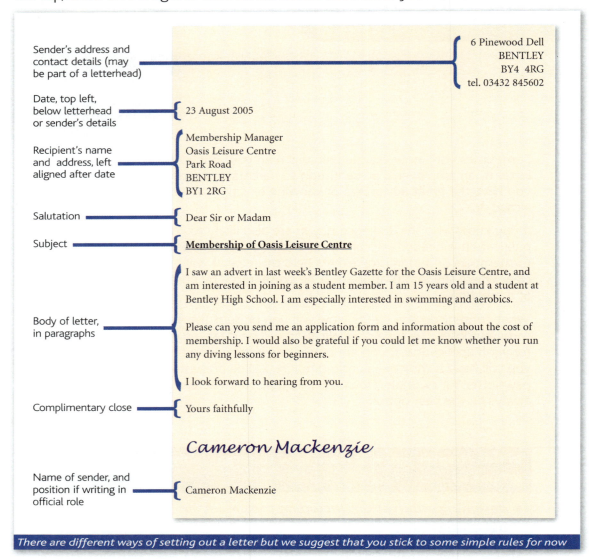

Sender's address and contact details (may be part of a letterhead)	6 Pinewood Dell BENTLEY BY4 4RG tel. 03432 845602
Date, top left, below letterhead or sender's details	23 August 2005
Recipient's name and address, left aligned after date	Membership Manager Oasis Leisure Centre Park Road BENTLEY BY1 2RG
Salutation	Dear Sir or Madam
Subject	**Membership of Oasis Leisure Centre**
Body of letter, in paragraphs	I saw an advert in last week's Bentley Gazette for the Oasis Leisure Centre, and am interested in joining as a student member. I am 15 years old and a student at Bentley High School. I am especially interested in swimming and aerobics. Please can you send me an application form and information about the cost of membership. I would also be grateful if you could let me know whether you run any diving lessons for beginners. I look forward to hearing from you.
Complimentary close	Yours faithfully *Cameron Mackenzie*
Name of sender, and position if writing in official role	Cameron Mackenzie

There are different ways of setting out a letter but we suggest that you stick to some simple rules for now

Date of letter

The date should come at the top left, below the sender's address. It can be inserted before or after the recipient's details.

This must include the month and the year. It should not include the day. There is no need to include *th* or *rd* after the number

✓ 4 April 2005 ✗ 4/4/05 ✗ Monday, 4th April 2005

Recipient's details

Do not use first name only or a nickname. Only use a title if you know what it should be.

✓ Mrs S Johnson ✓ Sheelagh Johnson ✗ Sheelagh

Include the recipient's full postal address, including postcode. Put the town in capital letters. Never put a full stop after a postcode and put it on a separate line.

The recipient's details should be exactly as they will appear on the envelope.

Salutation

You can use the person's title if you know what it is – Mr, Mrs, Ms, Miss, Dr, etc. Do not include the first name or initial as well as the title.

✓ Dear Mrs Johnson ✗ Dear Mrs S Johnson ✓ Dear Mrs Sheelagh Johnson
✓ Dear Sheelagh Johnson ✗ Dear S Johnson

If in doubt you can use Dear Sir or Dear Madam or, if you are not sure which is appropriate, use Dear Sir/Madam.

✓ Dear Madam ✓ Dear Sir/Madam

Sometimes you will know the recipient well enough to use the first name only.

✓ Dear Sheelagh

Subject

The subject should give an idea of what the letter is about. It should come after the opening salutation and before the body of the letter. It can include 'Re:' if you wish. It can also be bold or underlined.

✓ Re: Christmas Raffle ✓ **Christmas Raffle** ✓ <u>Christmas Raffle</u>

Body of letter

This includes the main content of the letter. It should be set out in paragraphs with correct punctuation. Leave a blank line between paragraphs.

You must make sure that it includes all required content.

Complimentary close

This depends on the opening salutation. If you have used a person's name, use Yours sincerely. If you have used Sir or Madam, use Yours faithfully.

✓ Dear Mrs Johnson → Yours sincerely ✗ Dear Mrs Johnson → Yours faithfully
✓ Dear Sheelagh Johnson → Yours sincerely ✓ Dear Madam → Yours faithfully

Notice that sincerely and faithfully do not start with capital letters, and are not followed by a comma.

✓ Yours sincerely ✗ Yours Sincerely

Sender's name and position

After leaving space for a signature, you should print your name on one line. If you are writing on behalf of an organisation or company, add your job title below your name.

> Once again, thank you for meeting with me. I look forward to hearing your response to this proposal.
>
> Yours sincerely
>
> *James Maccleton*
>
> James Maccleton
> Manager

Enc

You will often see 'Enc' at the end of a letter. It is short for 'Enclosure' and means that another document is included with it. Encs is used if there are two or more enclosures. Make sure that you add this if you are sending other documents with a letter.

Creating letters for an organisation or business

Most organisations use a standard letterhead on all their communications. It will include the organisation's logo, name, address and contact details. If you are given a letterhead to use you must *not* change it in any way even if you don't like it! All text that you enter should come below the letterhead.

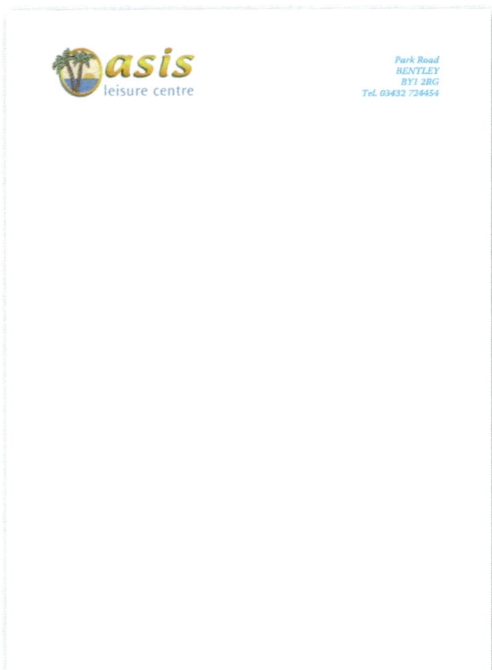

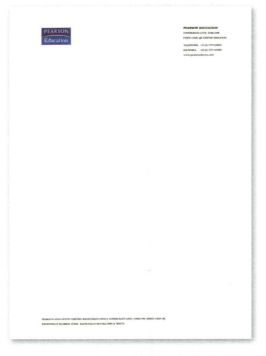

▸▸ Activity 8.1

Collect some examples of formal letters. These must include some that are from individuals like you as well as some from companies. How do they differ?

Activity 8.2

Create a formal letter using the components shown in the table. Click here to do this as a drag and drop exercise.

Yours sincerely	25 February 2005
I have enclosed a copy of my updated CV as requested and I look forward to seeing you on 8 March.	Dear Mr Bluestone
Enc	Further to our meeting last Thursday, I am writing to accept your offer of a work experience placement in your office next month.
I will report to the post room on Monday, 8 March 2005, at 8.30 am for my induction programme with Miss Shaw. Thank you for sending a copy of your staff handbook. I will make sure that I understand all the procedures before I start. I have read the office dress code and understand that I must not wear jeans or trainers.	Mr J Bluestone 17 Moorside Green Road Blythe Bridge STOKE ON TRENT ST21 4RF
25 Stoke Place Hanley BENTLEY BT25 5RP Telephone: 09782 3746910 E-mail: maggiesalt@etinternet.com	Margaret Salt (Miss)
	WORK EXPERIENCE

TALKING POINT 8.1

Look at these letters. Go through each of the features we have looked at and decide whether they are fit for purpose.

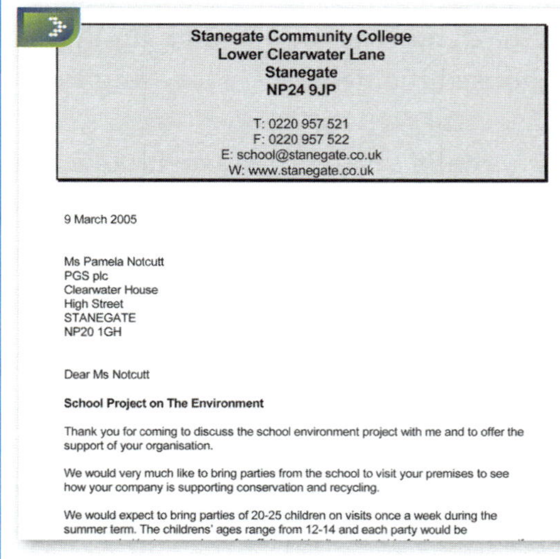

Stanegate Community College
Lower Clearwater Lane
Stanegate
NP24 9JP

T: 0220 957 521
F: 0220 957 522
E: school@stanegate.co.uk
W: www.stanegate.co.uk

9 March 2005

Ms Pamela Notcutt
PGS plc
Clearwater House
High Street
STANEGATE
NP20 1GH

Dear Ms Notcutt

School Project on The Environment

Thank you for coming to discuss the school environment project with me and to offer the support of your organisation.

We would very much like to bring parties from the school to visit your premises to see how your company is supporting conservation and recycling.

We would expect to bring parties of 20-25 children on visits once a week during the summer term. The childrens' ages range from 12-14 and each party would be

The Firs
29 Hexham Street
STANEGATE
NP15 6JW

15 March 2005

The Manager
Custom DIY Stores Ltd
Hexham Business Park
STANEGATE
NP25 3GU

Dear Sir

Summer holiday employment

I am writing to ask whether you have any vacancies for students during the long summer vacation.

I am a student at Stangate Community College and will be entering the Senior School in September to study for A and AS Levels. In the summer term I shall be taking GCSE exams in 10 subjects including English and Maths. I am also following a course for a DiDA (Diploma in Digital Applications) qualification.

I represent the College at soccer and cricket and keep myself fit so would not be afraid of hard work. The exams will end early in July and I would therefore be available to work any time after 25 July.

Proofreading

The computer does not pick up all spelling and grammar errors and it cannot check that information is accurate. Only you can do these things by proofreading. Print off a copy and check it. Ask someone else to read it and give you feedback. Make corrections and check again – it's surprising how often correcting one error introduces another one.

Park Road
BENTLEY
BY1 2RG
Tel. 03432 724454

Please insert name and address of member here

~~25 May~~ 1 June 2005

Dear Member

Oasis Leisure Centre – Swimming ~~faciitilities~~ facilities

I'm delighted to inform that we are improving our swimming facilities.

- The changing rooms will be refurbished and more large lockers will be added. Please insert a full stop here
- New more powerful showers will be installed.

So that this work can be accomplished, *the pool will be closed for three weeks from 1 to 21 July, inclusive.*

ted section should be Bold not

This letter has been annotated by a test user.

Is a letter fit for purpose?

Proofread the letter to check:

- sender's contact details
- recipient's contact details
- date
- salutation
- body text
- complimentary close
- spelling and grammar
- consistency of fonts and formatting.

Activity 8.3

Tamsin Whetstone has written to the local newspaper to complain about the ski slope. Read the letter and write a formal reply to the Editor putting your point of view.

Use the checklist to make sure that your letter is fit for purpose. Get feedback from others in your group.

NEW SKI-SLOPE

SIR – I see that the Oasis Leisure Centre has started to build a dry ski slope. Its construction involves the demolition of the old barn that until recently housed the Bentley Gallery, and the felling of several well established trees.

Having recently visited friends who live near another ski centre, I can also promise that local residents will be subjected to continuous noise while the chairlifts are in use.

What was the council thinking of when it accepted such a proposal?

Tamsin Whetstone
Bentley

Personalised mailings

Suppose you receive two letters in the post about similar things. One is addressed to you and mentions you by name in the letter. The other is addressed to 'The Occupier' and starts off 'Dear Resident'. Which one are you more likely to read?

Organisations often need to send out the same letter to many people – for example, a youth club with a hundred members. If you wanted to send a personalised letter, it would be very tiresome to have to create a letter for one person, and then change the name and address and print it again for each individual.

Mail merge allows you to create a standard letter which can be printed as many times as you like with some of the details changing on each one.

Mail merge using a database

This example uses the MEMBER table for Oasis Leisure Centre which you should have created in Chapter 5: Making use of databases. You won't be able to do the activities in this section if you have not completed Chapter 5.

Changing data

The changing data for each letter can be stored in a database table with a field for each different item. Here is an extract from the MEMBER table in the OASIS database.

Title	GivenName	FamilyName	Address1	Type
Mr	Dionysis	Kouroglou	13 Brookside Road	Day
Mr	Daniel	Clark	20 Windy Hill	Full

Standard letter

In the standard letter, the names of the fields are entered rather than the data itself. These are called merge fields. Merge fields will be displayed differently depending on what program you are using to create the letter. Here is part of Alistair Larsson's letter to all members – note the use of fields from the MEMBER table.

Park Road
BENTLEY
BY1 2RG
Tel. 03432 724454

16 September 2005

«Title» «GivenName» «FamilyName»
«Address»
«Town»
«Postcode»

Dear «Title» «FamilyName»

Slip down to our ski-slope opening

As you are currently a «Type» member at Oasis Leisure Centre, you are warmly invited to attend the official opening of our new dry ski slope next month on Friday, 7 October. The slope will be officially opened by the Mayor of Bentley at 6.30 p.m. This will be followed by a floodlit display of stunt skiing by this year's European championship winners.

On the same night our ski shop and booking centre will be staying open until 8 p.m. and will be offering a 15% discount on all members' purchases of clothing and equipment, plus a 10% discount on all lessons for October and November that are booked on opening night.

Merging the two together

When the mail merge is run, the program will insert the data from the database into the merge fields.

Park Road
BENTLEY
BY1 2RG
Tel. 03432 724454

16 September 2005

Mr Dionysis Kouroglou
13 Brookside Road
CHARWOOD
NP11 3LD

Dear Mr Kouroglou

Slip down to our ski-slope opening

As you are currently a Day member at Oasis Leisure Centre, you are warmly invited to attend the official opening of our new dry ski slope next month on Friday, 7 October. The slope will be officially opened by the Mayor of Bentley at 6.30 p.m. This will be followed by a floodlit display of stunt skiing by this year's European championship winners.

On the same night our ski shop and booking centre will be staying open until 8 p.m. and will be offering a 15% discount on all members' purchases of clothing and equipment, plus a 10% discount on all lessons for October and November that are booked on opening night.

I hope you will be able to join us for what promises to be a memorable evening.

Park Road
BENTLEY
BY1 2RG
Tel. 03432 724454

16 September 2005

Mr Daniel Clark
20 Windy Hill
GREENSTOKE
NP13 5RN

Dear Mr Clark

Slip down to our ski-slope opening

As you are currently a Full member at Oasis Leisure Centre, you are warmly invited to attend the official opening of our new dry ski slope next month on Friday, 7 October. The slope will be officially opened by the Mayor of Bentley at 6.30 p.m. This will be followed by a floodlit display of stunt skiing by this year's European championship winners.

On the same night our ski shop and booking centre will be staying open until 8 p.m. and will be offering a 15% discount on all members' purchases of clothing and equipment, plus a 10% discount on all lessons for October and November that are booked on opening night.

I hope you will be able to join us for what promises to be a memorable evening.

Yours sincerely

Here are two of the letters produced using mail merge.

Check that data from the MEMBER table has been inserted correctly.

Proofreading

Never print all the letters until you are confident that they are exactly what you want and fit for purpose. Print the first one and proofread it carefully making sure that it has all the features of a formal business letter and that the merge fields have worked correctly. A common error is to enter merge fields without spaces. For example:

Dear«Title»«FamilyName» results in DearMrKouroglou

Another is caused by inaccuracies in the database. If you find, for example, mixed capitals, this may not seem to matter in the database but it certainly does in the letter:

✗ Dear MR Kouroglou or ✗ Dear Mr KOUROGLOU

If you start looking, you will find many examples of poorly designed mail merge letters. Personalisation using mail merge can be very effective but only if the resulting letters are as good as they would have been if they had been individually created and checked.

Can I do this?

Using your mail merge tools, make sure you can:

Create a standard mail merge letter

Insert merge fields in a standard letter

Merge a letter with data from a database table

Print a sample merged letter

▸▸ Activity 8.4

The Youth Club is organising a charity raffle. As secretary, your task is to create personalised letters to all members of the Oasis Leisure Centre, asking them to sell tickets. You will enclose a book of five tickets with each letter.

Details of members are stored in the MEMBER table in the Oasis database.

Look carefully at the contents of the database table before you decide which merge fields should go in your letter. There is no need to print all the letters but you should print one copy for proofreading.

TALKING POINT 8.2

Work in groups and proofread each other's letters.

▸▸ Activity 8.5

You need to send a personalised letter to each youth member to tell them about activities offered by the Youth Club when the ski slope opens.

Create a contacts list by searching the MEMBER table. Save the search results as YOUTH.

Create a personalised letter to each youth member using mail merge.

Make use of feedback to ensure that your letter is fit for purpose.

Reports

Oh no, not reports! Reports are boring!

They certainly can be but what you have to remember is that the main aim of a report is to provide detailed information to people who want to read it. The most important thing is to get the content right and to make the information clear to the intended audience. As a report is likely to consist mainly of text it needs careful planning and design to make it effective.

TALKING POINT 8.3

Look at some examples of reports produced for different audiences and purposes. Discuss these features:

- *audience and purpose*
- *writing style and content*
- *colours and styles*
- *balance of text and images*
- *use of white space*

Who, why, where, what, how?

Whatever a report is for, it should be clear and complete. If it leaves too many questions unanswered it will be frustrating for the reader and certainly not fit for purpose.

As usual, you must start by identifying the target audience and the purpose of the report.

- Find out how the report will be distributed – by post, at a meeting, etc.
- Find out whether there are other publications to go with it, such as a presentation
- Decide what content must go in the report
- Decide how you will go about it – how many pages, what size, what software you will use.

Many of the design principles for posters, flyers and leaflets also apply to reports. Remind yourself of these if you need to.

Designing a report

What paper size?

Most reports are printed on A4 paper, sometimes double-sided, and some run to many pages.

Choosing colours

Keep it simple. Text is usually black on white. Only use something different if you have a good reason. Illustrations and charts may be more effective in colour and you should make sure that the colour combinations work when printed.

If you are printing in black and white, be particularly careful if you are including a chart from spreadsheet software. Different colours on screen often end up as the same shade of grey when printed, as shown on page 61.

Using text

Headings and subheadings

As the report is mostly text, you can help the reader by breaking it down into sections that can be read one at time.

- Use a sensible title that gives a clear idea of what the information is about.
- Use sub-headings to introduce each section of text.
- Make sure that the format and style of headings is consistent.

Fonts

- **Avoid word art** in formal reports – please!
- **Which fonts?** All the main text should be the same easy-to-read font. If you decide to use a different font for a heading, make sure that it works well with the rest of the text.
- **What sizes?** Choose the size according to the importance of the text but make sure that all the sizes are legible when printed, and be consistent.

1. Executive summary

The technology context
1. Digital technology is already changing how we do business and live our lives. Most schools – and every university and college – now have broadband access. Teachers increasingly use information and communications technology (ICT) to improve their own skills and knowledge – and to bring their lessons to life. People working with children, families, young people, and adults are testing out new and better ways to deliver services, with common processes supported by technology. The technology is making many administrative and assessment tasks easier.

2. Parents and carers use the internet to find advice and information to support their parenting role. Pupils use the internet for research: many have their own e-mail accounts. A growing number of schools keep parents informed online. Adults use online resources to improve their skills. The evidence is that where ICT is used effectively, lessons are better taught and students get better results.

3. These developments reflect government investment and local innovation. But their growth has also been haphazard: systems are often incompatible with each other. Each institution or organisation has the freedom to buy its own system and support services. The result is that they are often more expensive than they need be. There are too few economies of scale.

A strategic approach to ICT
4. That is why we need a more strategic approach to the future development of ICT in education, skills and children's services. By doing so, we believe we can:

- Transform teaching, learning and help to improve outcomes for children and young people, through shared ideas, more exciting lessons and online help for professionals
- Engage 'hard to reach' learners, with special needs support, more motivating ways of learning, and more choice about how and where to learn
- Build an open accessible system, with more information and services online for parents and carers, children, young people, adult learners and employers; and more cross-organisation collaboration to improve personalised support and choice
- Achieve greater efficiency and effectiveness, with online research, access to shared ideas and lessons plans, improved systems and processes in children's services, shared procurement and easier administration.

These are our four key objectives against which we will evaluate this strategy.

5. A greater focus on technology will produce real benefits for all. Parents could see more about what their children are learning in school through a school's website. Employers and communities

4 EDUCATION AND SKILLS HARNESSING TECHNOLOGY

Text alignment

Text should be left or fully aligned. You might consider centring main headings. Don't be tempted to use different alignments unless there's a good reason.

Numbered lists

If a list is in a particular order then it will make more sense to number the points rather than use bullets. For example, these results for a snowboarding competition are much clearer with numbers than they would be without.

Results

1. Harry Jackson
2. Martyn Edwards
3. Ashley Smith
4. Arvind Rafique
5. Siobhan Buchanan
6. Ann Watson
7. Adrian James
8. Chantal Porter
9. Annabel Porter
10. David de Vinney

Bullets

Bullets can be used to make a list of points easier to read but you must make sure that all the bullets in a list are consistent and in line. If this list of activities is to be included in a report about the Activity Day, it will be clearer if bulleted.

During the day participants can try out lots of activities:
Abseiling
Orienteering
Canoeing
Disco dancing
Swimming
Beginners' snowboarding
The choice is theirs.

During the day participants can try out lots of activities:

- Abseiling
- Orienteering
- Canoeing
- Disco dancing
- Swimming
- Beginners' snowboarding

The choice is theirs.

Using images

Images are one of the most effective ways to break up text in a report but *only if they are appropriate*. Reports are solely for information so you must choose images that help to get the message across – these will often be diagrams or charts.

Finding suitable images

Take care that an image is still effective when printed – that its size and quality are suitable. If you are printing in black and white, make sure that colour images print clearly.

Look critically at images when you print a prototype of your report. Ask yourself whether they are achieving anything. Never use images in a report just for the sake of it.

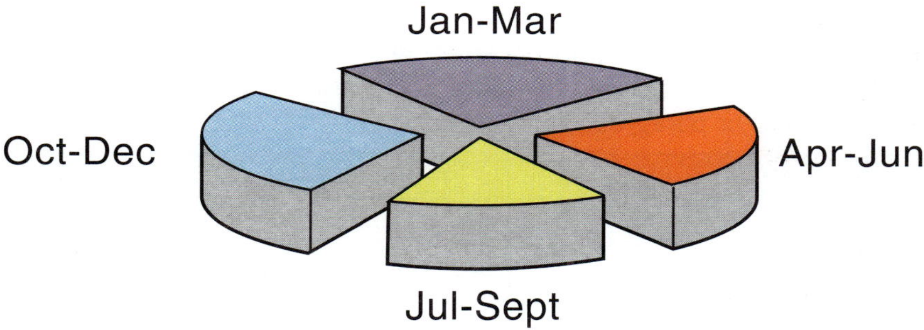

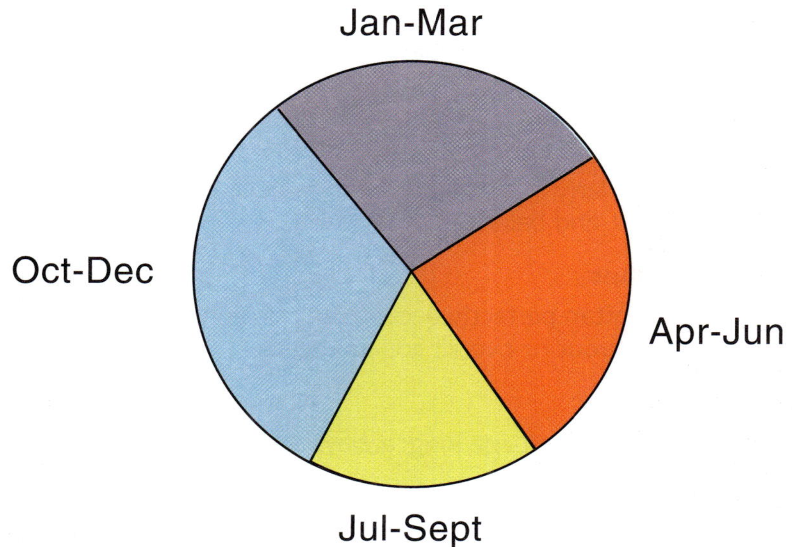

These charts were produced using the same data. Which one gives you accurate information?

Overview of the last 12 months

During the year, sales grew by 9.8% to nearly £9 million, an 8% increase compared to the previous year. In a tough trading year this meant we outperformed the competition and the market as a whole. This is a direct result of strategy of product innovation allied to improved marketing communications.

The new Aquat range of bathroom suites has spearheaded this improvement. Its fresh clean lines and innovative technical specification have been enthusiastically taken up by retailers and allowed us to break into direct sales to

initiatives during the year. The development of a new range of internet-based marketing communications has been enthusiastically embraced by our retailers. The improved the flow of information between the company and retailers, as well as our revitalised product range, has done much to support sales. It has also helped us to establish direct sales to builders.

Over the past year we have reviewed our supply chain, and over the next 12 months we will begin to benefit from the savings this will allow to us to make by streamlining

Overview of the last 12 months

During the year, sales grew by 9.8% to nearly £9 million, an 8% increase compared to the previous year. In a tough trading year this meant we outperformed the competition and the market as a whole. This is a direct result of strategy of product innovation allied to improved marketing communications.

The new Aquat range of bathroom suites has spearheaded this improvement. Its fresh clean lines and innovative technical specification have been enthusiastically taken up by retailers and allowed us to break into direct sales to developers of new homes. Over the coming year this range will be further developed by offering a wider range of sizes and finishes.

The expansion of the product range has been underpinned a number of efficiency initiatives during the year. The development of a new range of internet-based marketing communications has been enthusiastically embraced by our retailers. The improved the flow of information between the company and retailers, as well as our revitalised product range, has done much to support sales. It has also helped us to establish direct sales to builders.

Over the past year we have reviewed our supply chain, and over the next 12 months we will begin to benefit from the savings this will allow to us to make by streamlining our supplier base.

We look forward to next year being one with yet further improvements in performance as we capitalise on the innovations of this year.

Overview of the last 12 months

During the year, sales grew by 9.8% to nearly £9 million, an 8% increase compared to the previous year. In a tough trading year this meant we outperformed the competition and the market as a whole. This is a direct result of strategy of product innovation allied to improved marketing communications.

The new Aquat range of bathroom suites has spearheaded this improvement. Its fresh clean lines and innovative technical specification have been enthusiastically taken up by retailers and allowed us to break into direct sales to developers of new homes. Over the coming year this range will be further developed by offering a wider range of sizes and finishes.

The expansion of the product range has been underpinned a number of efficiency initiatives during the year. The development of a new range of internet-based marketing communications has been enthusiastically embraced by our retailers. The improved the flow of information between the company and retailers, as well as our revitalised product range, has done much to support sales. It has also helped us to establish direct sales to builders.

Over the past year we have reviewed our supply chain, and over the next 12 months we will begin to benefit from the savings this will allow to us to make by streamlining our supplier base.

We look forward to next year being one with yet further improvements in performance as we capitalise on the innovations of this year.

In the first example the text is difficult to read because the lines are so short and the spacing is poor. It would be better to make the image smaller or move it to one side

Deciding where to put them

Each image must relate to the text nearby, but there should be enough space around the image to separate it from the text. You may want to wrap text around an image but check that the text is not so broken up that it is difficult to read.

TALKING POINT 8.4

Have another look at the reports you discussed in Talking Point 8.3 and think about how you would improve them. Consider the text styles, images and other non-text components such as charts.

Using tables

If the information would be clearer in a grid of rows and columns, use a table, and formatting such as bold, underline or shading to emphasise column headings. For example, information about the popularity of different events would be much clearer set out in a table than in a list or paragraph.

Activity	Location	Age	Max per hour	Average per hour
Archery	Forest	10-16	12	4
Snowboard	Ski Slope	Over 10	20	20

Layout

Organise the information into manageable sections, each with a heading, and try to space things out evenly. If there is more than one page, make sure that the page breaks are sensible.

White space

White space is particularly important in reports because of the large amount of text. Use it to break up the text and balance the layout.

Margins and columns

Default margins are often perfectly acceptable but don't be afraid to change them a little if this improves the layout or overall appearance.

Page numbering

If a report is more than one page long, always insert page numbers.

TALKING POINT 8.5

Take another look at the reports. What do you think of the layout and use of white space?

Creating a report

Can I do this?

Using word processing tools, make sure you can:

- **Format text**
- **Align text**
- **Wrap text**
- **Import and position images**
- **Crop and resize images**
- **Use bullets**
- **Create a numbered list**
- **Change margins**
- **Use text boxes**
- **Create a table**
- **Insert page numbers**

Keep on checking!

Keep checking your work as you go along.

Create prototypes of your report and check them for

- mistakes in spelling or grammar
- readability
- consistency
- suitability of writing style
- sensible use of images and other non-text components
- layout and use of white space.

Ask others to check your prototypes and make use of their feedback. When you think you have the final version, try to find people who are similar to your target audience. Ask them whether they think the report is fit for purpose.

Don't forget about the production cycle. Use the loop back as many times as necessary – keep going back to the design until you are absolutely sure that it is fit for purpose.

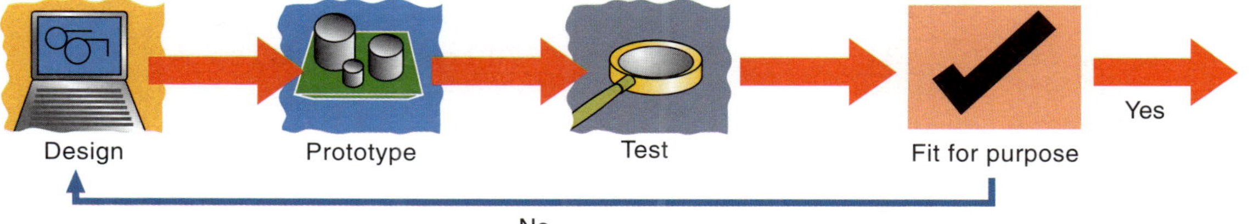

▸▸ Activity 8.6

Alistair Larsson has asked you to produce a report about the Youth Club. He wants to use this as part of a presentation to Bentley Council. His aim is to persuade councillors to increase their funding of the Leisure Centre. Your report should include information about the activities offered by the Youth Club and what you want to do in the future. Design and create this report using some of the information Alistair has stored in the folder. Include suitable images and other components.

Database reports

In chapter 5 you learned how to make use of a database to produce information using searches and sorts. In this section you will learn how to produce database reports that get the message across as effectively as possible.

This is part of a report produced by a student working on the Edexcel Specimen SPB. Read the relevant section of the SPB to find out the audience and purpose.

Heat Query

ID	Beds	HeatHours	email
1	3	95	heath@sunit23.co.uk
8	4	45	wilson@sunit23.co.uk
10	4	55	hussain@24gold.co.uk
21	2	45	wilson@life45000.com
22	4	90	ross@24gold3.co.uk
23	3	100	morrey@gyp2.co.uk
26	4	100	pal@sunit23.co.uk
32	2	45	yox@life45000.com
35	3	70	bourne@gyp2.co.uk
41	4	100	portertam@web5890.com
46	3	90	brookfield@sunit23.co.uk
49	4	60	khan@sunit23.co.uk
55	3	55	hashimi@life45000.com
59	4	95	canning@web5890.com
95	3	100	jameson@sunit23.co.uk
103	4	55	khan@web5890.com
105	2	70	ossy@web5890.com
119	2	70	phil@life45000.com
129	1	70	arm@sunit23.co.uk
134	1	70	bryant@24gold3.co.uk

What does it tell us? Why would we want to know how many beds there are? What does ID mean? Is it about houses? We really don't have any idea what this report is about!

TALKING POINT 8.6

What else should this report include? Make a note of all the questions you need to ask before you can be sure what it is all about. Look at the layout – what could be done to improve it?

Wizards are not magic!

This report was produced using a wizard. The trouble is that you can run the wizard, click *Next* a few times, fetch your report from the printer and think that's it! Believe it or not, that is NOT what wizards are for. They are meant to *help* you, not do the job for you.

Customising a report

Here is part of another report produced using the same database. It's not perfect but it makes much more sense. Although the wizard was used, the student has customised the report.

Households with double glazing and heating on for over 40 hours/week

ID	Title	Initial	Surname	Beds	HeatHours	email
1	Mr	A	Heathcote	3	95	heath@sunit23.co.uk
8	Mr	A	Wilson	4	45	wilson@sunit23.co.uk
10	Miss	F	Hussain	4	55	hussain@24gold.co.uk
21	Mr	A	Wilson	2	45	wilson@life45000.com
22	Mrs	C	Ross	4	90	ross@24gold3.co.uk
23	Ms	H	Morrey	3	100	morrey@gyp2.co.uk
26	Miss	F	Palmer	4	100	pal@sunit23.co.uk
32	Mr	A	Yoxall	2	45	yox@life45000.com
35	Mr	J	Bourne	3	70	bourne@gyp2.co.uk
41	Mrs	T	Porter	4	100	portertam@web5890.com
46	Miss	F	Brookfield	3	90	brookfield@sunit23.co.uk
49	Miss	F	Khan	4	60	khan@sunit23.co.uk
55	Mrs	D	Hashimi	3	55	hashimi@life45000.com
59	Mr	A	Canning	4	95	canning@web5890.com
64	Mr	A	Yip	4	45	yip@gyp2.co.uk
73	Miss	F	Finn	3	70	finn@sunit23.co.uk
75	Mrs	Y	Holdcroft	4	70	holdy@web5890.com
77	Mrs	T	Jasper	3	100	tinajasper@web5890.com
87	Mr	A	Carter	3	100	carter@web5890.com
88	Mrs	U	Joynson	2	70	joy@web5890.com
95	Mr	A	Jameson	3	100	jameson@sunit23.co.uk
103	Mrs	S	Khan	4	55	khan@web5890.com
105	Mrs	E	Osbourne	2	70	ossy@web5890.com
111	Mr	P	Woolley	3	70	woolley@sunit23.co.uk
113	Mr	A	Gibson	2	100	gibs@sunit23.co.uk
119	Mr	P	Phillips	2	70	phil@life45000.com
121	Mr	R	Reagan	3	70	reagan@life45000.com
127	Mrs	D	Marsh	3	70	marsh@life45000.com
129	Mrs	S	Armitage	1	70	arm@sunit23.co.uk
132	Mrs	F	James	3	45	james@sunit23.co.uk
134	Mrs	S	Bryant	1	70	bryant@24gold3.co.uk
135	Mr	A	Mohammed	3	45	mohammed1@sunit23.co.uk
143	Mrs	D	Barber	3	60	barber@sunit23.co.uk
162	Mrs	C	Neary	3	70	near@24gold3.co.uk
163	Mrs	C	Mohammed	3	45	mohammed@24gold3.co.uk
165	Mrs	D	Kemp	4	70	kemp@life45000.com

TALKING POINT 8.7

What features make this report better than the first example? What else would you do to improve it?

If you use a report wizard, you must be prepared to customise its output so that that the report is effective and the information is useful.

Heading

This should make it quite clear what the report is about. Don't let a wizard do it for you – it may enter the name you have used to save the report and the chances are that this will not be good enough. DB2 or Report1 or even HeatHoursOver40 don't make a lot of sense!

Column headings

The wizard will use the field names from the database. Field names are often abbreviations and only make sense to the person who created the database. Column headers need to be clear to the audience.

The database used to create the report on page 125 has a fieldname HeatHours which is the number of hours heating is used. In the report this could be replaced with anything sensible such as 'Hours Heating On' or 'Heating Hours'. This student has chosen 'Hours' because the meaning is clear from the title.

Layout

Check the spacing of the columns, especially if you have a right-aligned field next to a left-aligned one. This is something that could be done to improve the report on page 125 – the heating hours figures are too close to the email addresses. This makes them more difficult to read.

Footers

Page footers can be used to enter details of the author, date of report, etc. Be careful if you are using Access. This has two different kinds of footer: the report footer prints after the last record, not at the bottom of the page.

Can I do this?

Using database tools, make sure you can:

Create a report

Customise a report

Activity 8.7

Open the OASIS database you created in Activity 5.8 and create a report for each of the searches in Activity 5.11.

You will need to know what the searches are designed to find – look back at the activity if you need to.

Use the report wizard if you wish, but you must customise each report to make sure it is fit for purpose. Check all the features listed on this page. You may need to use landscape format if you are including a number of fields.

Presentations

Who is it for?

Most presentations are designed for a specific audience.

Ask yourself:

- Who will be sitting in front of you?
- Why do they need your presentation?
- How much do they already know?
- What style of language is suitable?

Why is it needed?

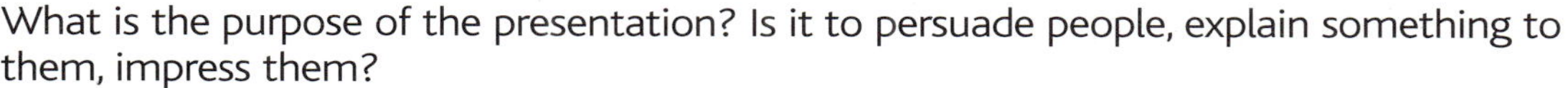

What is the purpose of the presentation? Is it to persuade people, explain something to them, impress them?

You should make sure that you are clear about audience and purpose before you start to think about what should go in a presentation.

The key message

Your presentation MUST have a key message. Leave your audience in absolutely no doubt what you came to tell them. You should aim to communicate your key message within the first 15 seconds.

A good key message for a presentation about DiDA for year 9 students might be:

> As you will be in year 10 from September, you will be the first students to take the new ICT course, DiDA. By the end of this 30 minute presentation I hope I will have convinced you that you will enjoy studying for DiDA. In fact, I think you may well find that your parents want to sign up as well!

As you can see, this message says:

- **Who** it is for – year 9 students
- **What** they will learn – find out about DiDA
- **Why** they need to know – so that they know why DiDA is being offered
- **When** they will do it – in the next 30 minutes.

This message is short but it says a lot and should keep students' attention. But why do we concentrate on what the speaker will say when this section is about slide presentations?

Using speaker notes

Most publications must contain all the information that is needed. Presentations that involve a speaker are very different. Slides should contain the key points but you will need to prepare speaker notes for the details. These remind the presenter what to say.

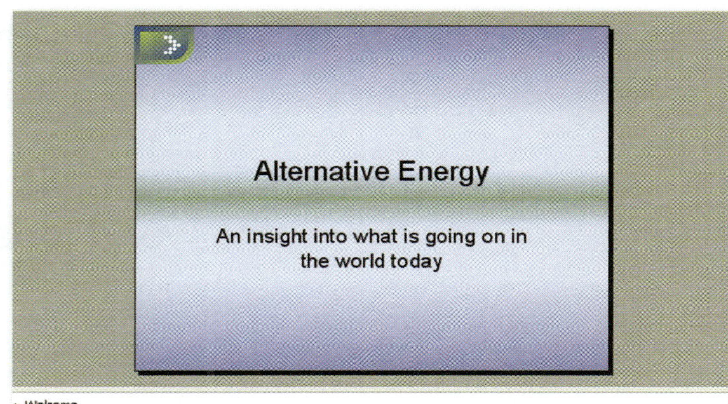

Alternative Energy
An insight into what is going on in the world today
• Welcome
• Presentation: encourage councillors to look at ways of motivating young people
• Shows results of survey carried out on 50 teenagers.
• Gives recommendations towards helping teenagers create a better future.

Most presentation software allows you enter the speaker notes below the slide so that you can print out pages like this

Designing a presentation

Storyboarding

Storyboards are useful when designing presentations as they allow you to capture your ideas, design each slide and how they link together.

Each slide should have a distinct purpose and message but the presentation should flow through from beginning to end. Not only do you have to think about individual slides, you also have to design the slides and links so that they are consistent. Your presentation must be designed to fill a certain amount of time and you should bear in mind that people generally remember best the things they hear last.

An outline storyboard will help you to plan

- how many slides you need
- the order of the slides
- what components will appear on each slide
- the position of components on each page
- the format and style
- the links between slides.

Use your storyboard to get feedback and to make sure that your presentation gets the message across. Look back at pages 101 and 102 to remind yourself about storyboards.

Choosing components

Too many presentations suffer from loud or unnecessary sound effects, boring clip art, too many colours and fonts or too much information. You will see many examples of poor design in the business world. DiDA students can do better!

Always remember that the most important part of your presentation is the message you are trying to communicate. Don't spend more time on special effects than on the real content. Remember that people near the back of the room need to be able to see all the content of the slides.

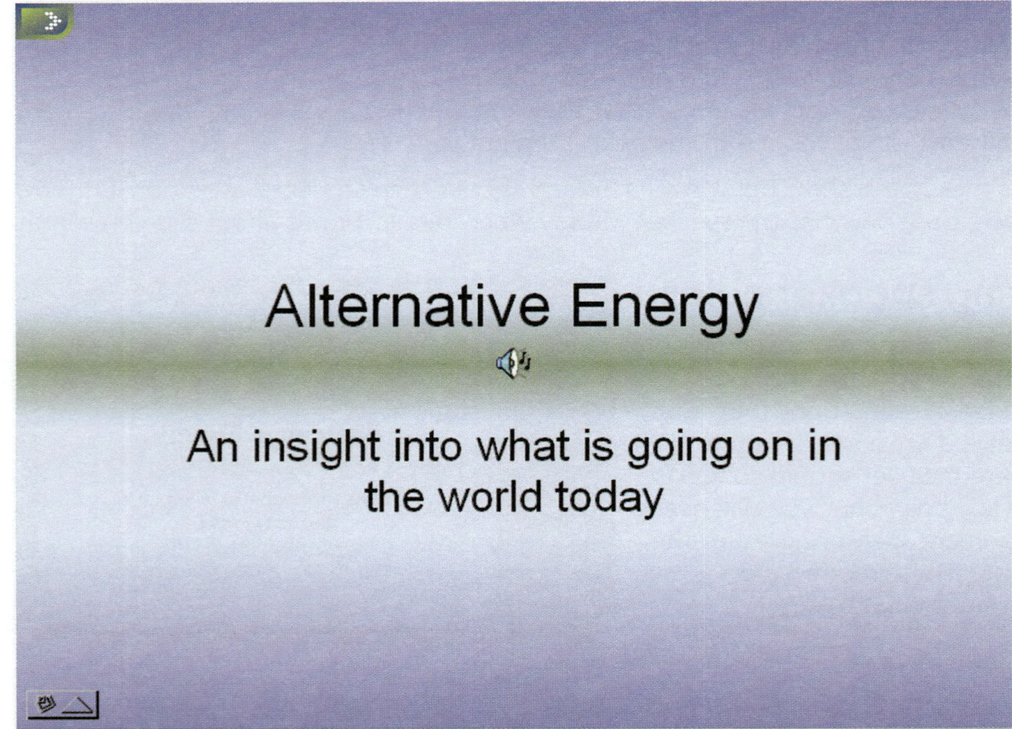
Alternative Energy
An insight into what is going on in the world today

Using text

Imagine that you are sitting listening to the key message. Which slide would you rather see behind the speaker?

> You all have children in year 9 and I know that you are concerned that we are starting a new ICT course from September. I think that by the end of this 30 minute presentation you will be as confident as we are that your children are lucky to be the first students to benefit from studying DiDA. In fact, I think you may well find yourself asking when you can sign up!

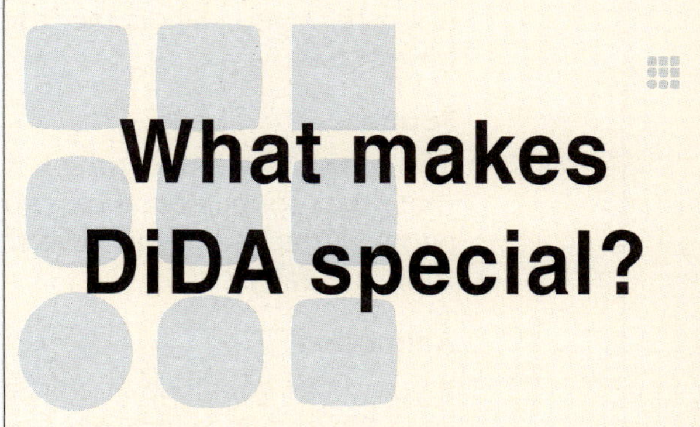

You must be clear about this – most of what you plan to say should not go on the slides.

- Stick to short, snappy bullets unless you are including a quotation.
- Limit the number of points on a slide, so that it is not crammed full.
- Avoid using capitals throughout as they are difficult to read.
- Experiment with different fonts and sizes, and try them out using a projector and screen.

Using images

Make sure that images are appropriate for the topic and send out the right messages. Use cartoons and clip art with extra care.

If you can't find something suitable, create your own, either by using a digital camera or by drawing something.

Introducing Aquat
selling tomorrow's bathroom suite today
Innovative technology
Wide range of sizes and styles
Easy to install

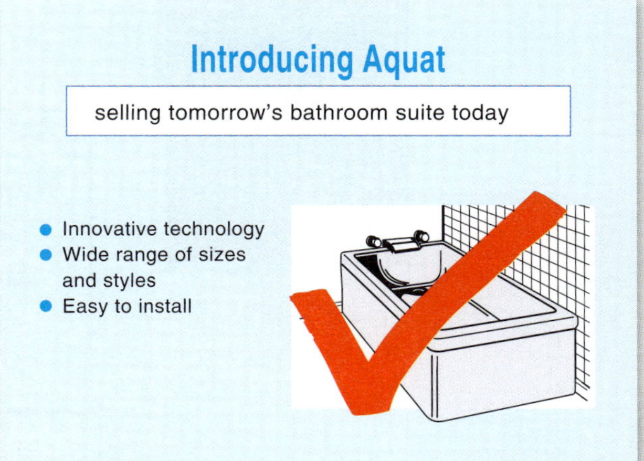

Introducing Aquat
selling tomorrow's bathroom suite today
Innovative technology
Wide range of sizes and styles
Easy to install

Using graphs and charts

Lists of numbers and spreadsheets can be even more to difficult to read on screen than they are on paper. Use graphs and charts wherever you want to highlight numerical information, especially when there are comparisons to be made.

8

Using other multimedia components

One of the reasons why people enjoy using presentation software is that they can make use of multimedia features such as sound and animation. Use them by all means but *only when it is appropriate*, for example when you want to emphasise a certain point. If you are not careful you will distract the audience rather than draw their attention to what you have to say.

Sound

Use sound if you really think it improves the quality of the presentation. Bear in mind that what sounds good on your laptop or PC may not work so well in a room full of people. Check that you have the equipment to play the sound loud enough for everyone to hear clearly.

Animation

If you make good use of animation it can help to keep the audience interested and demonstrate a sequence of events. The secret is to select just a few types and stick to them throughout a presentation. If you have things flying from all directions, your audience will be watching to see what happens next rather than listening to you!

Did you know...

- Burning petrol in your cars produces a great deal of smog and pollution
- By burning and wasting we are creating

Would you want to watch a long presentation in this style?

Links and buttons

These can be included to allow the presenter to jump to other slides or files. For example, if you were giving a presentation on web page design, you might want to link to an example of a website.

Choosing colours

You should experiment with different colours to see what works best on screen.

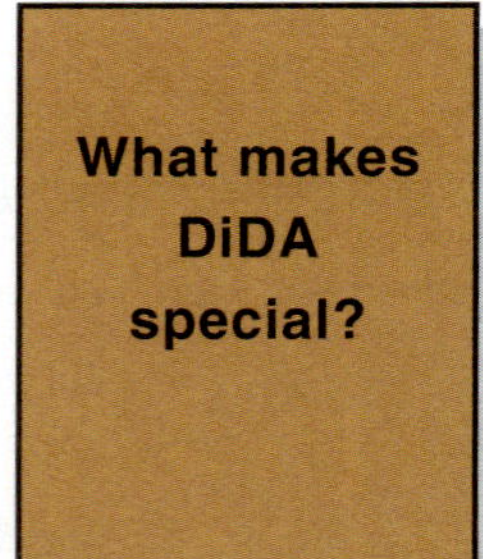
What makes
DiDA
special?

What makes DiDA special?

What makes
DiDA
special?

What makes DiDA special?

Consistency

Make sure you have some common features, such as:

- colour combinations
- font types and sizes
- bullets
- layout.

Master slides

You can make sure that your slides are consistent by creating a master slide. This is a template that contains all the features you want to use in every slide. Try it out using your presentation software.

Activity 8.8

Design a storyboard for a presentation for the Oasis management committee. It should give them information about Youth Club activities planned for the next season. Some resources can be found in the folder on your CD. The presentation should last for approximately 10 minutes. You must include speaker notes. Your design should include suitable multimedia components.

Transitions

Transitions are similar to animations in that they make images and text move on the screen but they also control:

- when one slide changes to the next, e.g.
  - on a mouse click
  - automatically after a set period of time
- how this happens, e.g.
  - one simply disappears and is replaced by the next
  - one fades out as the next appears
  - one dissolves as the next appears
- the speed at which one slide changes to the next.

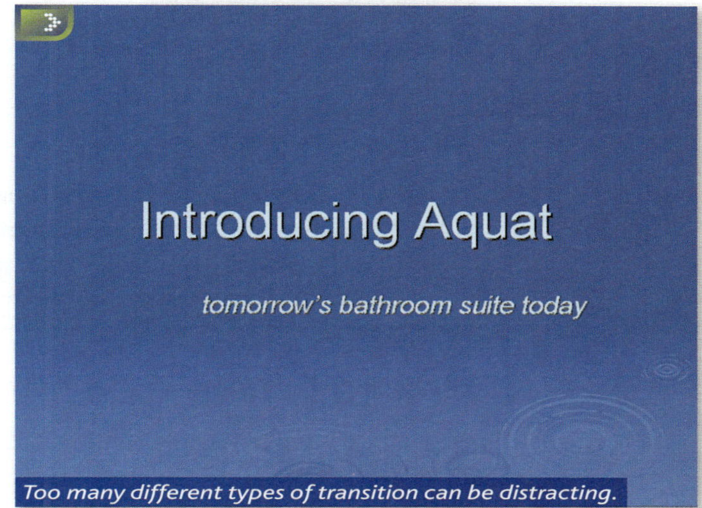

Too many different types of transition can be distracting.

Activity 8.9

Explore the features of your presentation tools, looking particularly at animation and transitions.

Proofreading

Spelling mistakes always create a poor impression but remember that on a slide they will be very big and everyone in the room will see them before you.

You cannot proofread too many times. Check, check, and check again!

Creating a presentation

Can I do this?

Using presentation tools, make sure you can:

- Create slides
- Create and use a master slide
- Use lines and borders
- Change colours
- Import and position images
- Align text and images
- Crop and resize images
- Include animation
- Include sound
- Insert links
- Create transitions

TALKING POINT 8.8

What else can you do to make sure that the slides are error-free?

Activity 8.10

Use your storyboard to create the presentation for the management committee at Oasis. Use information from the folder as well as multimedia components of your own. Your presentation should last for 10 minutes and you should prepare speaker notes to accompany the slides.

Making it more than just a slide show

No matter how well designed the slides are, a presentation is only as good as the presenter. You must practise your presentation in front of a test audience. Make sure that you know what you are going to say for each slide so that you can look at the audience when you are speaking. Don't keep turning round to look at the slides behind you and avoid just reading the speaker notes.

Sound enthusiastic about what you are saying and **never, ever stand there and read the slides out bullet by bullet**. The audience can read the slides for themselves. Your job is to fill in the details and get the full message across effectively.

Getting the timings right

Your audience will have been told how long the presentation will last. When you are practising, check that the presentation is the right length, allowing time for questions if appropriate. Don't talk for too long without involving the audience in an activity or a discussion.

You must also test your presentation to make sure that animations, sound and transitions work as intended. Use the prototype to get feedback from a test audience.

Other uses of presentation software

Scrolling presentations run without user interaction. These are often used in public areas such as a leisure centre reception area or an exhibition. Passers-by can stop and watch as much as they like.

Newsletters

First impressions

Whereas a report is likely to be read by the audience even if it is not very exciting, a newsletter is optional reading. If it is not designed well, they probably won't bother. It will come as no surprise that you cannot design a newsletter until you have answered these questions:

- **Who** it is for? How old are they? What sort of writing style can they cope with? Why are they interested in your topics? How much (or how little) do they already know?
- **Why** is it needed? Its purpose should be clear at a glance.
- **What** should go in it? Concentrate on what the audience will want to read, not on what you want to write about. They are not necessarily the same thing! When you design the pages, you will need to make sure that more important items stand out.

Sharing what we do

Have you ever wondered why a piece of furniture or a picture occupies any particular position in a historic house – by whom and how that decision was made?

This question was answered for visitors, volunteers and work placement students ... as the re-arrangement of the Drawing ... om took place in full view of the

"The curatorial process (making decisions about which objects are appropriate to the room and where and why they should be sited) we have gone through

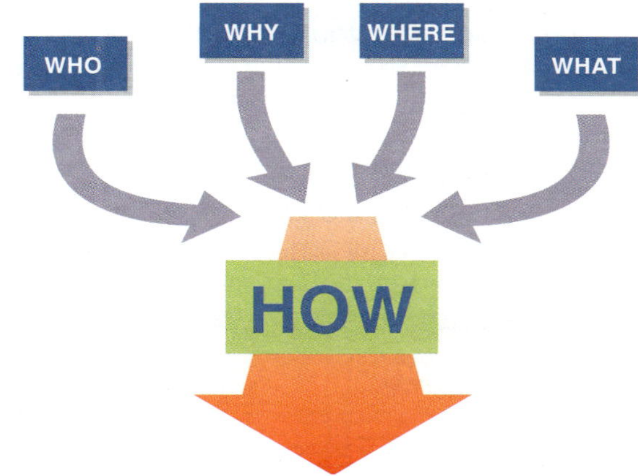

TALKING POINT 8.9

Look at these newsletters and comment on:

- *Audience and purpose*
- *Number and size of pages*
- *Colours (full colour/2 colour/b&w)*
- *Balance of text and images*
- *Title*
- *Writing style*
- *Content*
- *Use of white space*

kilmarnock edition

Quality Week scores on all fronts

Killie Writing Competition Breaks new Ground

On Track

Edition 2, February 2005

WAVERLEY RAILWAY PROJECT

Rail Supporters 'Rally' Round on Campaign March

This Month...

- Parliamentary Committee
- Safety benefits
- Addressing the alternatives: new roads

YOUTH PARTICIPATION

ETHIOPIAN STUDENTS CONDUCT CHILD-TO-CHILD SURVEY TO GET ALL CHILDREN IN SCHOOL

safer LONDON

March 2005 | Issue 9

News from London Fire and Emergency Planning Authority

Authority approves London Safety Plan

Designing a newsletter

Although leaflets have a different purpose – to make information available to an unknown audience – many of the design issues are the same as for newsletters. Rather than repeat all the information, you should refer to Chapter 7.

Common features include:

- Paper size and folds
- Colours
- Font types and styles
- Images
- Columns
- Alignment and bullets

Number of pages

You will need to consider how many pages you will need – a newsletter is likely to have at least four pages, often more. The front cover should persuade people to read on. Generally, you should save most of the detail for the inside pages. You will need to think about what size paper you are printing on and how you will fold it. For example, if your newsletter will be A5 size and you are printing on both sides of A4, each sheet will produce four pages. This means that the total number of pages must be a multiple of four or you will have blank pages.

Choosing a focus

Every page should give the reader a clear reason to stop and look. This focus could be a catchy title or an image. Build a page around this focal point – position it on the page and then place text and other components so that it stands out.

Columns

Make sure your columns are balanced – roughly the same amount in each. How you do this will depend on what software you are using. In Word, for instance, you can insert a continuous break at the end of the text on a page. Try it out.

Choosing your software

What software should you use? Desktop publishing software seems the obvious choice since this is specifically designed to produce publications such as newsletters. However, word processing software has become so sophisticated that it has all the features you need to create effective publications. For Unit 1, there is no requirement to use any particular type of software. The main thing is that it is capable of producing publications that are fit for purpose.

Creating a newsletter

Can I do this?

Using word processing or desktop publishing tools, make sure you can:

- **Use columns**
- **Format text**
- **Align text**
- **Wrap text**
- **Import and position images**
- **Align text and images**
- **Crop and resize images**
- **Use bullets**
- **Change margins**
- **Change colours**
- **Use text boxes**
- **Use lines and borders**
- **Create a table**
- **Insert page numbers**

Activity 8.11

Design and create a newsletter for youth members of the leisure club. The newsletter should give them information about current developments and future events. You may wish to use information from this folder. Think carefully about the content and the writing style you should use before designing the pages. Use two columns on each page.

Testing, testing!

Create a prototype of your newsletter and check it carefully for:

- mistakes in spelling or grammar
- readability of each section of text
- suitability of writing style
- consistency
- sensible use of images
- balance of columns
- layout and use of white space
- impact of front cover
- flow from one page to the next.

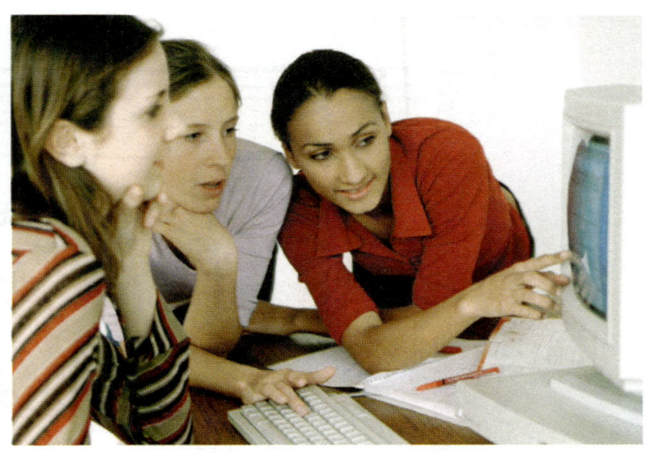

Activity 8.12

Test your newsletter by asking your peers for comments. Listen to what they have to say and make changes that improve the publication.

Alistair Larsson asks you to produce a similar newsletter for parents of youth members. Using your newsletter for youth as a guide, design and create a newsletter for adults. Think about what should be different – content, writing style, etc.

Tackling THE PROJECT

Now it is time to tackle 'Targeting a known audience' which concentrates on meeting the needs of specific people or groups.

Ask yourself

Have I got all the information I need?

Check your file WHICHPUBS and make sure you have all the information you need for each of the publications. Think carefully about the presentation to students which also requires some paper-based publications.

Carry out further research if you are not happy with the material you have collected.

Will people find the information useful? Does it make sense?

Since you know who your audience is, it should be easier to customise your publications to meet their needs.

For the presentation, are your speaker notes clear and concise? Do the slides summarise the main points? Is the style suitable for the audience?

A completely different style is required for the report. Have you got it right?

Your letter is to the newspaper editor but bear in mind that if it is published it will be read by many people with different language skills.

Make sure you save

- prototypes with user feedback
- final versions

9 Producing an eportfolio

At last – a chance to show off! An eportfolio is a very exciting way of presenting evidence of your achievements on screen. Instead of creating a mass of paper evidence, you build an eportfolio that can be viewed by anyone with a computer and an internet browser.

That really is all there is to it – a mini-website with links to various publications and evidence of how you did things. There is nothing magical about it – if you know how to create web pages and how to create links to different items, you can do it!

As you work through this chapter, you will learn how to design and build an eportfolio for the Unit 1 SPB and you will practise these skills by creating one for **The Project**.

Although you can work through the chapters in this book in any order and there are many links that take you back and forth, you should only tackle this chapter on eportfolios when you have completed Chapters 1 to 8.

In this chapter you will learn how to design and build an eportfolio by:

- *choosing the content*
- *designing the structure*
- *creating a folder structure to store the evidence*
- *designing the web pages using a storyboard*
- *converting the files into acceptable formats*
- *building the eportfolio*
- *testing that it works*

Who is it for and why is it needed?

An eportfolio can be used to present information about yourself or your work. It might be for a job application or for a record of all your achievements over a number of years. The audience might be a local employer or, if you decided to publish it on the web, anyone around the world could view your eportfolio via the internet.

Keeping the moderator happy

For all DiDA SPBs, the audience is clear – the eportfolio is for the moderator at Edexcel. The purpose is also clear – to show off what you have achieved when working on the SPB so that you can gain the marks you deserve.

You need to get the moderator on your side by making sure that your eportfolio is attractive and that all the evidence is easy to find.

What should go in it?

When you are sure that you have done everything you can for an SPB, you can make a start on your eportfolio. So how do you decide what to include?

Keep reminding yourself of the audience and asking yourself what you want them to see and how you can create the right impression. Don't automatically include everything you have stored as you went along – if you can't give a reason for including something, leave it out. Only include evidence that is going to help gain you marks. An eportfolio that seems to be full of any old work is going to put the moderator off straight away!

You should also be prepared to go back and make changes if you realise that something is not quite right.

TALKING POINT 9.1

The Project is similar to a real SPB but without the project planning. Imagine that you need to submit an eportfolio of your work on this project to a moderator. What does the moderator need to see? How can you create the right impression? Think about evidence of planning, gathering information and prototyping as well as the final products. What about project review?

Activity 9.1

Make a detailed list of the evidence you want to include in your eportfolio for The Project. You did not have to do any project planning so divide the evidence into three sections – gathering information, developing publications and project review. Go through everything you have stored to make sure that you don't miss anything out. Add The Project review documents to your list. You will produce these later.

Designing an eportfolio structure

The eportfolio consists of a series of web pages plus your evidence. In this chapter we will look at one possible structure for a Unit 1 eportfolio but you should bear in mind that there are many other possibilities and you are free to come up with your own design. The important thing is that the structure is logical so that users can move around the eportfolio and find what they want.

In our example, we divide the evidence into four main sections:

- how you got the information you needed
- your publications and how you developed them
- how you managed the project
- a review of the whole project.

A simple structure chart is a very good way of mapping out the structure of the eportfolio clearly. It can show the individual pages and how they link together. It can also show links to the evidence that you want to include.

It is best to start at the top with a **home page** and work down, adding more levels as you go. In our example, the home page introduces the eportfolio and allows the user to access a **menu page** for each of the main sections.

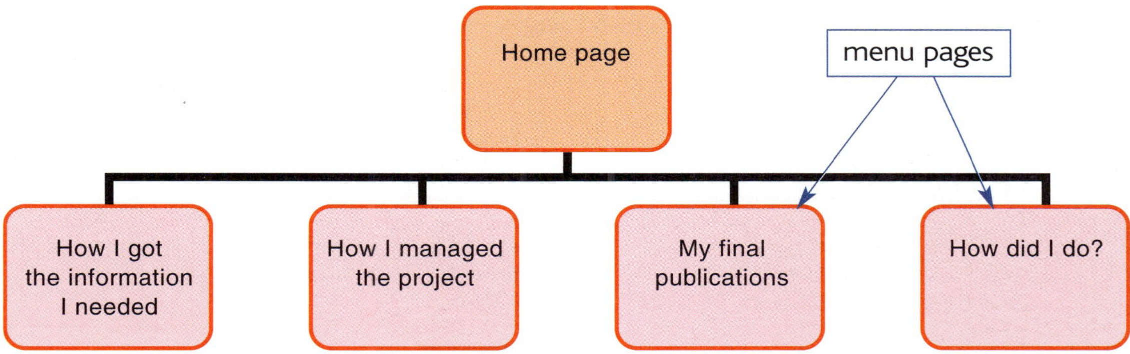

The connecting lines show that this page links to four menu pages, one for each main section. Note: All lines between web pages indicate two-way links.

Drilling down

From each menu page there are links that allow the moderator to drill down to **context pages**. This is where you provide a commentary and a link for each piece of evidence.

How I got the information I needed

This menu page provides links to context pages about gathering information.

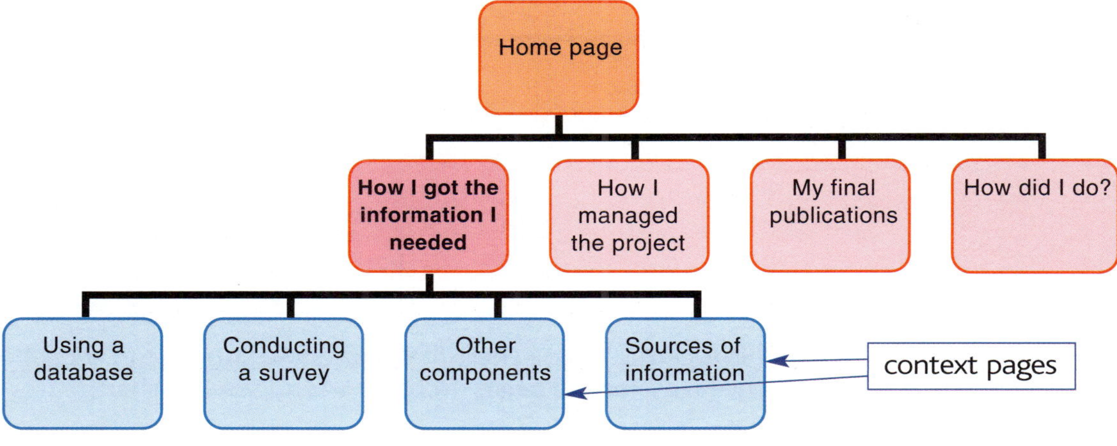

My final publications

This project brief requires four publications as shown. For each of the publications there is a context page introducing the evidence.

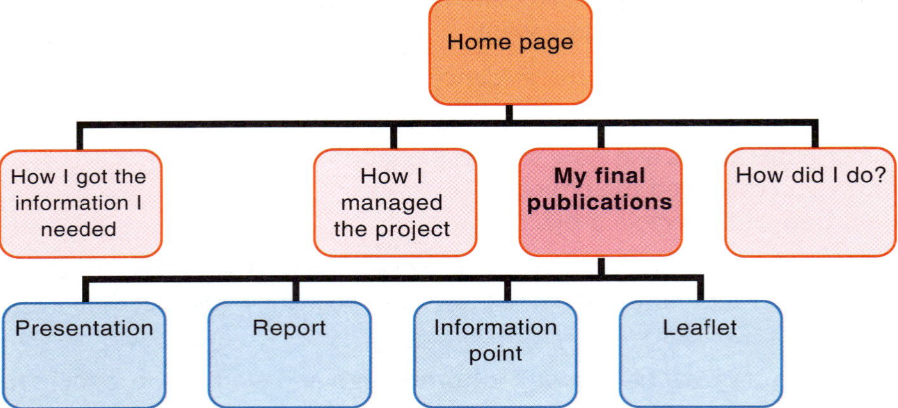

How I managed the project

This menu page links to two context pages – one for the project plan and the other for a project log.

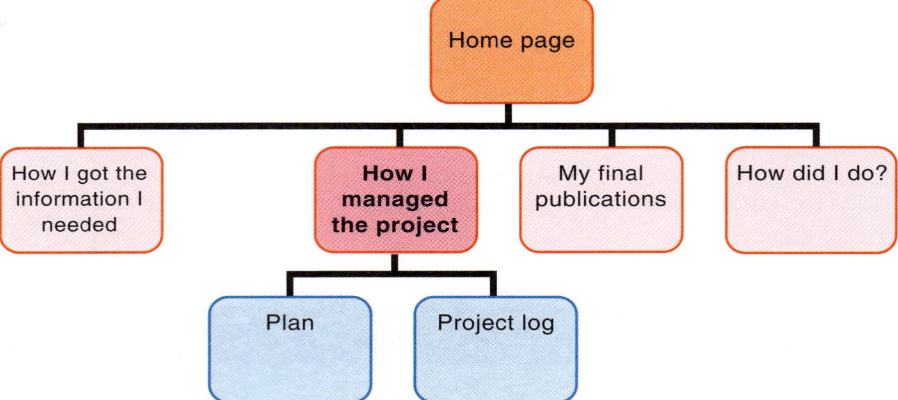

End of project review

This page links to two context pages, one for the student's review of the project and the other for reviewers' feedback.

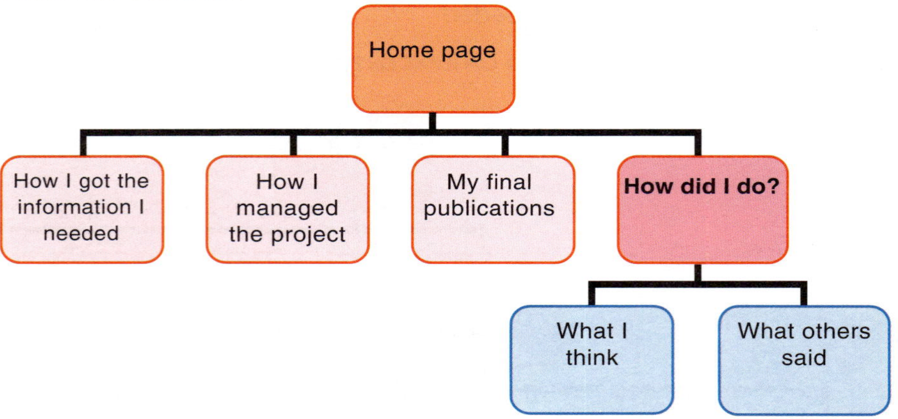

Now we can put all this together in one chart that shows the structure of the whole website and the evidence files. Turn to pages 142 and 143 to see this chart.

Navigation

Users need to be able to find their way around your eportfolio without wasting time searching for links on each web page – otherwise they may just give up!

The first rule is to keep the navigation simple and consistent. Some links will appear on every web page. Others will vary depending on what the page is for.

Navigation is indicated on the chart as follows:

- each connecting line between web pages is two-way so there must be a link back to the previous page
- each connecting line between a web page and an evidence file is one-way only
- the symbol **H** indicates a link back to the home page
- the symbol **M** indicates a link to each of the other menu pages.

This navigation structure will allow a user to move around without always going back up through the levels to the home page.

Your evidence files should **not** contain links to other parts of the eportfolio. Imagine what you would think if you were looking at the information point at Loughford School and there was a button saying 'Back to the eportfolio'. Clearly this is not fit for purpose and you must not do this in any of your publications.

So how does the moderator get back from looking at a publication in your eportfolio? It will depend on the type of publication – you should give the moderator instructions on the context page for each publication. For example, 'use the back button in your browser to return to this page'.

The same navigation bar appears on every screen.

TALKING POINT 9.2

Make sure that you understand the complete chart for our eportfolio structure. What is in it? How will a user move around? If they are at particular place, how can they get to a page or a file in another section? Our example is one possible structure. But there are plenty of others. What alternatives can you suggest?

▸▸ Activity 9.2

Create a structure chart for your eportfolio for The Project. Use your list of what must be included and think carefully about where users should be able to go from each page. Add clear navigation to the chart.

Note: You will not have a section for managing the project as you did not have to plan it!

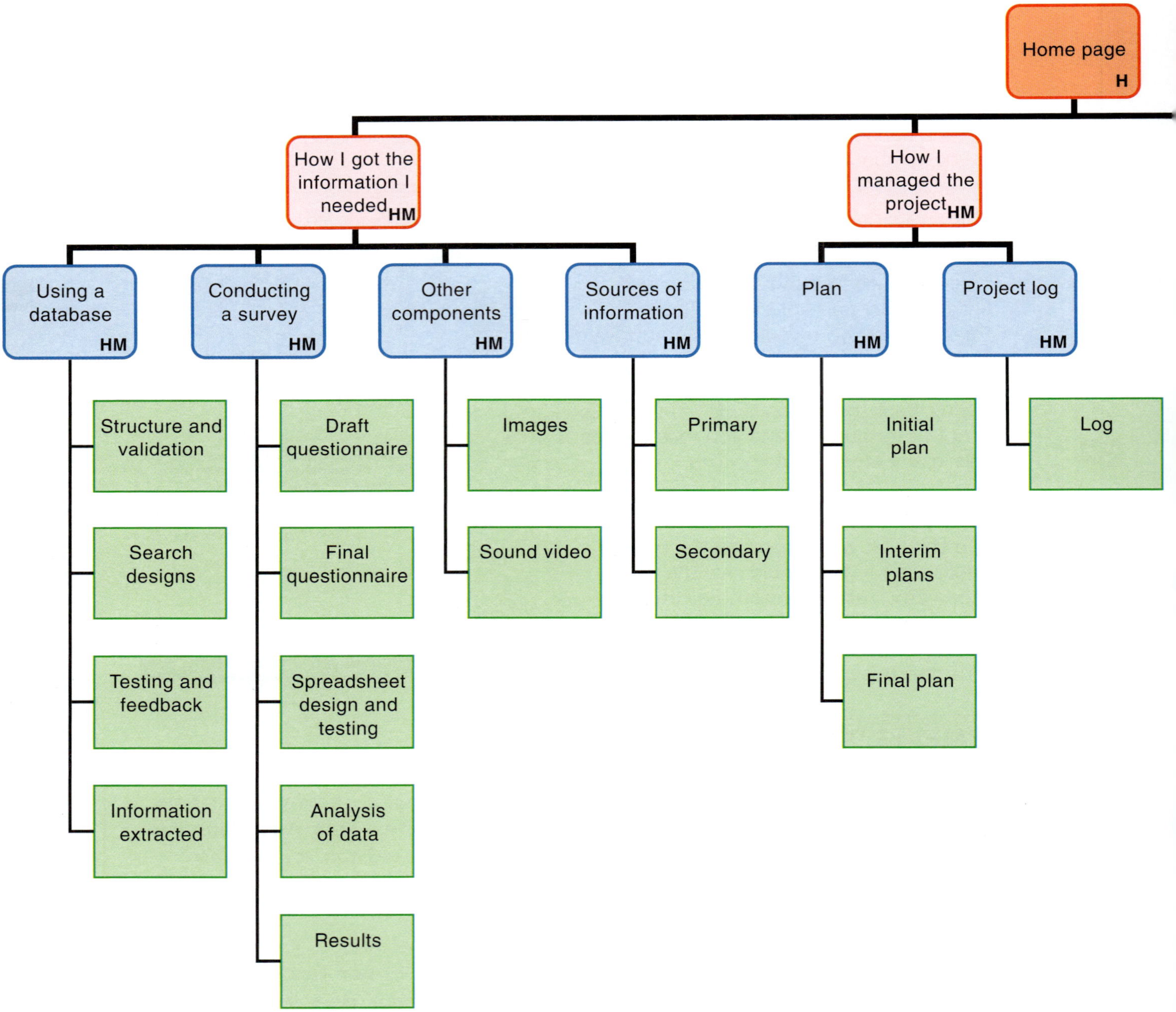

Home page H

How I got the information I needed HM

Using a database HM
- Structure and validation
- Search designs
- Testing and feedback
- Information extracted

Conducting a survey HM
- Draft questionnaire
- Final questionnaire
- Spreadsheet design and testing
- Analysis of data
- Results

Other components HM
- Images
- Sound video

Sources of information HM
- Primary
- Secondary

How I managed the project HM

Plan HM
- Initial plan
- Interim plans
- Final plan

Project log HM
- Log

Make sure that you understand how it fits together and where links must allow you to go. Remember that this is just one possible structure.

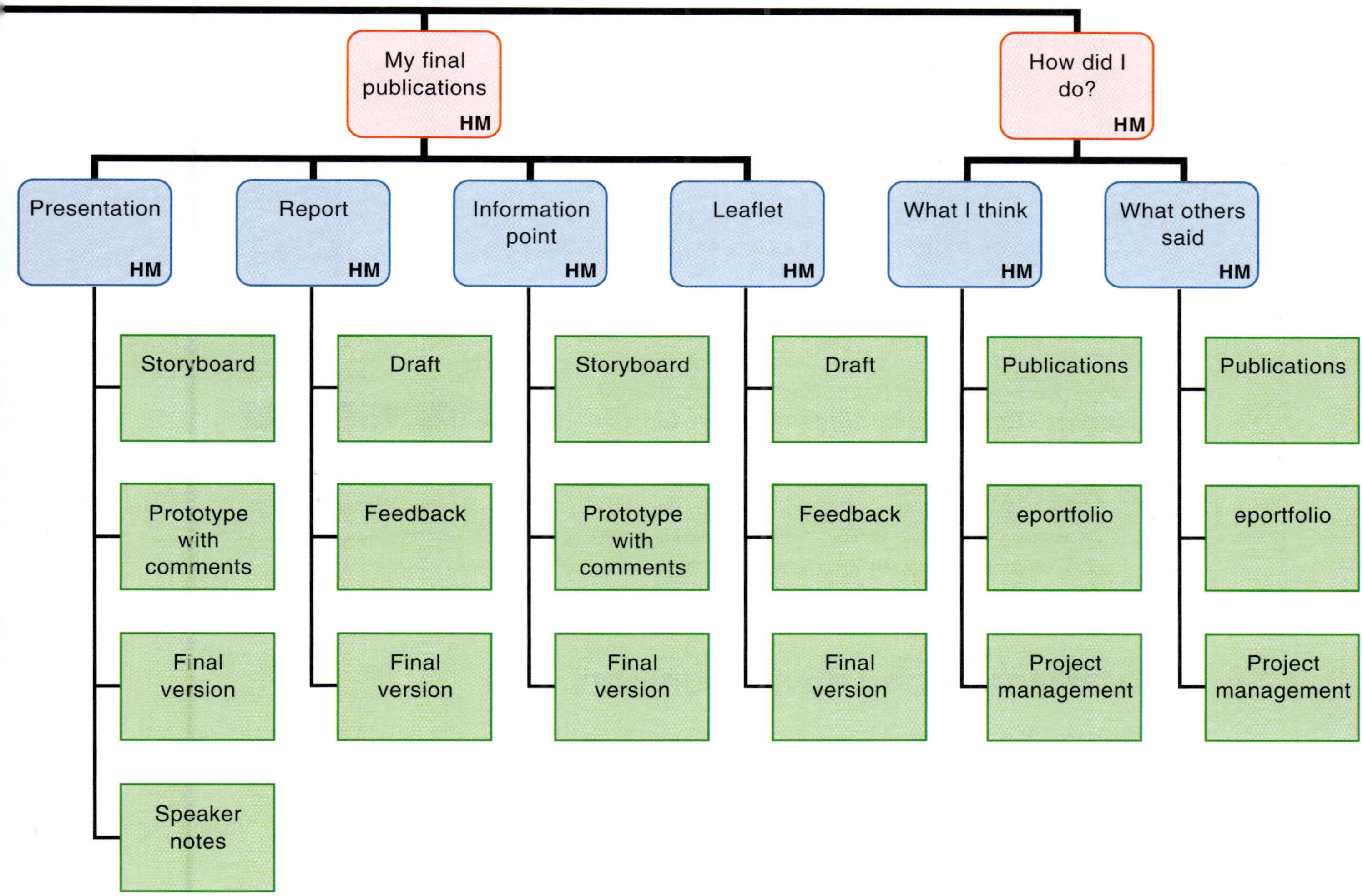

- My final publications **HM**
  - Presentation **HM**
    - Storyboard
    - Prototype with comments
    - Final version
    - Speaker notes
  - Report **HM**
    - Draft
    - Feedback
    - Final version
  - Information point **HM**
    - Storyboard
    - Prototype with comments
    - Final version
  - Leaflet **HM**
    - Draft
    - Feedback
    - Final version
- How did I do? **HM**
  - What I think **HM**
    - Publications
    - eportfolio
    - Project management
  - What others said **HM**
    - Publications
    - eportfolio
    - Project management

Designing the web pages

The home page, menu pages and context pages for your eportfolio need to be carefully designed. They must provide enough information for the user to know what the options are and include correct links that match your planned structure.

Before you can design the pages using a storyboard, you need to think some more about navigation – exactly how users will move around.

Make it obvious where the links are

There are a number of ways of including links in the eportfolio.

- **Text** is the simplest way to identify a link. Make sure that is clear what the user is linking to. If you say 'Click here', what does 'here' refer to? Make it more obvious than that. Use text that describes the evidence such as 'See what you think of my presentation to club members'.
- **Images and symbols** can be used to indicate links. These can be more attractive but take care to make them relevant.
- **Buttons** perform an action when you click them. They can be simple text or images or they can be made to change as you move over them or click them. These are called rollover buttons. Buttons can also be animated so that they appear to move or flash.

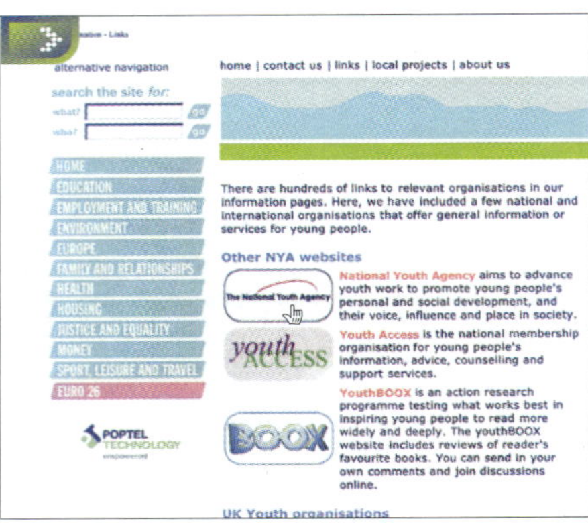

Examples of types of link

> **Activity 9.3**
>
> **Explore your web authoring software and try out different types of button. You can use ready-made buttons or create your own if you are feeling adventurous. Some simple examples can be found on the Macromedia website.**

Consistency and navigation bars

You will make life much easier for the user if navigation buttons and links look similar and are in the same area on every page. This can be achieved using a navigation bar that is the same on all main pages. Navigation bars are usually placed along the top or side of a web page. They consist of a series of text, graphical or animated buttons that link to other pages or files in the eportfolio.

If you are reading this page on screen you will see that there is a navigation bar of tabs along the top that stays the same when you change screens. Users can easily navigate between the main sections and find their way around.

Examples of navigation bars

The website for Wiltshire Farm Foods has a series of buttons across the top of the home page, each of which links to one of the main areas of the site. On each of these pages there is a navigation bar or menu on the left. This menu is the same on every page and allows you to move to other main pages without going back to the home page. You could easily navigate from the 'Home page' to 'Find your local outlet' to 'Frequently asked questions'.

⏩ Activity 9.4

Check out the websites for Wiltshire Farm Foods and for Hideaways. What do you like about each of the navigation designs? How does the home page differ between the two? Have a look at some other sites and think about how you could include a navigation bar in your eportfolio design.

The Home Page

The home page is the most important in your eportfolio. Think of it as a shop front – if the window display is good, visitors will open the door and see what is on offer.

Your home page must include:

- who you are, your registration number, centre name and number
- date completed
- a clear description of the purpose of the eportfolio
- a summary of what can be found inside
- links that enable the user to drill down (e.g. to menu pages or a contents page).

Make the page attractive – use a suitable image that illustrates the content or purpose. Don't be tempted to decorate the page with a variety of images that are not particularly relevant.

Call the homepage 'index.html'.

TALKING POINT 9.3

What features on a home page will persuade people to look at the rest of an eportfolio?

The menu pages

As soon as the user moves from the home page you will need to introduce them to one of the main sections in the eportfolio using a menu page (pink on the structure chart). Each of these pages should have a consistent look and feel and include:

- the purpose of the section and a brief description of what it includes
- links to the context pages for the various items in the section
- a link to the home page
- links to other menu pages, possibly using a navigation bar.

The context pages

Most of these pages are likely to include:

- a description of the collection of evidence
- some information about how you developed it
- a link to each item of evidence
- a link to the home page
- links to menu pages, possibly using a navigation bar.

Although each of these pages has a very different purpose you should still aim for consistency. Make sure that the navigation matches your structure chart.

⏩ Activity 9.5

Before designing your eportfolio in detail, get a feel for what is involved by looking at some of those published on the internet. Many colleges require students to publish their eportfolios on the web so that they can be easily accessed. Search for some examples. Note features that you like or dislike. Pay particular attention to the home page and the navigation.

Storyboarding

You should use a storyboard to design the web pages for your eportfolio. The storyboard should help you to ensure that your pages are consistent. There is more detail on storyboarding on page 102 and on web page design on page 128.

Each web page you create will have a different focus depending on its purpose and what it links to. Use a storyboard to help you decide:

- what will appear on each page
- the position of components
- how you will link to items in the eportfolio
- how you will link to other web pages in the eportfolio.

You should create a template for your menu pages to ensure that common elements such as the navigation bar look the same and are in the same position on each page. You should do the same for the context pages.

Your eportfolio must be complete if you are to gain as many marks as possible. You can use the storyboard to help make sure that you have not left anything important out.

⏩ Activity 9.6

Using your eportfolio structure chart for The Project, create storyboards for the web pages in the eportfolio. In Tackling The Project for this chapter you will use these storyboards to help you create the pages.

Building an eportfolio

Can I do this?

Using web authoring tools make sure you can:

- Create a logical file structure
- Convert files to other formats
- Create web pages
- Create a navigation bar
- Insert absolute links
- Insert relative links
- Use text and images for links
- Open a page or file in a new window

Folder structure

Now that you have designed your eportfolio, you can think about where you will store the evidence. You must create a folder structure that allows you to store all the various items so that you keep everything together and can easily find things and include correct links on the web pages. This may be similar to the folder structure you created at the beginning of the project but you should create a new one that will only contain the evidence you want the moderator to see. The more organised you are, the more time you can spend on making your eportfolio an exciting and effective publication. You won't waste time because you want to link to a file but you can't find it. Don't let this happen to you!

Here is a folder structure that matches our structure chart.

Within the eportfolio folder, there are four subfolders, one for each of the main sections. If you look at the column on the left you will see that within each main subfolder, there are folders of evidence.

▸▸ Activity 9.7

Create a folder structure for your eportfolio for THE PROJECT. Create this in your user area. Do not try to include any files yet.

Moving evidence into your eportfolio

Once you are happy with your folder structure, you can start to add content. Every item of evidence will need to be copied into the appropriate folder in your eportfolio. Some of the files will need to be converted into acceptable file formats.

If you look at this screenshot of our example eportfolio, you will see that the Presentation folder contains the draft and final versions of a presentation, the storyboard and the speaker notes. It also contains the context page for the presentation.

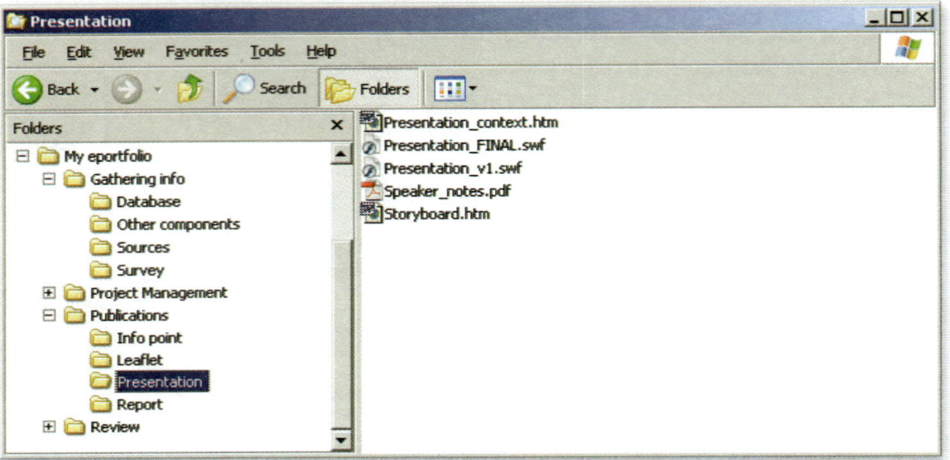

Using acceptable file formats

Have you ever seen a message like this when trying to open a new file?

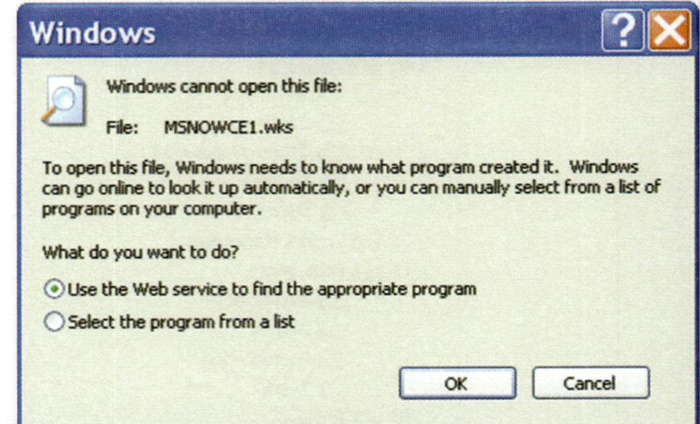

If not, then you are lucky! If someone sends you a file that was created in software that you don't have then you may not be able to open it. It depends on the file format or file type. You can tell the file type by the extension in the file name – .wks tells me that the file was created using Microsoft Works, which I don't have.

When you are building your eportfolio you must make sure that you only include file types that can be opened by everyone in your audience.

What to avoid

Some file formats cannot be viewed unless the user has installed the software that was used to create the files.

For the SPB there is a list of acceptable file types in the project brief. **You must NOT include file types that are not on the list.** If you do your eportfolio may be rejected and you won't get any marks!

Common file formats

There are some file formats that can be opened by just about everyone. The html format which is used for web pages can be read using any web browser. Rich text format (rtf) documents can be created from word processing or desktop publishing files and can be read by other software, but the resulting file sizes can be unmanageable.

Free software and viewers

Some software readers or players are freely available – such as Windows Media Player for wmv files, Adobe Acrobat for pdf files – and files created in these formats are not a problem.

There are also free downloadable viewers for some file types although these often do not allow users to see any of the design. If a file requires a free viewer you might want to include a link to it for users who need to download it.

You must not include a file type that is not in the list for the SPB even if a viewer is freely available.

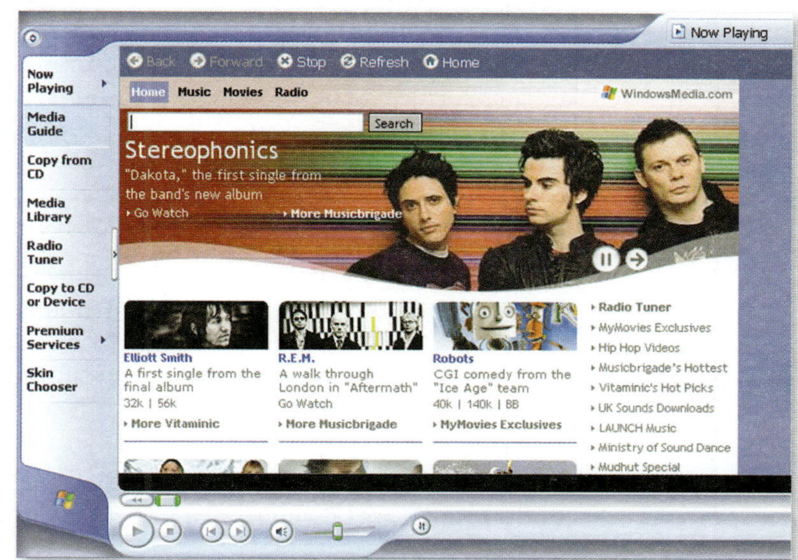

Creating acceptable file formats

For each piece of evidence you want to include, you must check that it is saved in an acceptable format.

In many software applications there are options to save files in a number of different formats. In some instances, you may need to use a converter program to convert publications to acceptable formats.

This table gives some file formats that can be used in Unit 1 eportfolios.

File type	Used for
html	web pages, word processing, desktop publishing
txt	data sets, word processing
pdf	word processing, desktop publishing
swf	movies, presentations, screen recording
mov, avi, wmv	video
wav, midi, mp3	sound
jpg, png, gif	images

▸▸ Activity 9.8

Open the file and save a copy as FORMATS in an appropriate folder in your user area. Check that the contents match the list in the THE PROJECT brief and amend your file if necessary.

TALKING POINT 9.4

Which file types do you use that you will not be able to include in an eportfolio? What facilities do you have in your centre to deal with this problem?

Activity 9.9

It is time to copy your evidence of work on THE PROJECT into your folder structure for the eportfolio. You do not yet have files for the project review section 'How did I do?' as you cannot create these until you have finished everything else. Convert files into acceptable formats and make sure that you store each item in the correct folder. You will create the introductory web pages later.

Creating links that work – absolute vs relative

There is nothing more frustrating than a link that doesn't work. Even if you have included a first-class publication in your eportfolio, if no-one can get to it, it will not do you a lot of good. Although you did some work on simple web pages in Chapter 7 you did not have to create a complete website structure. It is now vital that you understand how links work so that you can use them appropriately.

Every link must have a path (address) – absolute or relative. **Now don't switch off, this is really important!** If the moderator can't see all your work you will lose marks!

TALKING POINT 9.5

*Look at these two pieces of information about the location of Salisbury Museum. The envelope has an **absolute** address – the exact full address for the museum. The second gives some directions to the museum – these instructions are **relative** to the cinema. When would each be useful?*

Salisbury Museum
The King's House
65 Cathedral Close
Salisbury
Wiltshire
SP1 2EN

'from the cinema, walk along the pavement until you reach Waterstones Bookshop turn left until you enter the Cathedral Close. Follow the road to the right and you will reach the museum on your right'

External links

An **external** link has an absolute path which is the exact full address of a file. For example, http://dida.edexcel.org.uk/home/aboutDiDA/ takes you straight to an information page on the DiDA microsite. It doesn't matter where you are so long as you are online.

Links to web-based secondary sources you have used should be absolute links so that the user can go straight to them via the internet.

You MUST use an absolute path if you want to link to a site on the web.

If you used the link C:\\MyDocuments/Myeportfolio/Publications/publications_menu.htm in your eportfolio it would be a different matter. If you clicked on this link it would take you to *your* C: drive and follow the path through the MyDocuments folder to the correct page – no problem!

But – if you were to send me your eportfolio, what would happen? If I clicked on the link it would go straight to *my* C: drive to look for MyDocuments and then Myeportfolio and, surprise, surprise, it would not find it! It would not look on the CD and it certainly would not look on your computer.

Do NOT use absolute paths to go to pages or files within your eportfolio.

Relative links

An **internal** link should use a **relative** path.

Relative paths in your eportfolio do not include the drive name or folders outside your eportfolio such as My Documents or the address of another website. For example, here is an outline for the publications menu page for our sample eportfolio (the screen shot shows the structure to remind you).

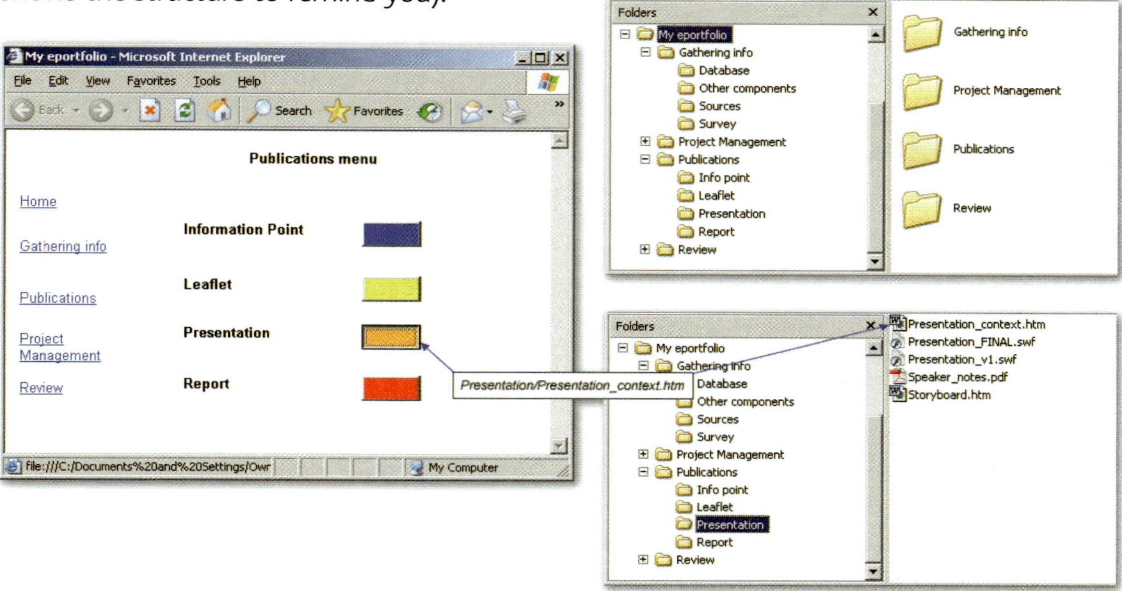

The main Publications folder contains a menu page for the publications (publications_menu.htm). This page has a link to the context page for each publication. The relative path for the presentation context page is shown. There is just enough information to get from the menu page to the correct file in the folder Presentation.

Clicking the link above will open the presentation context page. Now look at this outline of the presentation context page and the folder structure next to it.

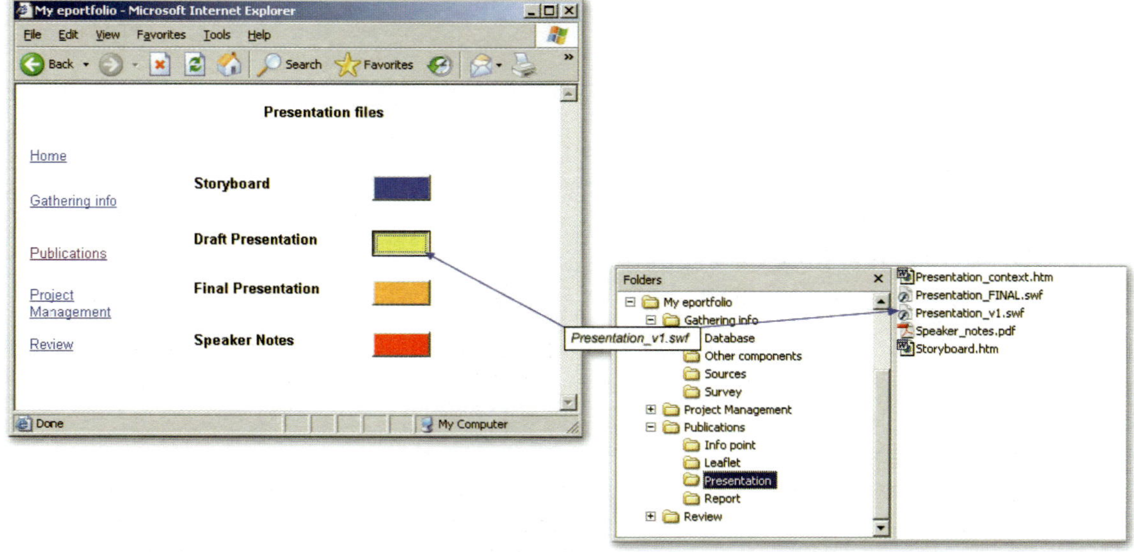

The context page has links to each of the files relating to the presentation. The relative path for the draft presentation is presentation_v1.swf. That's it! There is no need for any more information because the file is in the same folder as the page containing the link.

This method works for all links inside the eportfolio. A link to a different section of the eportfolio will need to include more details. The link to the project review context page is shown. Use the structure chart on pages 142 and 143 to make sure you understand how this works.

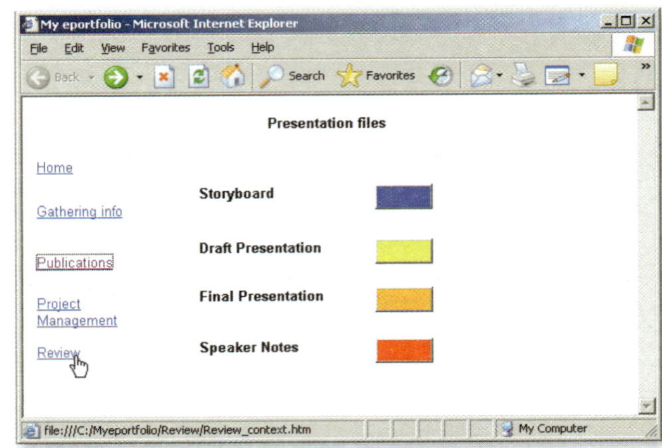

TALKING POINT 9.6

Look at the full structure chart on pages 142 and 143 and work out the relative paths for some of the links. Make sure you understand how they work.

How you create relative links will depend on what software you are using but usually you do not have to type the address yourself. For example, in Macromedia Dreamweaver, these links are called document-relative paths and they can be entered by dragging or pointing to the file you want to link to.

Activity 9.10

Open your web authoring tools and use the help menu to find information about relative and absolute links. Make sure that you understand what they are and how to create them using your software. Get this right and you will be able to move your complete eportfolio to different locations without breaking the links.

Keeping it all together

Hopefully you will have got the message by now – it's no good spending time making your pages attractive if users then get the dreaded 'File not found' message. Your eportfolio is meant to be portable and will be viewed on other computers by people who do not have access to your system.

Check, and check again, that all the pages, images and files are stored inside your eportfolio folder structure before you create the relative links. It is very easy to include a link to another area on your system that works perfectly well when you test it.

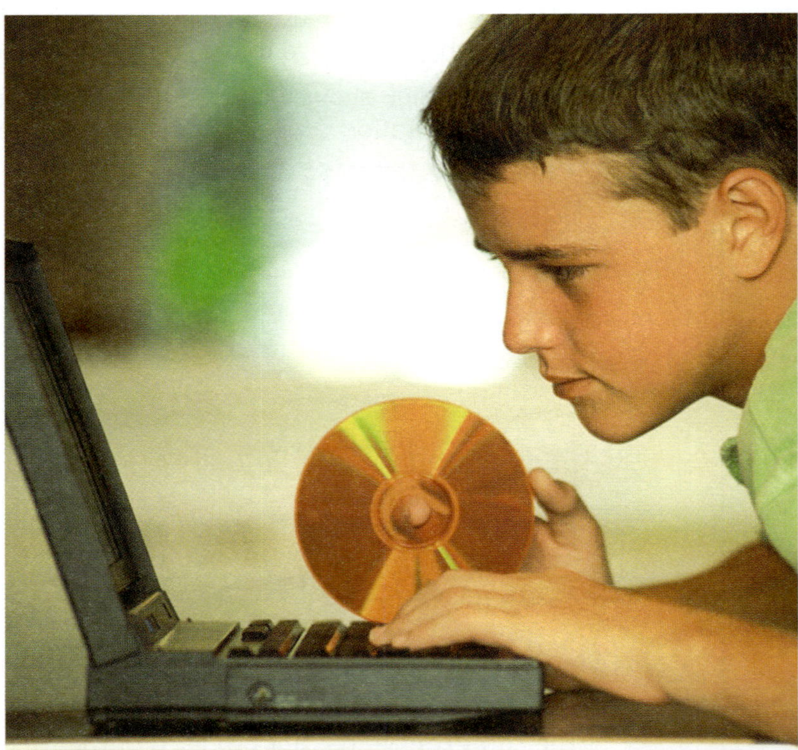

It is a good idea to load your eportfolio onto another system, a standalone PC or laptop, and check that everything works as it should.

Getting the size right

If an eportfolio is too big, it will take too long to download and people may be put off reading it. More importantly, for DiDA SPBs there will always be a maximum file size specified. If you submit an eportfolio that is bigger than this maximum then your work may not be accepted.

How do you find out the size of your eportfolio?

This will depend on the software you are using. For example, in Windows Explorer, you can right click on any folder and select properties. This will display information about the folder including its size. The maximum for a Unit 1 SPB is likely to be around 15MB so this example is clearly way too big!

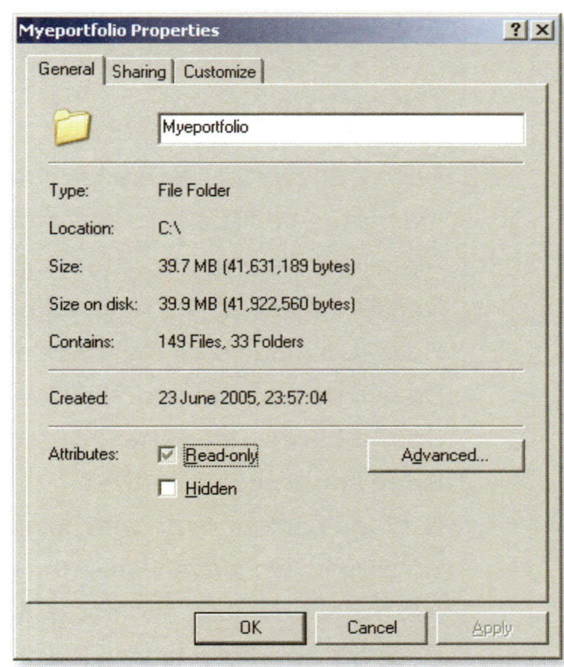

What do you do if your eportfolio is too big?

There are various techniques you can use to reduce the size of your eportfolio.

Optimise components

Multimedia components generally take up quite a lot of space. If you are including video or sound, you may need to make the clip shorter. The file sizes of images can be dramatically reduced by changing the resolution or cropping the picture (see chapter 7).

Changing the file formats

Some file formats take up far more space than others. Look what happened when I saved the draft version of this chapter in pdf and then in rtf!

Chapter 9 Producing an eportfolio v4.doc	2,082 KB	Microsoft Word Document	05/05/2005 20:05
Chapter 9 Producing an eportfolio v4.pdf	404 KB	Adobe Acrobat Document	05/05/2005 20:05
Chapter 9 Producing an eportfolio v4.rtf	86,831 KB	Rich Text Format	05/05/2005 20:06

No wonder rtf is not an acceptable file format for DiDA eportfolios!

An alternative format for documents that takes up far less space is pdf. It is a read-only format but this is fine as your eportfolio is intended for viewing only.

If you are unhappy with the size of a file or the time it takes to open, check what other formats may be suitable and see if you can convert it to a smaller size. Use your file FORMATS to help you.

Leave things out

This is a bit drastic but if all else fails, you will have to find things such as images that are not absolutely necessary and get rid of them!

Prototyping and testing

You must test your eportfolio to ensure that it functions properly. One of the tests must be to ensure that it works on a different computer.

You should also ask peer reviewers and your teacher to test it and give you feedback.

You and your test users should ask yourselves these questions:

Checklist

Does it show clear awareness of the audience and purpose?
If a maximum file size is specified, is the eportfolio within the limit?
Are all the file formats acceptable?
Does it include all the required evidence?
Have you made sure that there are no unnecessary files included?
Does it demonstrate your achievements?
Does it have a good user interface?
Is the home page effective?
Is all the content error-free? Is all spelling and grammar correct?
Do all links work even when the eportfolio is viewed on another system?
Are the appearance and navigation clear and consistent?
Does the eportfolio have a logical structure and navigation route that makes it easy for users to find their way around?
Are the images good enough quality without making the files too big?
Is all text readable – font types, sizes, colour combinations?
Are all the web pages well designed?
Are all sources acknowledged correctly?
Does it include evidence of process, with commentaries?
Does the eportfolio display correctly in different browsers?

If the answer to any of these questions is 'No', do something about it! If you agree with your reviewers, make the changes and then test it again.

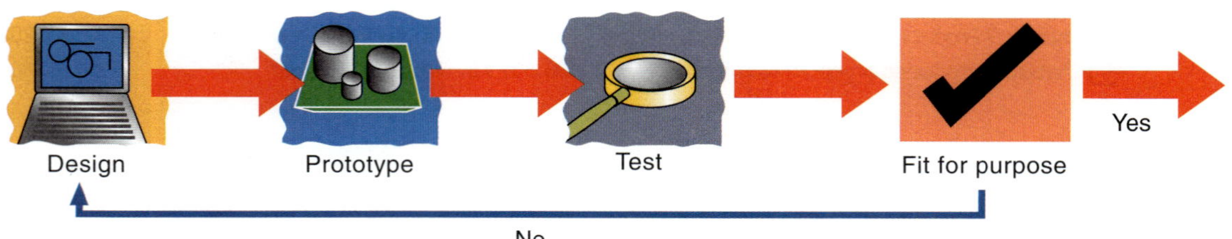

▸▸ Activity 9.11

Open the file and customise it for use by your eportfolio test users. Add space for details including the name of the reviewer, date of review, reviewer's comments etc. You may want to change the wording of questions and add some more of your own.

Creating an effective eportfolio

There is a lot to take in, isn't there? All the more reason to design and build your eportfolio in a logical order. As you reach each stage remind yourself of what is involved. Here is a summary of the main stages.

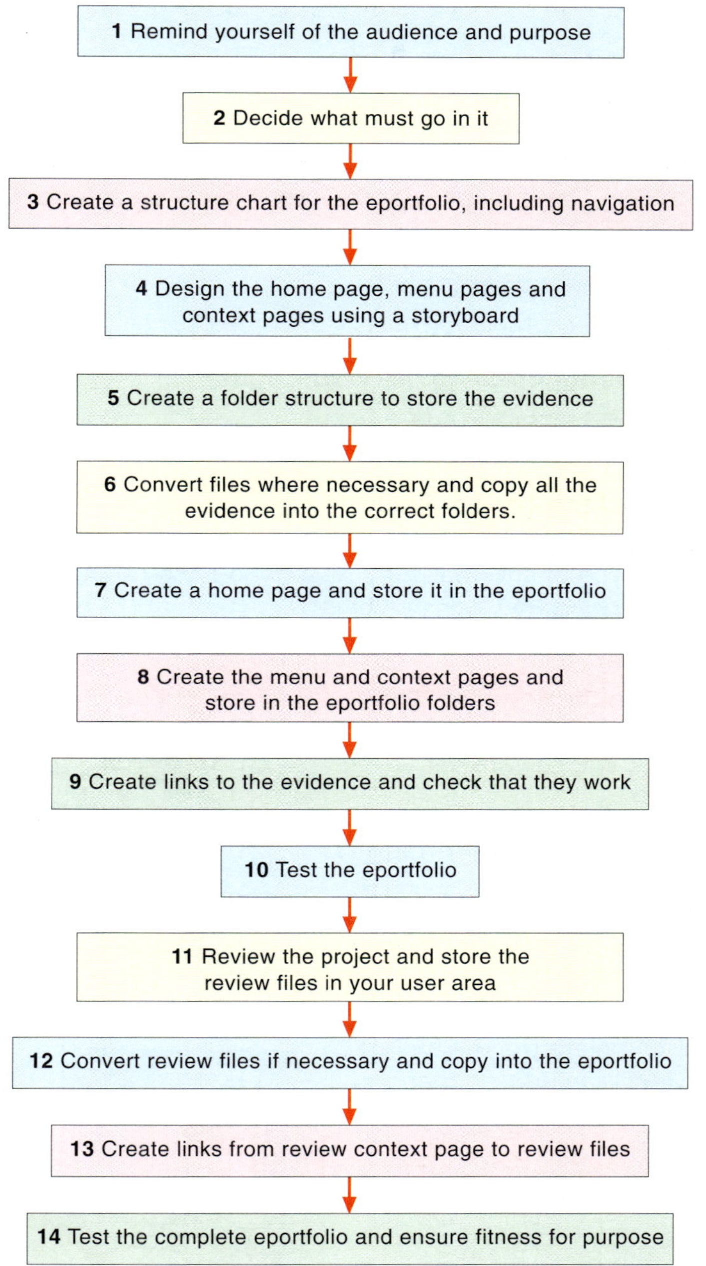

1 Remind yourself of the audience and purpose
2 Decide what must go in it
3 Create a structure chart for the eportfolio, including navigation
4 Design the home page, menu pages and context pages using a storyboard
5 Create a folder structure to store the evidence
6 Convert files where necessary and copy all the evidence into the correct folders.
7 Create a home page and store it in the eportfolio
8 Create the menu and context pages and store in the eportfolio folders
9 Create links to the evidence and check that they work
10 Test the eportfolio
11 Review the project and store the review files in your user area
12 Convert review files if necessary and copy into the eportfolio
13 Create links from review context page to review files
14 Test the complete eportfolio and ensure fitness for purpose

Activity 9.12

Before you move on to Tackling The Project, check through steps 1 to 6 and make sure that you are happy with what you have done so far. You should not think about creating the web pages and links until you are sure that all the evidence is where it should be.

Tackling THE PROJECT

THE PROJECT is well on the way to completion! Check where you are on the flowchart. You should find that you have completed the first six stages. What next?

Read the eportfolio page of THE PROJECT and keep this in mind as you move on to steps 7 to 10 on the chart.

Ask yourself:

Have I got all the evidence I need?

Check that you have copied absolutely everything you need into the appropriate eportfolio folders. Don't forget that the user will not be able to find evidence that is sitting in your user area!

Are my file formats acceptable?

Check the list of acceptable formats in the project brief.

How will I go about creating the web pages?

The key to success now is to make full use of your storyboard. Make sure that your home page makes the user want to look further.

Have I included the correct links?

You should refer to your structure chart when creating the links. Make sure that you have used the right type of link, that they all go where they should and that you can move easily between pages and look at all items.

Does it all work?

This is Step 9 on the flowchart. Refer to the checklist on page 154 and make sure that you can answer yes to every question.

Have I told the moderator enough?

Check that the commentary on each context page makes sense and includes enough detail.

What about the review?

You cannot complete the review just yet. The review is an add-on that you will work on in Chapter 10.

Make sure you save

- every single item that is part of your eportfolio inside the correct folder in your eportfolio structure

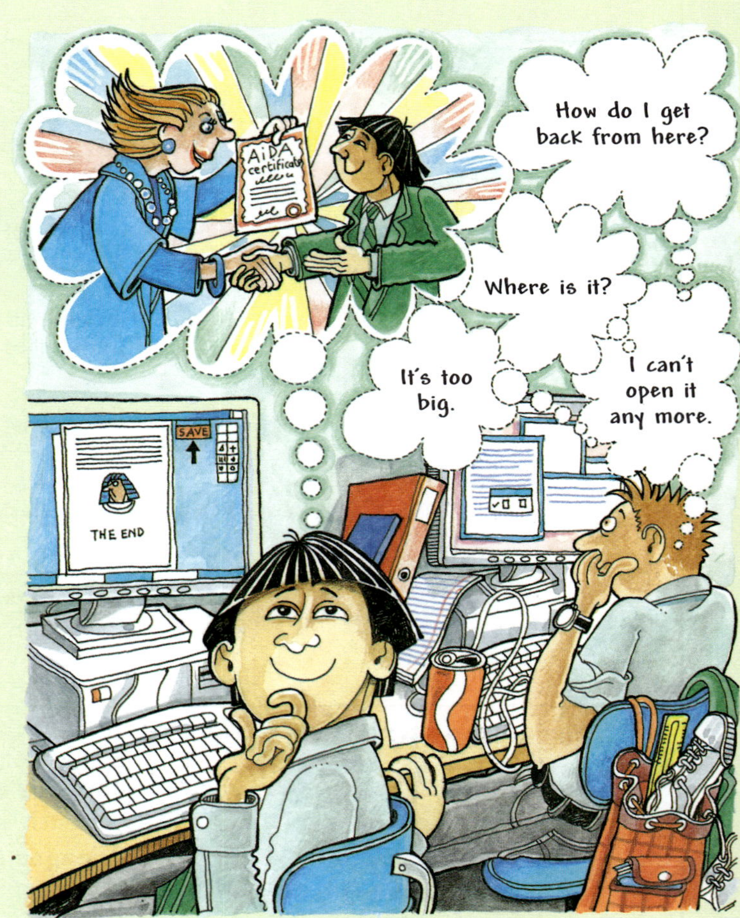

10 Managing a project

Digimodule

It's easy to lose your way in a big project like the SPB. How will you manage your time? How will you avoid getting carried away doing the bits that you like and not doing the bits you don't like? How will you make sure you finish on time?

What you need is a plan! This will help you to break the project down into a number of smaller tasks and to allocate a sensible amount of time to each. A plan is a bit like a road map in that it helps you to find your way from start to finish.

You will learn how to produce a plan and use it to help you manage the project and produce everything on time.

So let's assume that you use a plan and meet the deadline. Can you breathe a sigh of relief? Not just yet!

You must ask yourself some questions. Has the project been a success? Did you do everything that was required? Are the final publications effective? What do other people think? What could you have done better? This is all part of a project review where you can look back on what you have done and think about lessons learnt.

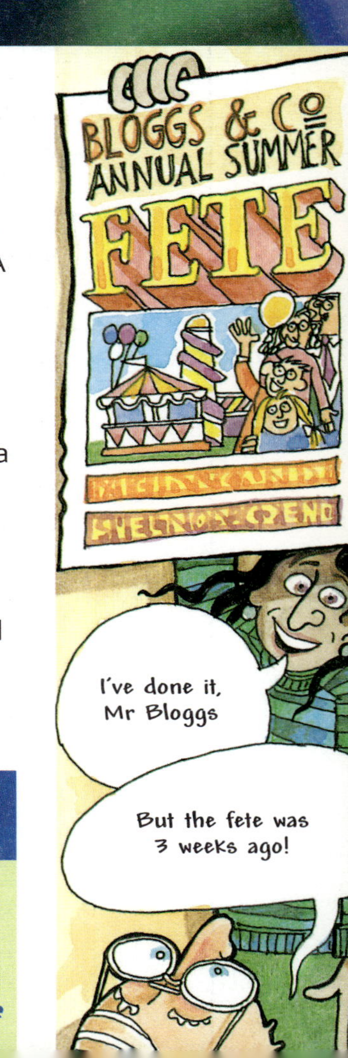

In this chapter you will learn how to manage and review a project by:

- *producing a project plan using appropriate software*
- *using your plan to monitor your progress*
- *recording changes that you make to your plan*
- *reviewing the outcomes of the project and your own performance*

Failing to plan is planning to fail!

If you are going to stand any chance of completing a project on time, you need to plan. This is not as bad as it sounds, you do it all the time.

I need to hand in my Geography coursework by midday tomorrow. I just need to get that map I produced printed off at school
I will get up 15 minutes earlier in the morning and go to the IT room before registration. I can then hand my folder in at break time

A simple plan, but it should work. You may not like the idea, but your plan tells you that you have no choice.

When it comes to the SPB for Unit 1, things are a good deal more complicated than this example. For a start, it will take around 30 hours to complete and this is probably the first time you have tackled such a huge project on your own.

Working out what is required

You first task is to work out exactly what needs to be done. You will need to break the main tasks down into smaller sub-tasks. Mind mapping is one way of doing this and you will find more information on this on page 32.

You need to identify:

- exactly what is required for the whole project: who, why where, what, how
- all the main tasks and sub-tasks including project planning, file management and end-of-project review
- the order in which you will carry out the tasks.

▶▶ Activity 10.1

Find the Unit 1 specimen SPB on the Edexcel website. Read the brief and use a mind map to work out what is required.

Getting feedback – peer reviewers and other test users

Getting feedback is an important part of the prototyping process and this needs to be built into your plan.

You and your peers can help each other out. You can work in pairs or in groups and offer constructive comments on each other's work.

You will also need to make sure that you get feedback from test users who are similar to your target audience.

You need to:

- decide who you will ask for feedback
- find out when they are available
- decide when to ask them to look at your work
- include these review points in your plan.

'Guesstimating' the time

Estimating the time needed for each task is a real problem for you if you have no experience of this type of project. You need to:

- decide how much time you will need for each task and sub-task
- check that you have allowed enough time
- check that you will meet the deadline.

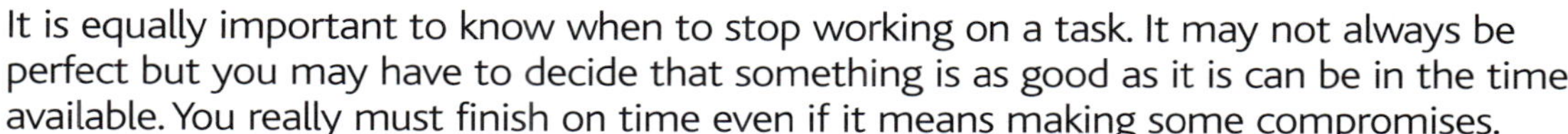

It is equally important to know when to stop working on a task. It may not always be perfect but you may have to decide that something is as good as it is can be in the time available. You really must finish on time even if it means making some compromises.

To start with you will have to 'guesstimate'. You may not get it right first time but once you have a plan you will be able to discuss it with others and improve the timings. You can make changes to your plan at any time.

Before you go on to produce your plan, you should discuss your timings with your teacher who may be able to help you reduce the amount of guesswork.

If you do another SPB for DiDA you should be able to learn from your experience with Unit 1 and turn your 'guesstimates' into realistic estimates – so long as you have updated your plan and recorded the reasons why you made changes.

Working towards a plan

You should use your mind map to produce an outline plan of tasks and sub-tasks and decide roughly how long each will take. You can also start to think about which tasks depend on others being finished first and which can be worked on at the same time.

To summarise, you need to decide:

- exactly what is required for the whole project
  - who, why where, what, how
- all the main tasks and sub-tasks
- the order in which you will carry out the tasks
- how you will get feedback
  - who will you ask for feedback?
  - when will you ask them?
  - how will you ask them to do it?

For example, the section for a survey might look something like this.

	Task		Sub-tasks	Time needed	Comments
7	Prepare questionnaire				
		7.1	Draft		Waiting for feedback on poster
		7.2	Feedback and changes		
8	Prepare spreadsheet				
		8.1	Draft		Can start at the same time as questionnaire
		8.2	Testing and changes		
		8.3	Testing with questionnaire		
		8.4	Feedback and changes		
9	Survey				
		9.1	Conduct survey		Must follow 7 and 8 Make changes to poster in class
		9.2	Collate data		
		9.3	Analyse results		

> **Activity 10.2**
> **Produce an outline plan for the Edexcel specimen SPB.**

Producing a project plan

Having created an outline, you are almost ready to produce a detailed project plan. There are just a couple of other things to think about.

Leaving nothing to chance

If something takes time, even a very short time, it should appear in your plan. Don't be tempted to leave things out because they seem too obvious or too small to worry about.

Creating checkpoints

Checkpoints need to be included to make you stop from time to time and review your progress so far. For the SPB you should use your checkpoints to discuss progress with your teacher and agree any changes you need to make. You should make a new version of the plan at these points if you and your teacher agree that changes are necessary.

Allowing time for things to go wrong

Network failure, illness, reviewers not giving feedback quickly, a task taking you much longer than you expected. Recognise any of these? Things do go wrong unless you are very lucky. Bear this in mind when you are planning and allow extra time where you can.

For Unit 1, there are no rules about what your project plan should look like but it should clearly show:

- a start date and finish date for the project
  - plan how you are going to meet the deadline
- the project broken down into manageable tasks
  - identify the main tasks and the sub-tasks
- time for file management, user feedback and review
  - these are all essential and carry marks!
- a logical order for the tasks and sub-tasks
  - which items need to be completed before others begin
  - which things can be worked on at the same time
  - which things depend on availability of a resource such as a camera
- enough time for each task and sub-task with start and finish dates for each
  - allow realistic amounts of time and stick to them
  - allow for contingencies, things can go wrong
- checkpoints where you discuss progress with your teacher
  - if your plan is going wrong, be open about it. Talk to your teacher. Now is the time to sort it out!
- changes you needed to make as you went along
  - keep a record that you can refer back to. Use comment boxes, a project log, etc.

Here is an extract from a simple project plan produced as a Gantt chart:

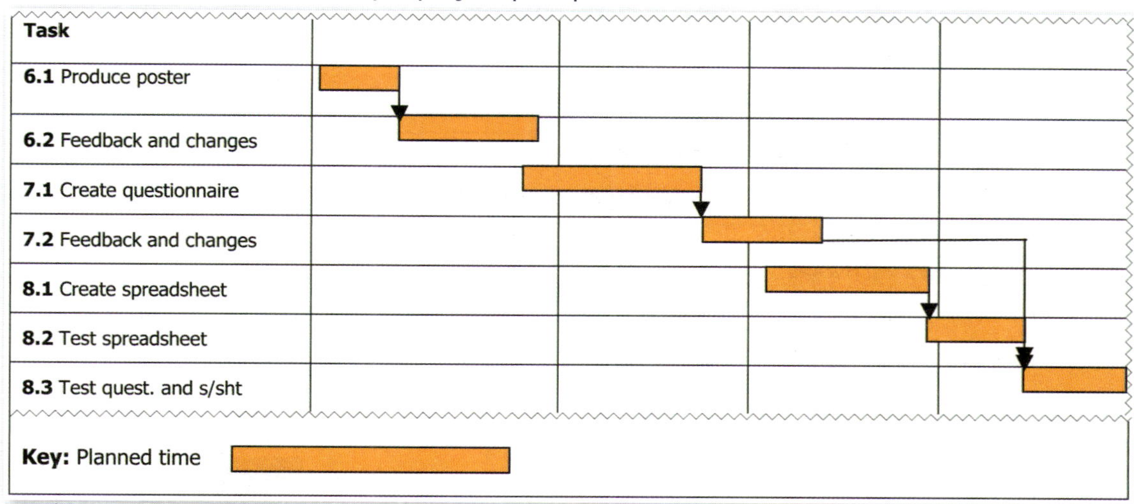

The chart shows a time line for each task and clearly shows the order of the tasks. The orange bars show the time allowed for each task. On the complete chart, dates and times appear as column headings.

The arrows show when a task must be finished before the next one can be carried out – for example, the questionnaire must be finished before it can be tested, the questionnaire and spreadsheet must both be tested separately before they can be tested together. Feedback on the poster does not affect the design of the survey so there is no arrow.

▸▸ Activity 10.3

Use the internet to find examples of Gantt charts.

Plan your work and work your plan!

There is no point in spending time drawing up a plan if you do not use it to help you achieve your objectives and meet the deadlines. The plan is not cast in stone – it can and will change. You should use it to monitor your progress so that you can anticipate problems or delays and take action. You can also give yourself a boost by ticking things off as you go along! You may want to consider keeping an audio/video project log to comment on what you have done at different stages.

The Gantt chart can be used to monitor progress. Use two rows for each task, one for the planned times (the orange bars on the chart below) and one to show what actually happened (the green bars).

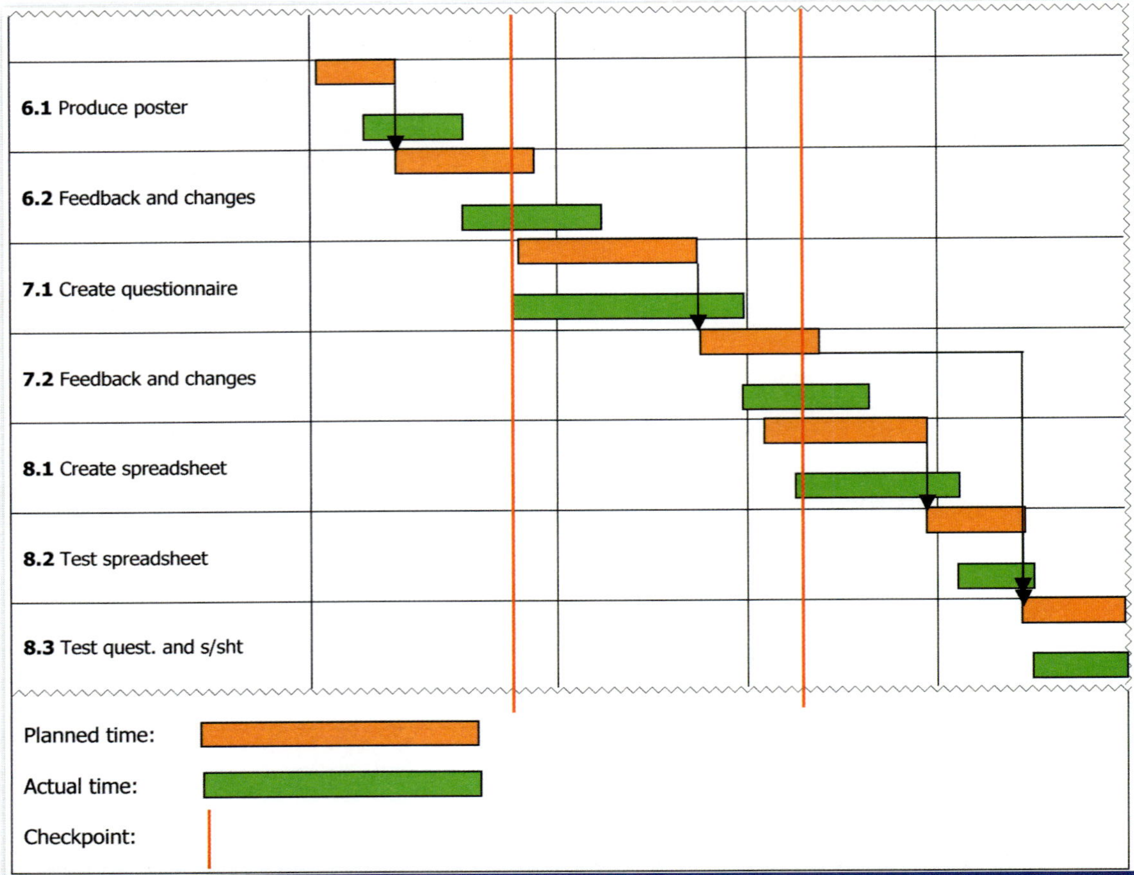

The first green bar shows that the poster started behind schedule and took longer than planned – this held up the feedback task. The red line indicates a checkpoint where the student discussed progress with the teacher. As a result, the student started the questionnaire design earlier than planned because it did not depend on the poster completion.

TALKING POINT 10.1

Discuss the rest of the project plan. What did the student originally intend to do (the orange bars) – can you find any errors? What did he actually do and why did he make the changes? Where are the comments?

If this project had been carried out without a plan, the chances are that it would have continued to be behind schedule all the way. By monitoring progress it has been possible to make changes that ensure that the project gets back on track. Don't panic if your plan shows that you are getting behind! It is almost always possible to do something about it if you monitor progress regularly.

Explaining the changes

Gantt charts are very popular because they are a type of graph and it is easy to spot where you are at any time. However, you must make notes about progress and changes you make. How will you do it? You can add text to the chart either by writing in the bars or by adding rows but you might want to consider making use of your ICT skills by using links to a comments document stored separately. Over to you!

Using a table

If you prefer, you can produce a project plan as a table using word processing or spreadsheet software, for example:

PROJECT PLAN

Task	Sub-task	Time needed	Planned start date	Actual start date	Planned finish date	Actual finish date	Comments

You would need to design the table to show tasks, sub-tasks and checkpoints clearly. Comments can easily be recorded on the chart but again you can link to other documents if you wish.

The important thing is that you create a plan which is complete and which you can use throughout your work on a project. You must be able to use it to monitor progress and to record any changes that may be necessary. Don't forget that other people will need to be able to make sense of your plan.

Choosing your software

There are many specialist programs for project planning and you may use one of these if you wish. However, this is not a requirement for Unit 1. Gantt charts and tables can be produced using standard word processing or spreadsheet software. There are also other types of project plan you might want to consider, such as PERT charts.

TALKING POINT 10.2

Discuss which application you will use to produce your project plan. If you use a Gantt or PERT chart how could you add comments?

Always remember it is the content that matters. Your plan must be clear to read and easy to use – dates, times and comments must all be clear if the plan is to make sense.

How did it go?

Project review

Assuming you have planned the project, carried it out, got feedback as you went along and finished all the tasks, what next?

You must carry out a review of the whole project so that you can be sure that you really have finished and so that you can think about what went well and what went badly.

You should incorporate feedback from others, such as:

- test users
- your peers
- your teacher
- a focus group.

Using email to gather feedback

Email can be a very efficient way of gathering feedback, both as you go along and at the end. You need to keep emails well organised.

Can I do this?

Using email tools, make sure you can:

Receive an email
Reply to an email
Send an email
Send an attachment
Use folders to organise emails and attachments

TALKING POINT 10.3

What are the advantages and disadvantages of using email rather than a face-to-face meeting to get feedback from others?

Reviewing the project outcomes

At this point you must consider the project as a whole as well as the individual publications.

You will need to look back at the project brief to remind yourself of what was required. In your review you should consider the project, the publications and your performance.

The project as a whole

- What did the project set out to achieve?
- To what extent have you met the objectives?
- How well did your plan work?
- How well did you manage your time?
- Did you meet the deadlines?
- Did you choose the right people as your test users and reviewers?
- What, if anything, went wrong?
- What improvements would you make if you had time?
- What you would do differently if you did the project again?
- What have you learned from working on the project?

TALKING POINT 10.4

This student is talking about his use of his project plan. What do you think of this method of review? How would you improve it?

The publications

- Does each of the final publications get the right messages across to the intended audiences?
- How could the final publications be improved?
- To what extent is the eportfolio well structured and easy to use?
- Is the information well presented and well organised?
- Did you include enough evidence to show how you developed your publications?

How did you perform?

The whole point of this part of the review is to get you to learn from your experiences. It is sometimes difficult to get started but you must remember that it is all about YOU!

What will you say?

What you must not do is include general statements such as these:

My mum says I worked very hard on this.

I think I am brilliant and I would do exactly the same next time.

The review of your performance does not have to be very long. Try to focus on questions like these – and be honest!

- What do you think of your final publications?
- What do you think about your performance on the project?
- What could you have done better?
- Has your work on this project improved your performance in other areas of study??
- How have you benefited from working on the project?
- Are you proud of your achievements?

How will you go about it?

Your review could be any combination of:

- a report
- a verbal evaluation recorded in sound or video
- a presentation.

You could include links to relevant areas of the eportfolio to illustrate points you are making.

Completing your eportfolio

As soon as you have finished your review you can complete your eportfolio. You must make sure that all your review files are in acceptable formats and copy them to the correct folders in your eportfolio. Check that the overall size is still acceptable and then create links from the web pages to the review files. Check that the links work and then re-test the whole eportfolio. You must be quite sure that your eportfolio is fully portable – that all the links will work on another machine. Try saving yours onto a CD and running it on a stand-alone computer.

Tackling THE PROJECT

The end is in sight! When you have finished patting yourself on the back you need to take a realistic look at how well you did. Be honest with yourself!

Reviewing the project as a whole

You can carry out a review of THE PROJECT:

- To what extent have you met the objectives of THE PROJECT?
- What, if anything, went wrong?
- What have you learned from working on THE PROJECT?

You were not asked to produce a project plan for THE PROJECT so of course you will not be able to comment on the use of one!

Reviewing project outcomes

You should be able to carry out a full review of the final publications.

Reviewing your own performance

You should review your performance on THE PROJECT (Step 11) by thinking about:

- how well you worked on sections of THE PROJECT
- what others have to say about your performance
- how this work has helped you in other areas
- ways that you have benefited
- what you would do differently another time.

Try to be creative in your use of ICT tools to present this review. Don't just rely on text, try out video, sound, graphics or a presentation.

Finishing the eportfolio

Remind yourself of the steps to an effective eportfolio by looking at the flowchart on page 155 . You should now have completed step 11.

The next step is to add the review files to your eportfolio for THE PROJECT, making sure that they are in acceptable file formats.

Create and check links from the web pages to the review files

And the final stage is to test, test and test again. This really is it and it is all down to you to make sure that everything works both on your computer and when loaded on to another one.

Work in groups with your peers and test the final eportfolios for each other. Check again that yours works on a different computer.

And finally...

Your eportfolio for THE PROJECT is not going to be marked but if you have worked hard on it, why not show it off? You could save it to CD and give a copy to anyone who might be interested. You could zip it and email it to people but you might want to check first that they are happy to receive such a big attachment! You might even consider publishing it on the web.

11 The SPB and beyond

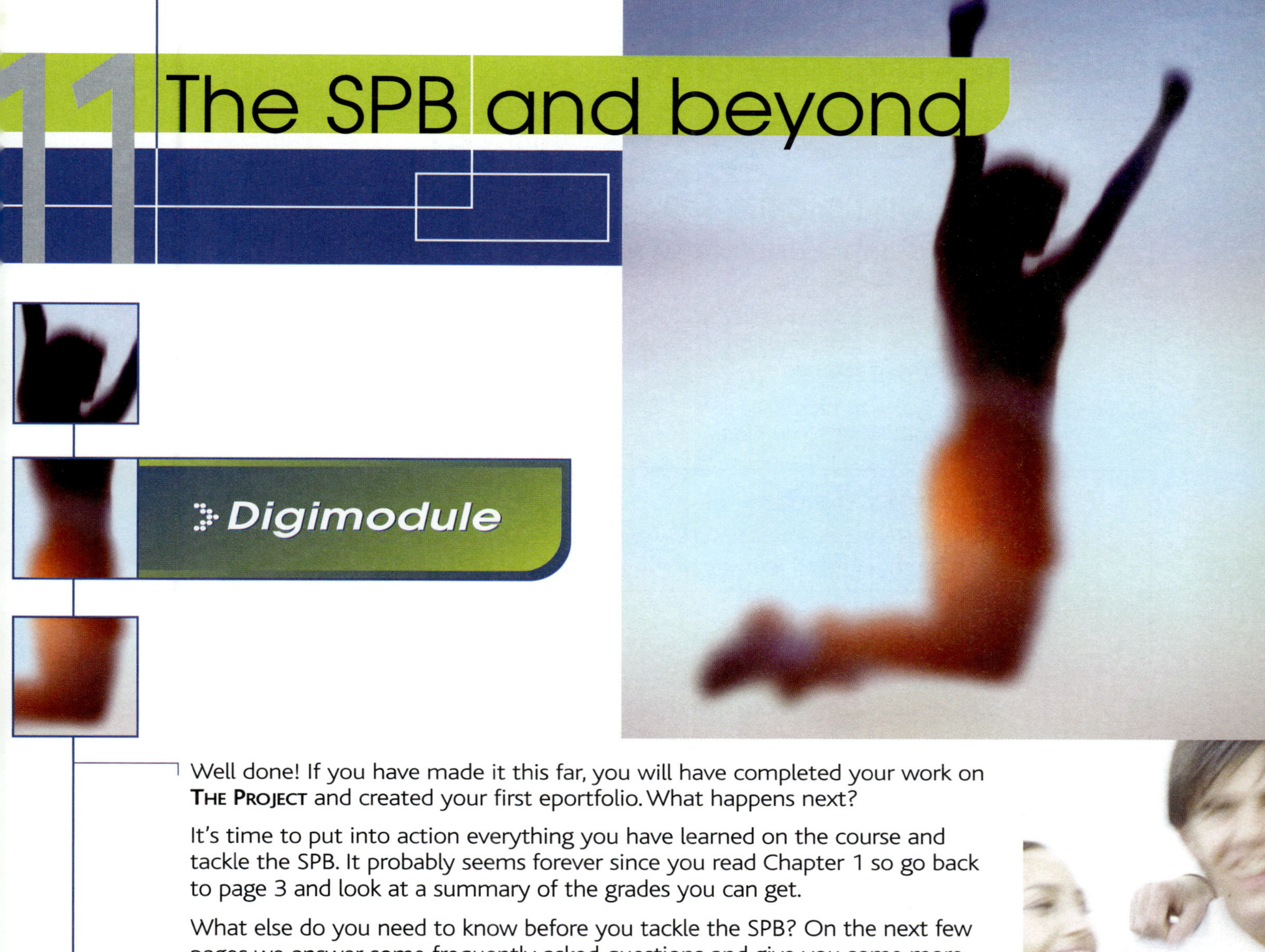

Well done! If you have made it this far, you will have completed your work on **THE PROJECT** and created your first eportfolio. What happens next?

It's time to put into action everything you have learned on the course and tackle the SPB. It probably seems forever since you read Chapter 1 so go back to page 3 and look at a summary of the grades you can get.

What else do you need to know before you tackle the SPB? On the next few pages we answer some frequently asked questions and give you some more information about how to gain as many marks as possible.

You are probably already starting to think about what you will be doing once the SPB is over. If you are continuing as a DiDA student, you will be making a start on another unit. Are you aiming for CiDA or DiDA? Remind yourself of what the possibilities are by revisiting page 2.

In the final pages in this chapter we take a look at some of the options and how you will be able to build on your achievements in Unit 1.

In this chapter, you will prepare for the next stage by:

- ***learning more about tackling the SPB***
- ***exploring what else DiDA has to offer***

Tackling the SPB

This is for real, marks are involved at every stage, so here are answers to some of the questions DiDA students ask.

Where will I find the SPB?

Look on the Edexcel website for DiDA Summative Project Briefs. You will find a number of them with different codes and dates so which is yours?

For Unit 1, level 2 you should look for D201. There may be more than one available – which one you do depends on when you will submit your eportfolio to the moderator – check with your teacher.

If you are going to tackle the level 1 SPB, you need D101 but you should talk to your teacher about what to do next.

Activity 11.1

Find the SPBs on the Edexcel website. Ask your teacher when your eportfolio will be moderated and see if you can find the correct SPB.

How long will I get?

You will have at least 30 hours of lesson time to work on the SPB. This is not a fixed amount of time and you can spend longer if your teacher agrees.

How much help will I get?

- You cannot work in groups (except to collect data for the survey if your teacher agrees).
- You must not copy what anyone else is doing.

Level 2 only

- You can only gain marks in your SPB for work that you have done yourself.
- When you were working on **The Project** and other practice materials you could ask for help as often as you liked but for the level 2 SPB, you are on your own.

This does not mean that you cannot discuss your progress with your teacher or reviewers but they can only give you feedback. They must not give you the answers.

Level 1 only

- You can ask for help with some parts of the SPB. The less help you need, the more marks you can get.

Can I work on it at home?

Most of the work for the SPB must be carried out under supervision. You cannot take it away and work on it at home. If you do, your teacher may not be able to confirm that all the work is your own. However, there is nothing to stop you thinking about it, carrying out research or asking for feedback.

Who assesses it?

Your teacher will assess (mark) your eportfolio using a mark scheme provided by Edexcel.

Why do I need an eportfolio if my teacher is marking my work?

The skills you need to create an eportfolio are part of the course – over 20% of the marks are for the eportfolio itself.

DiDA is a paperless qualification and your work must be sent to the moderator at Edexcel electronically. If you didn't create an eportfolio, you would have to send lots of files separately and the moderator would have no idea what was what!

What is a moderator?

A moderator is a DiDA expert employed by Edexcel to make sure that all teachers mark to the same standard. This means that everyone gets the marks they deserve.

Will the publications be the same as in THE PROJECT?

Not necessarily. THE PROJECT is actually quite big because you need to practise all the different skills and produce a wide range of publications. Each SPB has a different scenario and requires you to produce a different set of publications. Look at the SPBs on the Edexcel website to see how they vary.

Will I need to produce a plan this time?

Definitely! You will need a detailed project plan and you must use it. This is where project planning comes into its own. How else can you hope to get so much work done in the right order and still meet the deadline?

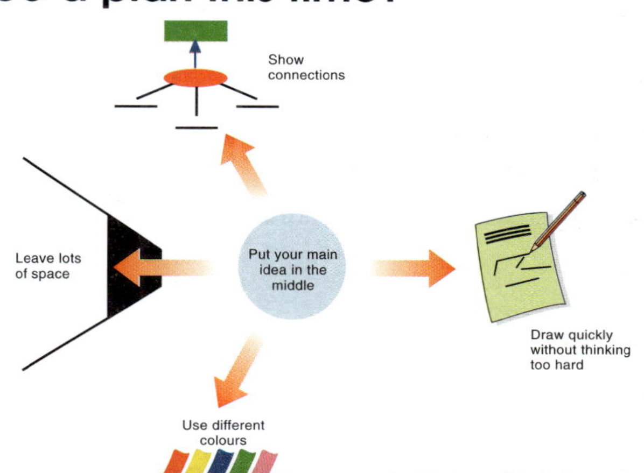
Show connections
Leave lots of space
Put your main idea in the middle
Draw quickly without thinking too hard
Use different colours

Before you produce the plan, you should consider drawing a mind map to help you work out what is required and how one task is related to another (see page 32)

Can I use components from the SPB in my own publications?

Of course you can, if they are relevant to what you have to say – but don't forget to acknowledge your sources!

How will I know if I'm doing well?

Your project plan must include times when you talk to your teacher and times when your test users and peer reviewers take a look and give you feedback. Make sure that you choose reliable test users who are as similar to the target audience as possible and peer reviewers who will be honest and do a good job. You need them to be critical but helpful and you need them to take it seriously. One thing you can do is pair up with someone else in your group and help each other out.

What do I do if I'm running out of time?

If you have produced a good plan and you have been making use of it, then hopefully this won't happen to you. You must avoid spending too long on some tasks at the expense of others. You may have to be satisfied with a less than perfect job if it is taking too long. Whatever you do, don't leave things out.

What will the moderator need to see?

The moderator will not know you and will not have seen you working on the SPB. He or she can only give you marks based on what they can see in your eportfolio. This is why it is so important to include all the required content. Check, check and check again!

What if some of my links don't work properly?

Even if the teacher has given you marks for something, the moderator cannot allow those marks if he or she cannot see the evidence. You must check that all your links work as they should. Test, test and test again!

How many marks are there?

The Level 2 SPB carries a maximum of 42 marks. You need 18 to achieve a pass which is equivalent to a grade C at GCSE. The Level 1 SPB also has 42 marks. This table summarises things for you:

Level 2			Level 1		
Mark out of 42	AiDA	Equivalent GCSE grade	Mark out of 42	AiDA	Equivalent GCSE grade
36 – 42	Distinction	A*	36 – 42	Distinction	C
30 – 35	Merit	A	30 – 35	Merit	D
24 – 29	Credit	B	24 – 29	Credit	E
18 – 23	Pass	C	18 – 23	Pass	F/G

So how do I get marks?

Look at the marking grid in the specification. The grid is divided into 6 sections, (a) to (f). To get a particular mark in a section you must achieve everything listed for that mark. Your teacher will mark each of these sections separately so you can do very well on one section and not so well on another. All six marks are added up to give the total.

TALKING POINT 11.1

Have a look at the marking grid in groups and see what you have to do to get marks in each section. Look at the mark alerts in the SPB for helpful hints on how to improve your marks – and how to avoid losing them.

What if I leave something out?

You will almost certainly lose marks! How many you lose depends on what you have left out. If you look at the requirements for one mark in each section of the marking grid, you will see what you have to do to get any marks in that section.

For example, look at Level 2 strand (c) – if you don't create and use both a database *and* a spreadsheet you will get zero in this section. Similarly, in strand (d) you must produce *all* the publications listed in the SPB.

TALKING POINT 11.2

Look at strands (a), (b), (e) and (f) to see what you must do to gain marks in these sections, or look at the grids for Level 1.

What if I'm really good at databases but not spreadsheets?

Or you think you are a real whizz at spreadsheets but useless at databases? As you saw earlier, you must not ditch one in favour of the other. The marking grid shows that the mark you get will depend on the quality of both of these. Do your best on them both and try to even things out – it's better to get 3 marks overall than to produce a spreadsheet that heads for 7 marks when the database is going to restrict you to 1 mark.

What happens if I don't capture images or sound?

Look at the marking grid for *(b)* – you can only get 3, or possibly 4 marks.

What happens if I don't acknowledge my sources?

This is section *(b)* of the marking grid again. For 5 marks, you must acknowledge all sources so you will only be eligible for 1-4 marks if you do not acknowledge them all, even if you have done everything else.

TALKING POINT 11.3

What happens if you don't acknowledge any sources? What do you have to do to get 1 or 3 marks? What about full marks for (b)?

What happens if someone copies my work?

Tell your teacher – you don't want to risk being accused of cheating – moderators are trained to spot possible cases.

Can I resit an SPB?

Yes you can – but don't bank on it! It's much better to put every effort in doing well the first time round.

Will I get AiDA even though I am going to do another unit?

You're only eligible for a certificate if you are claiming AiDA rather than doing Unit 1 as part of a CiDA or DiDA.

Where next?

If you are going to work towards CiDA or DiDA you will need to make a start on one of the optional units.

Each unit is assessed by an SPB and you must submit your work in an eportfolio. As you will see, the eportfolio has a different emphasis each time – a showcase, a gallery, a business proposal.

All units build on Unit 1, so whichever one you do, you will have a head start – apart from anything else you already have experience of project management and of building an eportfolio.

We are going to take a look at the first three units available – if you want to find out more about them, you will need to visit the Edexcel website. While you are there, check out what other units are available – by the time you read this there may well be more options.

Unit 2: Multimedia

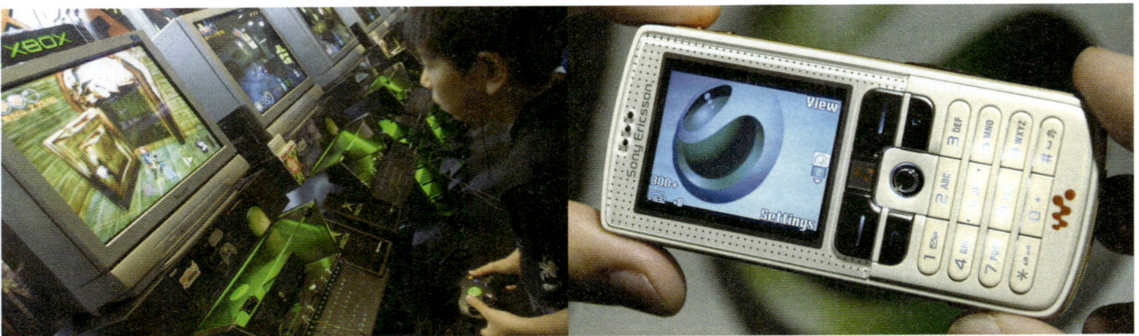

You are surrounded by multimedia – when you browse a website, play a video game, download an MP3 file, use a mobile phone or watch a DVD. Multimedia is any combination of text, images, sound, video and interactive components such as buttons.

You already have some experience of producing simple multimedia products – for example, the presentation and web pages you produced for **THE PROJECT**.

TALKING POINT 11.4

Why is multimedia used? Think of all the times you have worked with multimedia and how it helped to communicate information.

▸▸ Activity 11.2

Look at the list of skills you will need before you tackle the SPB for Unit 2 – what do you know already?

If you study Unit 2, you will learn how to plan, design, build and test more complex multimedia products – not only websites and presentations, but other products such as virtual tours, interactive quizzes, movie trailers, presentations and e-books.

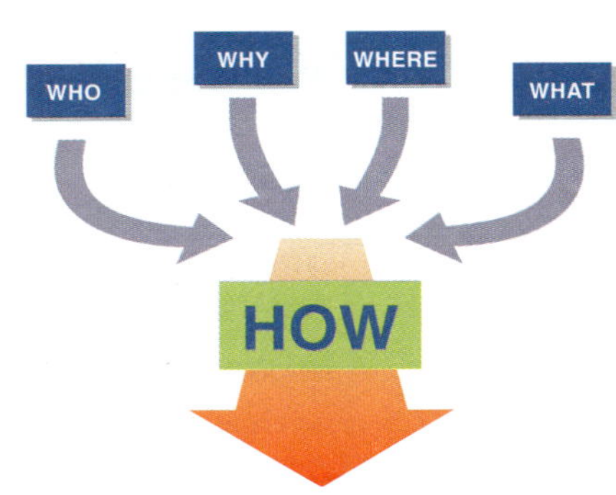

Every multimedia product must have an audience and a purpose. If your products are to be fit for purpose you will need to consider the same questions as you did for your publications in Unit 1 – who, why, what, where, how! How could you forget?

TALKING POINT 11.5

What is already out there? What multimedia products have you used during the past week?

The production cycle is just the same. You will be able to use your skills to produce mind maps, structure charts and storyboards and you will know that prototyping is essential to check that you are on track with your designs.

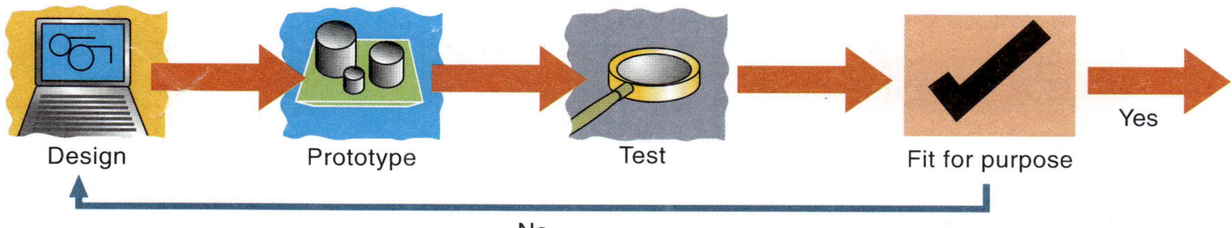

When it comes to the SPB, you will create different types of multimedia products.

And the eportfolio? With all your new skills you will be able to make it much more attractive, interactive and user-friendly – and give the moderator an unforgettable experience!

Unit 3: Graphics

Can you imagine a world without images? Think of how they are used to promote products, clothes and services in the worlds of fashion, advertising and marketing. Where would computer games and the internet be without them?

Again you will be able to build on your experiences in Unit 1. You have learned a little about selecting and capturing images and how to prepare them for use on screen and in print.

▸▸ Activity 11.3

Look at the list of skills you will need before you tackle the SPB for Unit 3 – what do you know already?

If you study Unit 3 you will learn more techniques so that you can use graphics software creatively. You should not underestimate what is involved here. Ask yourself why there is a whole unit devoted to graphics – but don't panic, you do not have to be an artist to do this unit!

⏩ Activity 11.4

Producing graphics is a complex business. Have a look at some of the computer art and graphics magazines at the newsagents. Think about what you have already learned about working with graphics. Have you created publications that have little or no text?

If you study this unit, you will learn to plan, design and create graphics components for use in various products and publications.

TALKING POINT 11.6

Choose a group or organisation that interests you – a pop group, football team, well-known brand of food or drink, etc. – how are images used to promote them? As you walk along the street, what images are instantly recognisable? If you want an image to communicate information, what issues do you need to consider?

Whether you aspire to producing stunning computer art or simply want to have the skills necessary to get your message across without words, this unit is for you.

Not only will your eportfolio be a gallery for your work on the SPB, your home page, menu pages and context pages will all give you further opportunities to use your new skills to enhance the eportfolio itself. You should revisit your reviews of your other eportfolios and make sure that this one is the best yet.

TALKING POINT 11.7

How does the content of this unit relate to other areas of your work? If you are an art or design student, the connections may be obvious, but what about other subjects?

Unit 4: ICT in Enterprise

Have you ever thought about starting your own business? Or organising a big event? You might not need to make a profit but you would certainly need to make sure that you didn't get into debt. Enterprise is about identifying and exploring opportunities to make sure that you turn an idea into a successful venture.

⏩ Activity 11.5

Look at the list of skills you will need before you tackle the SPB for Unit 4 – what do you know already?

Successful enterprises, from organising a school disco to building up a multi-million pound company, depend on careful investigation and planning.

TALKING POINT 11.5

What is already out there? What multimedia products have you used during the past week?

The production cycle is just the same. You will be able to use your skills to produce mind maps, structure charts and storyboards and you will know that prototyping is essential to check that you are on track with your designs.

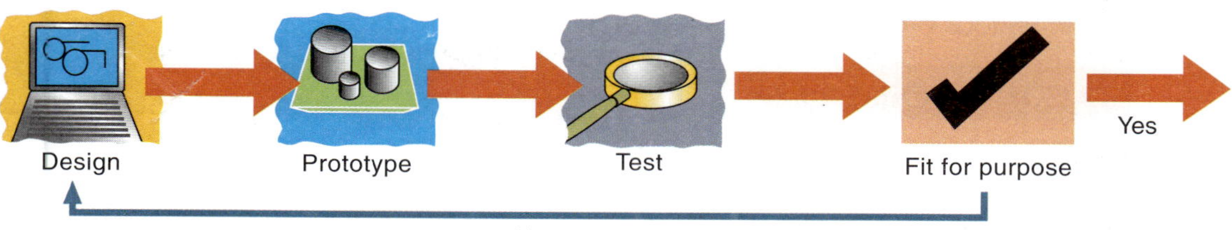

When it comes to the SPB, you will create different types of multimedia products.

And the eportfolio? With all your new skills you will be able to make it much more attractive, interactive and user-friendly – and give the moderator an unforgettable experience!

Unit 3: Graphics

Can you imagine a world without images? Think of how they are used to promote products, clothes and services in the worlds of fashion, advertising and marketing. Where would computer games and the internet be without them?

Again you will be able to build on your experiences in Unit 1. You have learned a little about selecting and capturing images and how to prepare them for use on screen and in print.

▸▸ Activity 11.3

Look at the list of skills you will need before you tackle the SPB for Unit 3 – what do you know already?

If you study Unit 3 you will learn more techniques so that you can use graphics software creatively. You should not underestimate what is involved here. Ask yourself why there is a whole unit devoted to graphics – but don't panic, you do not have to be an artist to do this unit!

▸▸ Activity 11.4

Producing graphics is a complex business. Have a look at some of the computer art and graphics magazines at the newsagents. Think about what you have already learned about working with graphics. Have you created publications that have little or no text?

If you study this unit, you will learn to plan, design and create graphics components for use in various products and publications.

TALKING POINT 11.6

Choose a group or organisation that interests you – a pop group, football team, well-known brand of food or drink, etc. – how are images used to promote them? As you walk along the street, what images are instantly recognisable? If you want an image to communicate information, what issues do you need to consider?

Whether you aspire to producing stunning computer art or simply want to have the skills necessary to get your message across without words, this unit is for you.

Not only will your eportfolio be a gallery for your work on the SPB, your home page, menu pages and context pages will all give you further opportunities to use your new skills to enhance the eportfolio itself. You should revisit your reviews of your other eportfolios and make sure that this one is the best yet.

TALKING POINT 11.7

How does the content of this unit relate to other areas of your work? If you are an art or design student, the connections may be obvious, but what about other subjects?

Unit 4: ICT in Enterprise

Have you ever thought about starting your own business? Or organising a big event? You might not need to make a profit but you would certainly need to make sure that you didn't get into debt. Enterprise is about identifying and exploring opportunities to make sure that you turn an idea into a successful venture.

▸▸ Activity 11.5

Look at the list of skills you will need before you tackle the SPB for Unit 4 – what do you know already?

Successful enterprises, from organising a school disco to building up a multi-million pound company, depend on careful investigation and planning.

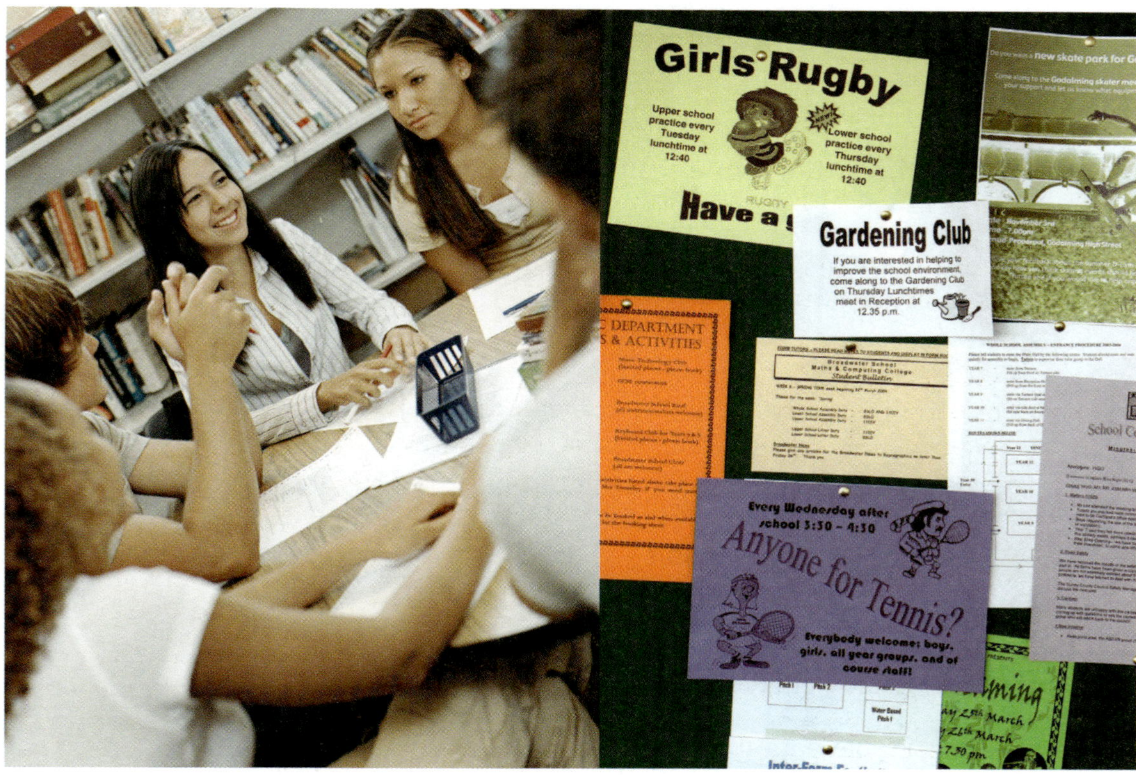

TALKING POINT 11.8

Think about some successful enterprises, some that are intended to make a profit and some that are not. What makes them work? Think about different aspects – finance, marketing, image, customer service, etc.

If you study Unit 4, you will learn how to explore enterprise opportunities using ICT. You will be able to build on the skills you already have to conduct market research and to produce marketing materials and other publications. You will need to develop your spreadsheet skills so that you can check out what will happen in different situations – more customers, higher prices, etc. – to make sure that you don't make a loss.

TALKING POINT 11.9

Remember the Bentley Charity Ball on page 88? Imagine that you have been asked to organise an event like this for your local community. What would you need to consider? What would you need to spend money on? How would you decide how much to charge? What could go wrong? What publications would you need? How could you make use of your ICT skills?

For the SPB you will research and plan for the launch of a business enterprise. Your eportfolio will be an e-business plan – everything you need to convince someone that your enterprise can be a success. The eportfolio itself will need to be professional and relevant so that the moderator knows that you are on to a winner!

TALKING POINT 11.10

How does the content of this unit relate to other areas of your work?

Skills list

Artwork and imaging tools

Database tools

Internet and intranets

Presentation tools

Word processing tools

Index

Edexcel
190 High Holborn
London WC1V 7BH

Second impression 2005

The right of Elaine Topping and Ann Weidmann to be identified as the authors of this work has been asserted by them in accordance with the Copyright, Designs and Patents Act of 1988.

ISBN -10: 1-903133-11-4
ISBN -13: 978-1-903133-11-8

Designed by Roarrdesign
Picture research by Ann Thomson
Illustrated by David Shenton and Tony Wilkins

Printed in Great Britain by Scotprint, Haddington

The publisher's policy is to use paper manufactured from sustainable forests.

Acknowledgements

The publisher and authors would like to thank Stuart Thompson of Boots Group plc and Deborah Harrison.

We are grateful to the following for permission to reproduce photographs and illustrations:

A1pix: pg 27, pg 92, pg 123, pg 135 (J. Alexandre); **Abode:** pg 122 (T. Imrie); **Alamy:** pg 13 (Design Pics Inc.), pg 17(t) (Black Star), pg 21(t) (D. Hoffman Photo Library), pg 85 (t), pg 90(t) (Shoosh/Up The Res), pg 137(b) (Ace Stock Ltd), pg 152 (Dynamic Graphics Group/Creatas); **BAA Aviation Picture Library:** pg 1(t); **Camera Press:** pg 172(l) (H. Miyata), pg 172(r) (C. Bresciani); **Corbis:** pg 4, pg 36, pg 47(b), pg 73, pg 80 (Royalty-Free), pg 5(r) (LWA-D. Tardif), pg17(b) (H. Rune/Sygma), pg 18(b), pg 35(t) (R. Hamilton-Smith), pg 24(r) (R. Klune), pg 45(r) (Owaki-Kulla); **Dorling Kindersley:** pg 24(l) (M. Alexander), pg 91; **Education Photos:** pg 175(r) (J. Walmsley); **Empics:** pg 48 (F. Matthew-Fearn); **Epson UK Ltd:** pg 173(r); **Getty Images:** pg 23(t) (R. Estakhrian), pg 31(br) (C. Zachariasen), pg 47(t) (Sparky), pg 65(t) (J.W. Banagan), pg 65(br) (M. Schlossman), pg 85(br) (T. Page), pg 95(t) (S. Johnson), pg 111(t) (VCL/S. Rowell), pg 137(t) (T. Anderson), pg 157(t) (Photodisc), pg 159 (M. York), pg 167(t) (S. McAlister); **Guzelian:** pg 173(l) (J. Russell); **Hideaways:** pg 68; **Image Source Ltd:** pg 167(b); **Masterfile:** pg 23(b) (H. Vu); **Pearson Education:** pg 18(t) (*Digitexts: The Lost Boy*); **Photographersdirect.com:** pg 12 (S. Kujawa Images), pg 22 (P. Glendell Photography); **Punchstock:** pg 40, pg 99 (Digital Vision), pg 98 (Photodisc); **Robertharding:** pg 175(l) (BananaStock); **Superstock:** pg 31(t) (Digital Vision Ltd), pg 111(b) (age fotostock); **Topfoto:** pg 53 (J. Greenberg/The Image Works).

Cover photograph: Getty Images/Steve McAlister

The following photographs were taken on commission © **Pearson Education Ltd:** pg 1(br), pg 20 (t), pg 50, pg 52, pg 85(br), pg 95(br), pg 104(b), **(By Trevor Clifford):** pg 38(b), pg 39, pg 66, pg 67(t)

We wish to thank the following sources for the use of their website information and other copyright material:

adultlearning.co.uk; The BBC; beetrootblue.com; Boots Group plc; Broadway Cinema Ltd; Clarity Business Solutions in Writing Ltd; Lewes District Council; The Countryside Agency; Cresta Hospitality Hotel Group; Currys; Andy Darvill; Dicoll Limited; Food Standards Agency; gastroblog.com; Glasgow Museums; Google Inc.; Hideaways; Inform; Interflora; Klmarnock College; King's College Hospital; London Fire Brigade; Microsoft Corporation; The National Trust; Northumberland National Park Authority; NSPCC; scream.co.uk Ltd; Scrimsign Micro-Electronics Ltd; Shropshire County Council; Office for National Statistics; Stevenage Borough Council; Stourport Town Centre Forum; Tesco Stores Ltd; UNICEF; VSO; Waverley Railway Project; Wiltshire Farm Foods; Yellow Pages; The National Youth Agency